# Fighting Theory

Selected Works by Avital Ronell

*Dictations: On Haunted Writing.* Bloomington: Indiana University Press, 1986; repr. Lincoln: University of Nebraska Press, 1993.

*The Telephone Book: Technology, Schizophrenia, Electric Speech.* Lincoln: University of Nebraska Press, 1989.

*Crack Wars: Literature, Addiction, Mania.* Lincoln: University of Nebraska Press, 1992. In French as *Addict: Fixions et narcotextes,* trans. Daniel Loayza. Paris: Bayard, 2009.

"Deviant Payback: The Aims of Valerie Solanas." Introduction to *SCUM Manifesto,* by Valerie Solanas, 1–35. London: Verso, 2004.

*Finitude's Score: Essays for the End of the Millennium.* Lincoln: University of Nebraska Press, 1994.

*Stupidity.* Urbana: University of Illinois Press, 2001.

*The Test Drive.* Urbana: University of Illinois Press, 2005.

*The ÜberReader: Selected Works by Avital Ronell.* Ed. Diane Davis. Urbana: University of Illinois Press, 2008.

# Fighting Theory

## Avital Ronell

in conversation with
Anne Dufourmantelle

Translated by
Catherine Porter

University of Illinois Press
Urbana, Chicago, and Springfield

Library of Congress Cataloging-in-Publication Data
Ronell, Avital.
[American philo. English]
Fighting theory / Avital Ronell in conversation
with Anne Dufourmantelle ;
translated by Catherine Porter.
p.   cm.
Translation of: American philo. Paris : Stock, c2006.
Includes bibliographical references and index.
ISBN 978-0-252-03414-5 (cloth : alk. paper)
ISBN 978-0-252-07623-7 (pbk. : alk. paper)
1. Ronell, Avital—Interviews.
2. Philosophy, American—20th century.
I. Dufourmantelle, Anne.
II. Porter, Catherine, 1941–
III. Title.
B945.R49A3      2010
191—dc22      2010009714

# Contents

# Preface
## The Scene of Fighting

This work began at the invitation of French philosopher Anne Dufour-mantelle in her capacity as editor with the French publishing house, Édi-tions Stock. She wondered if I would be willing to present myself and de-scribe my work so that it could make sense to a French readership. After some back and forth in my mind (Could I make the work make sense to any group or ensemble of purported readers? Should I assist in this sense-making project or refuse to participate? What does it mean to "present" oneself when one has spent one's life disarticulating and dispersing the self? Was I not, after all, categorically opposed to any form of so-called self-presentation or quasi-memoir writing? Could I handle the pressure of self-evaluation in French? Who in their right mind would address themselves to the highly invested army of French readers, the Paristocrats? How many meetings were we talking about?)—I said I would do it. I contemplated the dare and set out to meet the challenge of critically unfolding the orientation and possible implications of my work to date. We pulled out our calendars and penciled each other in. That did not mean that the matter was settled. I was concerned and characteristically anxious about the assignment, but remained very impressed by what Anne had done with the motif of hospi-tality when she published her discussions with my mentor.

Anne Dufourmantelle, who has conducted extensive interviews with Jacques Derrida, Antonio Negri, Alessandro Baricco, and others, has pub-lished a number of outstanding books under her own name. She is both a highly regarded philosopher and a practicing psychoanalyst in Paris. Each interview lasted from two to three hours as we discussed different facets of the questions that she felt would illuminate my writing and locate my intentions. In preparation for our meetings I would study, meditate, clean the apartment, exercise, go food shopping, wash my hair, study, listen to France Culture (to get French phrasing in my head), wait for her to ring the bell. She was always on time, on French time.

One would think that by now I would have some control over what can be said about the work I do, but that hope flew out the window immediately after our initial salutations. Perhaps because she is a psychoanalyst, I quickly lost all control and transferential restraint. Soon after the first session I loosened my native gag orders—and my tongue: against my better instincts, some of our discussions delved into deeply personal aspects of my writing, my life. I could not have anticipated the outcome, nor could I have prepped myself to deliver some of the trajectories and explanatory phrases that emerged to account for my relation to thought.

I was being asked to work on a double register of description and critique, in some instances to double back and rethink the premises of my practice as a critical theorist. My responses form the contours of a self-evaluation that arose both from a psychoanalytic *demande* and specific philosophical cues. Peculiar figures emerged to account for a history of solitary feints and rigorous apprenticeship. My reflections were guided by the understanding that I had always been in training, always responding to the squeeze of some sort of full-court press. Or, staying in the arena but switching matches, maybe it would be fairer to say that I engaged a practice (if this is imaginable, and it should be, as I am telling you it is the way my scholarly life went) that placed me in a site of struggle, often on a losing streak yet not entirely down for the count. Still, I kept fighting, and sometimes my friends or inner voices would ask me why. But I stuck it out, if often with stubborn persistence, as if I were fighting *for* something beyond my comprehension. I was often guided by the inescapable prompt of a "rope-a-dope" technique—I have for the most part found myself on the wrong end of a rope-a-dope; I could build on this to say something about a lifelong involvement with a kind of "trope-a-dope" pedagogy, often ducking out of harassing situations by playing numb and dumb, backing down where necessary, taking a beating until a sudden turn seemed possible—I have documented this relation to the Other, to the world, to my teachers in the book *Stupidity,* following de Man's analysis of Hellenic comedy where the dope actually triumphs and proves able to outwit the smart adversary.

But the dialectical turnover does not stop in my story, and I will not say that I can claim a triumphalist moment in any of the scenes that I lay out in this book. I did not come out of episodes of humiliation as a winner. I do know what it is to be academically beaten down and humiliated, how to maneuver and play dead when you find yourself at the wrong end of a rope-a-dope (OK, so there is no wrong end—or there is *only* the wrong end, and I have lived both ends and many ends; let us continue, remembering that Muhammad Ali prided himself on being a "pretty boy," meaning that he nearly never let himself get hit in the face: he was sensitive to disfigurement and he *danced*).

Themes came up in my conversations with Dufourmantelle that took me by surprise, and whose invested qualities I had not been aware of before our meetings. For this reason I would be tempted to recommend that everyone go through such a process of critical evaluation, however disruptive and jolting, however alien and, at times, necessarily dispiriting the process turns out to be. Everyone should partner up with the questioning other whose smile one cannot entirely decipher. At no point, however, should one expect a synthesis or any kind of dialectical summation to emerge from the jarring rhetorical consequences of such an encounter. Anne Dufourmantelle brought all sorts of unanticipated lifelines and ligatures into our reciprocal reflections on a work that still has no easy access code or settled place in our shared intellectual worlds. Of course one could peg me as a *Derridienne,* but would that be clarifying enough? Not for a French audience that wanted to see an American philosophical adventure unfold. I tried to keep the American accent alive in our conversations, even though I am as foreign—Europe, the Middle East, New York, Czernowitz—as the next writerly creature.

Some emphases in our conversation really took me by surprise.

I did not expect the athletic emphasis on working and thinking through; I did not know that Muhammad Ali would become the intellectual's hero; I was fairly surprised to learn that I continue to carry some wounded memories from graduate school and that childhood brooding about racist exclusion has not been stilled. I recognize that anti-Semitism does not qualify strictly alongside racist anxiety, but I do not know where else to locate it in the expository registers of persistent shaming. The bruises of misogyny I know about, but I didn't necessarily expect to find them still pulsing in my narratives. I admit that some of the ways I chose to engage Anne's questions and assertions involved my calibration of what was right to say to the French, so returning to America may invite some warping, the inevitable conceptual snag and a sense of permanent jet lag.

And so I am deeply moved to find my work routed differently, this time from the other side, from France, translated with extraordinary sensitivity and competence by Catherine Porter, whom I have long admired for everything she has brought to our shores, for her relation of *justesse* to every phrase and syntactical enigma. The generosity of Dr. Regier, who has housed my work and allowed for its ever dislocated bearings, has given me a solid and abiding sense of support, to the extent that I am capable of giving refuge to such a sense. Here, I have to interrupt myself. Something calls out for further elucidation before we wrap.

I should probably add a word about the persistent recourse to philosophy that marks these discussions. A good part of my training is philosophical. In the United States the concern with rhetorical and poetic dimensions of language lands you in literature departments, which is fine by me. In Europe, educated and written up as I have been, one is considered a philosopher unless proven otherwise. My European teachers have for the most part been stellar philosophers. I have no problem being associated with literary criticism or with what has come to be known, according to an ambivalent calculus, "literary theory" or "critical theory" or "critical thought," or "Continental philosophy," or "theory," all of which remains incongruent with the discipline of philosophy that is protected by institutionally sanctioned forms. So much for trying to find a homeroom. I just didn't want the reader to think I was running around with a fake ID—unless every kind of ID is inevitably fake, even those guaranteed by institutional borders and common academic policing practices. The concern with finding a proper place for a work and signature brings us to the crux of this effort, which I hope one quickly understands must break off where any identity or identitarian politics begins to solidify. I have never been less continuous with myself than when I tried to birth a historical narrative and critical overview of my "work to date." Surprisingly little of my own story is available to me. The episodes, frolics, crashes, and moods I narrate did happen, but who can say for sure what happened to a traumatized being whose existence pivots on her chronic sense of innocence? So much remains inassimilable, a blur, blanks, dazzling light, emergency calls, and rejected passwords.

We could have called this work "Chockerlebnis" (Shock-Experience) after Walter Benjamin's complicated description of the spare experienceability of experience in modernity—but maybe I should quit here before deconstructive velocities overtake me, tempting me to erase and reverse everything that was said and duly noted. The temptation is always great to delete and then flee from the scene of one's own undoing.

• • •

OK. One last remark, one last instruction before I peel away. I have decided to put the word "Theory" front and center, perhaps as a provocation from elsewhere and to flash a hint of street sensibility, a beat from which I have never shied. Theory, as I know and practice it, always teeters on the edge of legitimacy. This does not scare me. It is theory that always picks up death threats, even though philosophy deserves to be put up against the wall, having in many ways exhausted meaning and depleted its astonishing resources, disturbed so many viable dreams of vitality. Being of mixed origin and in its own way homeless, hybridized, illicit, off center, theory gets routinely pounced upon. "Theory" was targeted from day one, even by its practitioners who bore the stain of its nonbelonging within the higher classes of academic jurisdiction. I guess I decided to go with the distressed term of theory, in part because that is my habit: to pick up and move with what has been discarded, ridiculed, scarified. Even more attractive, it arrived on my beat with a DOA tag, institutionally shunned yet irreversible. Being DOA, it came upon us with a stealth population of phantoms and ghostly disarticulations: my kind of colloquy.

In some sections of these conversations you may wonder how I got away with some of what I say or do. I don't think I have gotten away with much—I am still paying taxes, so to speak, for the attacks I have permitted myself, for certain skirmishes and minor outrages that I initiated or did not end. At the time of their clocking, these interventions or deviant skids did not at all seem minor and cost me, on several occasions, my livelihood if not my feeble sense of dignity. I have paid with my health for facing down some of the harsher edges of an academic life. But I do not want to register a complaint here—not my style, unless we say that my entire work is one long complaint, a shriek along the lines of the *Schreiben/Schrei,* the *gritto escrito* or *cri/écrit* scroll (my laments turn to many languages): the famous inscribing/cry on which I was suckled.

When people asked me how I fueled my fresh departures, I do not stand on heroic mythemes or self-bloating tropes. (Rhetorically, this moment is hard to navigate because I do not want to let these statements sound, by some shrewd manipulation, like boasts, which they are not: please set this entire prefatory remark on pianissimo and, where possible, slow it down to a calculated anti-rant, toned down and reserved.) Anyway, if I have gotten away with something—this feeling of getting away with something, of being in trouble, corresponds to the sense of the abused—I would like to think that my stances and moods, the pitch at which I argue (I do argue) are, on good days, tribute to something like the divine insolence of the poet. Throwing punches or humbled by finitude, the poet fights, even when it is a matter of shadow boxing, in the neighborhood of that which escapes a firm linguistic hold.

For reasons of poetic probity, I would like to remember in this work a beloved student who is no longer with us and who every year on my birthday offered me a book of American poetry, a fresh stash of sacred insolence. Patrick Helikson was also an intense sports fan, a graceful poet-athlete, who could describe and critically break down every possible play. He still talks to me about my work and the moves I make or fail to achieve. He has always had a keen sense of the assist in basketball or of some of the sacrificial decisions in the metaphysics of sports.

Nonetheless, I am nearly certain that Pat would have issued a strong peril advisory about my tendency to overinvest the figure of the classical athlete. Pat was always on my side, even as he talked me down from certain positions I took. I imagine that in this case my introjected friend would have cautioned me against going overboard with my enthusiasm for a good fight. Essentially affirming my choices, he would have also instructed me on some of the downsides of finding an idol in Ali: that was Pat's way, to find the downsides, to operate a quasi-dialectics and turn things around or to the advantage of another, more hidden facet of a problem, structure, or image. I am supposing that he would have seen something other in Ali than an exemplary athlete; perhaps he would have pointed to the one who refused his debt to Frasier: in my head I hear Pat relating Ali's disavowal of indebtedness to the way Heidegger turned away from his mentor, Husserl, when he was down for the count. Then Patrick Helikson would have taken the relationship between Ali and Frasier, Heidegger and Husserl, and others locked in the adversarial embrace, for another round, pursuing his customary logic of exhaustion, until the conversation stalled and one of us would be KO'd. (The following morning, after our conversations, I would habitually go to rewrite.)

# Translator's Note

Translating a work into a language that the author can claim as a mother tongue entails a supplementary challenge: how to find expressive means that will satisfy not only the anticipated target-language audience but also the one reader who could have written the text directly. The task is all the more daunting when the author in question has established her own quite distinctive voice in numerous major publications in English. To the extent that the translated text has managed to capture that voice, much credit must go to the author herself. As Avital Ronell read through my final English-language draft, she occasionally added material to clarify or extend an argument, once in a while deleted passages she had come to deem superfluous, and frequently made small adjustments in the language. While the resulting book is thus in some sense not as faithful to the source text as translatorial conventions might dictate, the cotranslation is much the richer for the author's willingness to expand and help reshape the thinking launched in her French original for her new English-reading audience.

# Fighting Theory

# When Philosophy Meant
the Love of Wisdom

The etymology of philosophy is "love of wisdom." Do you think this still applies today?

If philosophy resembles in the first place a love story, then the love in question would have to be a little perverse for me to be comfortable with it. People will claim that philosophy borrows from love stories—their narrative structure, their need to be told, their need to be embodied in words. As for wisdom, that strange salvation we turn to when we no longer know what else to look for, what meaning can it have for us? It's true that in French you talk about *la sagesse*, but it's hard for me to conceive of philosophy as having feminine features, since in English it has no gender. And if I look at it through bifocals, I see philosophy in all its brutality, especially when it's set against literature and poetry. Also, in English, a certain sexual warfare is implied in the coupling of philosophy and literature, while in French I'm not so sure. What the act of philosophizing evokes for me in the first place isn't wisdom or love, but rather combat: the resumption of vital hostilities. More than a space for lovers, philosophy as I see it marks out a hostile territory—and this is not necessarily contradictory.

Where I come from, philosophy scarcely exists, or at least it no longer has the determining role that it was credited with for a long time, or the aura of grandeur that set it apart. What you and I understand as "philosophy" can no longer count on shelter or space in any Anglo-American zone of academic thought. Roadblocks and avowedly underhanded schemes have led to its devaluation and exile. And if I talk about plots, it's not because I'm after some great villain in the matter, but because I'm trying to understand how the most virulent forces of resistance operate and cooperate.

What you and I call philosophy is disappearing, but I'm interested mainly in the designs of those who are making that happen and in the delegitimizing velocities that still require a reading.

Let's go back to the love of wisdom. If there is love in this story, we would have to understand it starting with Freud, that is, we would have to think through its essential ambivalence, discern the contradictory values it harbors. The meaning of the word "love" wasn't the same for the Greeks (in whose literature different essential types of love are announced), or for the Latins, or in the time of the troubadours, or at the beginning of the twenty-first century. Love has all sorts of modalities; that's in part why it's hard for me to address the question of love in and with philosophy, unless I conceive of it in its essentially sadomasochistic dimension, at once degraded and upgraded, according to a highly sensitive grid. For, contrary to what people might still have been able to believe in preceding centuries, philosophy may not be as radiant, as openly positive, as its etymology seems to indicate. It is not necessarily on the side of life. It does not guarantee a mobilizing energy, it does not affirm, it does not respond, or it no longer responds, to our vital needs. Besides, who knows whether that was ever its job or its function?

Heidegger had already designated the last philosopher long ago: Nietzsche. And it seems to me that since then we've consigned philosophy to oblivion and even to something less poetic than oblivion and perversely much more attractive to me: we've consigned it to *ridicule*. In my own philosophical work, I urge awareness of a class struggle, and the "prole" that slumbers in me considers that the Heideggerian oblivion remains terribly elitist, the ruse of a false peasant. "Oblivion" strikes me as still too exalted, too noble, and too optimistic. Oblivion is promising. It makes a tacit deal with return, with memory. And I think that what is happening right now in philosophy is much more serious than oblivion, than what oblivion promises. I happen to be attracted by things that are ridiculous, even lamentable; one could even call this attraction "philosophy." I started considering the figure of the ridiculous philosopher in the registers of Kant's anxieties. He has a real sense of what it means to *sich lächerlich machen*, to produce oneself as ridiculous—it's quite a performance of inescapable abjection.

Philosophy, if it still exists, is worn out; it's threadbare. Our culture—I'm taking a shortcut when I say "our culture," as if there were one and as if we knew what that meant—is marked by deficit, exhaustion, chronic fatigue. Metaphorically, our culture can be said to be directly threatened by one of those autoimmune diseases that we generate ourselves, and this is what interests me: regions, territories, bodies, corpuses, discourses that attack and defeat themselves. I'm attracted by what rejects me, what rejects the immunity of a vaccine. Moreover, I studied HIV/AIDS very soon after it appeared, as a terrible and singular disease but also as a philosophical problem inscribed within a social logic.

Do you think that philosophy has made itself ill?

Philosophy began in relation to failing health and, to this day, issues statements that often parallel doctor's orders, prescriptive ordinances, a rhetoric of wholesomeness. In my research and teaching, I interrogate relations of self-destruction, hostile zones that undermine being. Of course, one type of "vigorous" philosophy continues to be practiced and taught in universities. We find completely healthy philosophical exercises that do not appear to have been affected yet by the disease. This global autoimmune disease and the way it operates internally are experiencing a sort of repression. I won't say that everything ended with the pre-Socratics; this would be to adopt a false, possibly nostalgic attitude. But a very brutal, physical way of putting things would lead to an observation like this: "Ah, philosophy has been over for a long time now, there's nothing left." Even when I seem to be mimicking this discourse, I'm actually totally distancing myself from it.

Nostalgia is always a mistake. We have to trust the machine that transvalues values, the Nietzschean machine. Let's say that a good and a bad decadence most likely coexist. The decadence of health is the one that Heidegger designates later on as marking the difference between destruction and devastation. Destruction is connected with the future, after all; it is positive in that it makes it possible to open up fields, to bury what is destructive or unhealthy. But we have to be careful: this discourse might have somewhat fascistic resonances. So destruction is dedicated to the future, while devastation for its part is absolutely futureless: it's a collapse, it comes when one has gone too far, and it's possible that we have gone too far. Yes, it's possible. Is the end, if we have actually entered an "end of philosophy," is this end a definitive closing off, or merely a boundary? We have to continue to interrogate the figures used to designate the end, and to recognize the difference among such terms as closure, finality, terminus.

Today, it's crucial to keep reflecting on technology. Because philosophy also entails thinking about what's coming. And what is coming is often already here. From this perspective, wisdom and even love become secondary. Besides, technology, which tends to invade everything, has also colonized the field of love. There is a rhetoric of everyday words (at least in English and German) that borrows its terms from technology itself. In English, one is "turned on," "plugged in," "having a blast," "connected" (in French, *branché*). Even words that signify interiority, or that designate some characteristic of subjectivity, have been annexed by technology. In this sense, Heidegger's prediction has come true: technology has extended its hold on language and inflected our very existence. For Freud, too, love, which is linked to affects, is first of all informed by a technological notion, that of a libidinal "economy." The German term that designates libidinal investment evokes an electrical structure (*Besetzung*). Transference, the word designating the relation between the analyst and the analysand, is structured, like the unconscious, in homology with a telephonic device. We continue to be invaded in our bodies and in language itself by the parasitic means of technology. We must constantly come back to affects. To sensations. To what has bound together the body, love, and thought since Spinoza. And we have to question ourselves about this mutation of our relation to love and to language starting from what Heidegger calls the essence of technology.

Is what you call "technology" the same thing as what Heidegger meant by "technology," insofar as it affects our way of thinking?

No, not exactly. Well, yes, maybe. Heidegger is very ambivalent when it's a matter of characterizing the essence of technology, even though he's among those who have gone the farthest in pointing out its contradictions and the incalculable range of our fascination with it. He asserts that the essence of technology poses the greatest danger to our future democracies. In the ineluctable and increasingly rapid development of technology, against all odds, he was able to detect a very serious event. When I connect Heidegger to the question of democracy, I recognize that we end up with a distorted trajectory. A sort of perversion. In one of my books, I show that, in the same way that Heidegger was blinded or rendered naive by technology, he let himself be ensnared by Nazism. In any case, it would be necessary to examine the relations between Heideggerian thought and democracy as attentively as we have done with Nazism.

How do you perceive this danger?

First, not everything is homogeneous; as in geology, there are multiple strata. We can go ahead and inveigh against the media—we've been doing it since Mirabeau—but this doesn't solve anything. The problems raised by excessive mediatization were already foretold by Plato and rebooted by Aristotle. What interests me is not so much the positivity of objects or the everyday invention of new technological gems, but the fact that technology responds to the needs of what Heidegger has called the "essence of technology." And finding out to what extent this process puts democracy in danger. I've done so much work on this topic that I have trouble summing up the problematic in a few hours of dialogue. For Heidegger, one of the dangers began showing with man's first step on the moon. This step destroyed the world, symbolically; it destroyed the essentiality of the world. But Heidegger tended to think somewhat naively that some space in the world could escape technology, that there could be a "safety" zone. Poetry, for him, was one such space. He also seemed to retain a belief in the protected space emblematized, materially and symbolically, by the Black Forest. If technology was one of the moments of revelation of being, at the same time Heidegger signaled (and when I use the word "signaled," I am using yet another technological term in spite of myself) that there was a possibility of being much more anterior and authentic than the possibility embraced and dominated by technology.

The question we face is this: for what destructions is technology responsible, and exactly what does it endanger? Because I don't believe that there are any "protected zones," of the sort we have in national forests. A particular wave of destruction, still in force, began with the Nazis' terrorist state, which was a state explicitly invested in technology, even the *technology* of mass murder. All the rhetoric, the so-called theory of Nazism, was devoted to technology. Robert Musil said that there was no theory of Nazism, that it was the movement the most lacking in intellectuals, books, or texts that had ever existed on the planet. Apart from Hitler's *Mein Kampf*, a poorly written tract, by the way, there was not even the pretense of any theoretical justification whatsoever. Even Mao had his *Little Red Book*! Whereas Nazism was characterized both by its exaltation of technology, in connection with the Nazi myths, and its contemptuous refusal to support its own so-called political ideas.

But here too we have to be careful: even though I think that there is no such thing as a space free of any relation to technology, technology must not be viewed in a solely negative light, precisely because, as a good Nietzschean, I have to take note of all its facets and complexities, including the fact that it is our "destiny." We can't get away from it. So why complain that technology has no meaning, if meaning itself is what has to be interrogated?

Certain moments in the history of technology have been liberating, especially for women, and technologies have been put in place through

5

women. And here I am no doubt going to shock you by speaking of positive technologies, inventions that have often been very "feminine." Every new bomb bore a woman's name, every airplane, every ship. Canning, for example, was one of the first objects of industrialization that brought about real change. For the first time, a whole population of women was no longer confined to the kitchen, no longer had to do the canning or cooking herself, and the new situation constituted a threat to traditional patriarchal society. This is why, with the invention of every positive technology, an antifeminist discourse sprang up, as a warning.

# II

# The Finite but Unending
# Goethe Loop

You began with the Germanic world, with Goethe. Have you also met
with hostility there?

Yes, unquestionably. My first thesis was rejected by my dis-
sertation director at Princeton. Because it didn't deal either
with a famous writer or an established philosopher, my
thesis struck him as useless: I wanted to work on a certain
Walter Benjamin, who was unknown at the time. Hannah
Arendt herself had said only a few years earlier that it was all a rumor:
Benjamin was only a phantom, not even an acknowledged philosopher
or a writer. And yet I had spent two years working on his writings. Into
the trash. I then turned to Goethe, Hölderlin, and Kafka, somewhat better
known. But here, too, there were problems. My graduate directors told me
to eliminate the passages where I discussed temporality and to weave in the
idea of nature instead. What was really behind this maneuver was the allergy
to French philosophical terminology characteristic of a certain American
milieu that saw itself as having been "colonized" by Derrida, Foucault, and
their ilk. In my thesis I dealt only with German texts, but these texts were
nevertheless viewed as corrupted by the French and the analyses peculiar
to their idiom. And the allergy to my own work appeared at the outset. I
had been initially trained as a Germanist, and the readings of German texts
that were being produced in France interested me a great deal. But a sort
of patrol was doing its job at that time, and perhaps it was right, after all,
to guard the border, because since then French philosophers have never
stopped invading the Germanists' territory. Here, in German studies in
American universities, people don't tend to venture further than hermeneutics! The opening to French theories scarcely belongs to their "horizon

of expectation," as it's called. . . . Anyway, my own itinerary, at once phobic and intimate, is somewhat more complicated. The German texts owe their current vitality to the French sentinels, to those who have devoted themselves to restoring meaning—or the process of unmeaning—within different registers of classical German texts and other, more contemporary ones.

So you launched your "career" by writing about Goethe . . .

I thought that my attentiveness to Goethe would be greeted with enthusiasm, whereas in fact my career as a Germanist was practically destroyed on that score alone. It was naive to think that one could attack with impunity the literary monument that immunized an entire people against the castration of "national" carriers of pride and imagination. Goethe's signature is the privileged figure of everything seen as good, abiding, and necessary in "German" culture. I thought I had discovered very important things, and I was attacking the work not frontally but structurally; I unleashed significant hostilities without meaning to. I was interested in Goethe's status as monster as well as in the imaginary fiction around which his legend had been built, a legend that was far more widespread than knowledge of his texts and his discoveries. I don't deny that we owe him works as magistral as *The Sorrows of Young Werther* or *Elective Affinities*. Goethe is altogether very transgressive, very courageous; but what interested me from the start was the way he had been able to penetrate the unconscious of every German-speaking writer and thinker, from Nietzsche, Marx, and Freud to Benjamin, Kafka, and Heidegger among many others.

Freud saw in Goethe the source and starting point of psychoanalysis, but when Freud designates a father we know that there will be reprisals! Moreover, Freud turned out to be ensnared by his own limitless admiration for Goethe; his writings were extremely ambivalent in that respect—at least that is what he shows us, if I may say so, unconsciously. Goethe is not only designated as the initiator of numerous concepts and texts of master narratives, the source of so much good (but then Freud is not so sure that there is that much good in civilization . . .), but also as a "father" of psychoanalysis who became in turn a threat and a weapon. Freud said that he couldn't write anything while he was reading or close to Goethe. He frequently associated Goethe's name with a sort of paralysis, or even, as I try to show, an illness in its terminal phase. Walter Benjamin, for his part, had dreams about Goethe from which he awakened in tears. It's interesting to see how Goethe inhabits people who try to write in German. Goethe acts as a destructive force and at the same time as someone who inspires a feeling of endless indebtedness—so he represents a specific configuration of

8

guilt in regard to language and history. His position as infinite creditor has instigated some of my analyses of the way he arrives on the scene of writing in order to collect with interest what he has also given. On a thematic level, he appears to be beyond reproach, an object of simple and unburdened admiration. But writers do not simply admire their predecessors. They chow down on them, introject them, and sometimes don't manage to spit them out in time. Then the drama of incorporation takes hold and the undead exact their revenge.

This is how I began my research, by retracing the destructive links, the conscious or unconscious episodes in the letters and texts of German philosophy that referred to Goethe. It all starts very nicely, with Goethe eluding all sorts of snares. When Nietzsche wants to designate the singularity of the individual who escapes *ressentiment,* he names Goethe, whereas *ressentiment* can be said to snag most texts by thinkers from the same period. And even Goethe's best friend, Schiller, who lived across from him in Weimar and who constructed his own texts in a naive and sentimental writing style, said of Goethe that he belonged to the Greek world, that is, that there had not yet been any rupture or caesura in his being or in his writing, that there was in him an unbroken totality.

Is this what you have called "monstrous"?

Yes, in part, in terms of his special status that works over those who seem to be attached to his corpus. From this starting point Goethe becomes a sort of destructive weapon smashing those who come within reach. "Goethe will not be forgiven for having escaped the shipwreck that the others experienced," Blanchot says. There were Hölderlin, Kleist, Lenz, and more . . . those who broke down around him and often through contact with him. When Hölderlin met Goethe together with Schiller, it was a traumatic event for him. And Goethe advised him to write differently, he told him his writing was shit, that it made no sense. Everyone suffered, felt judged, even phantasmatically, but Goethe kept right on. He recovered from his crashes, while others were limp, scattered casualties in comparison. He was almost an Übermensch, a superman or transhuman, in the Nietzschean sense: he knew how to cast off his skin, transform himself, and persevere. Some of his writings were scandalous objects. Even today some of Goethe's texts and poems are only beginning to be published, so "transgressive" were they deemed to be: these are erotic, often almost pedophilic poems. When I mention this sort of thing, the official or normative Germanists— the ones still in power in academia—are not pleased. He is their comfort food—what can I say?

9

Goethe has an absolutely perverse imagination. He broke with his mother very early and never saw her again. Their collected correspondence is fabulous; every time he sent her some smutty text—for example in his first play, where he says "the emperor can kiss my ass"—his mother wrote back: "but you're marvelous, my boy, I'm so proud of you, I imagine that the profes sors have heart attacks when they read you." She was very encouraging by mail! He never saw her again after he was twenty-four years old. He left Frankfurt for Weimar and never turned back.

Nietzsche, who had so much trouble breaking off relations with his sister, his friends, Nietzsche, who kept breaking with Wagner in his texts while constantly attesting to his friendship in his letters, must have been fascinated by the way Goethe broke radically with the people from his past. Goethe may have been on the brink of suicide with each separation, but once he managed to resolve to go ahead and break off relations he did so with utter self-domination, and that must have seduced Nietzsche. In any case, they collaborated in the almost insurmountable anguish of surmounted separation, and they wrote gigantic books about that abyss they had had to clear.

> Was Goethe one of the reasons for your interest in deviant, marginal figures?

Certainly, to the extent that I've been led to explore the secret places and sites of deviance within Goethe's life and work, the "rogue state" that he embodied all on his own and that was "ennobled" when he was turned into a national monument. He was the least obvious place to go for sleuthing the margins. Nonetheless, he managed to trip up colossally, and lived to tell about it. The serious crises of depression, the quasi-psychotic episodes, and the mechanisms of denial that kept the Goethe machinery in good working order really excited me, even if my interest in what is inscribed in the margins, in the uninhabitable and hostile zones we were talking about earlier, and to which the figures of the monstrous, of genius, foolishness, and stupidity belong, is by no means limited to Goethe. He was a great host for those concerns, though. He could handle my inquisitiveness, my intrusive snooping, and I did not feel that I was unwelcome or capable of weakening anything in the mammoth composition that contains his-life-his-works. He could handle me, and I felt that he was possibly relieved to get dusted off by a perv who understood one part of him so often pushed away and canceled out by his largely prudish handlers, the legitimate custodians of his legacy.

To come back to the way my work of critical investigation began, I asked myself how Goethe, as a body of work and as a prestigious signature, had come to be invented and commemorated. To my great surprise, every time someone mentioned Goethe or cited him, I discovered in the archives that the text in question was signed "Eckermann." And I wondered, as I pursued my thesis research: who *is* this person or placeholder who pops up around every corner? Why does the truth of Goethe pass through him? Was he a sort of surveillance camera, a witness, a voyeur, an unstoppable admirer, a live-in or love-in or seer? Why was it necessary to go through this Eckermann every time someone wanted to check out what Goethe had said about art, about Caspar David Friedrich, about the French, about war, science, or indeed literature and his own poetic production? In the library, I discovered that the book so often cited, the book described by Nietzsche as the best text in the German language, was Goethe's *Conversations with Eckermann*. Heine was reading it on his deathbed. I understood that Goethe's best book was signed Eckermann! At the library, the *Conversations* with Goethe turn out to be stored on the Goethe shelf, as his last work. In Germany, in the United States, in France, in Spain, this is now a book signed by Goethe. What a fine trick of legerdemain!

Eckermann was thus obliterated behind Goethe's posterity and the mercantile sense of publishers in all countries, even though one can still find copies (I have one) actually signed by Eckermann. What a prodigiously interesting and revealing event, this foreign body introduced into Goethe's corpus! Eckermann was a young man, illiterate until the age of thirteen, who set out on foot from Göttingen for Weimar to introduce himself to Goethe. He was a protoschizophrenic—I spoke about this to Félix Guattari, who expressed enthusiasm over adding him to the roster of a schizopoetics. Well, I paid a fine price for my own enthusiasm about Mr. Eckermann. Henceforth I was a certified kook—I had signed my own pink slip, what was I thinking? Maybe I *was* thinking (Heidegger asks, "What is called thinking?"), and that is not always the way to go in universities where you are asked to convey and transmit and package, not unwrap, a codified bulk of knowledge. I was fired a first time from the German department in which I was teaching, apparently for having discovered and demonstrated that Eckermann had stimulated a special eck-onomy and was the hidden price tag of the Goethe monument, an "eckonomonument," if you will. In any case, while everyone was bowing down before Goethe's image in our then twentieth century, Goethe's desire—the desire that led him to choose a near psychopath as his assistant—intrigued me a lot. The choice (Goethe's, not mine) was a good one—if it can be evaluated this way—since Eckermann was able to imitate Goethe's style to the extent of blending in completely. It was he who concluded Goethe's autobiography, wrote letters in his hand, and it was he again who told Goethe, at the end of his life, what he was to do and what texts were worth finishing.

Even so, he was incredibly cultivated for an illiterate!

A quick study, Eckermann learned things starting at age thirteen, entirely on his own, in the countryside. To read, to play music, to imitate thought. Eckermann arrived at Goethe's house at the end of a long journey and virtually never left him after that. He never believed, for example, in Goethe's death, because after that event he continued to have conversations with Goethe, at night. That's why my book on that question is called *Dictations: On Haunted Writing*. Eckermann received Goethe phantomatically; he took dictation every night, in the dark. Eckermann was interested in birds, and he lived near Goethe's house, in a confined space, with forty birds, including predators and raptors, and these birds often damaged his manuscripts. Apparently, people said that Eckermann himself—"le petit docteur" Eckermann, as he was called—resembled a bird, had gradually taken on that morphology. Goethe chose that broken being who identified with him and lived in small quarters with dangerous birds. I would have liked to consult Hitchcock on their story and its avian traces. They flutter throughout the conversations. But Goethe himself was a tough bird and kept Eckermann caged, making him a carceral subject, one (or two, because Eckermann was hosting a phantom, he was body-snatched before Goethe captured him—but that's another story) who tried to get away only a couple of times. One day, for example, Eckermann said to Goethe that he had met a girl he liked, and Goethe responded that it was out of the question for him to get involved with her. "We don't have the time!" he is said to have exclaimed. "We have neither the time nor the wish that you marry. Nor do we have time for the articles you want to write. We don't need money." (Eckermann received practically no pay.) And in the book Eckermann wrote (some *Entretiens infinis*—infinite conversations—before Blanchot), he began by caressing Goethe's corpse. But he couldn't bring himself, it seems, to accept Goethe's death. Goethe was not dead, not for Eckermann (I call this particular crypt-formation Eckermania). He will never be entirely dead. And I see now that there is a sort of trajectory in my work on Eckermann that leads all the way to the idiots and innocents in poetry and literature, the mute witnesses of the philosophical trek, the freaks and misfits to whom so much is owed, including my identificatory path and passage . . .

There are also some quasi-dialectical moments when things are reversed, when Eckermann dictates to Goethe and gives him orders. Certain bird allegories are marvelous, and show Goethe's homegrown perversity. For example, their conversation about the legendary pelican functions as an allegory for their relationship (the pelican is a large bird that allows itself to be devoured by its young), but Goethe adds: and what if that bird wanted, *needed*, to have himself devoured? What if this were the pelican's desire? We see here a typically Goethean form of maneuver that enchanted Nietzsche, a maneuver thanks to which Goethe keeps on escaping a fateful lure. Every time Eckermann tried to put *him* in a cage, Goethe slipped away. He is a powerful songbird who wants to be devoured, but it is *his* power and *his* desire to be devoured. And we also understand why Goethe was so important in Freud's eyes: there are beings whose desire strongly undermines the supposed difference between sadism and masochism. For Freud, it was Goethe who had been able to inscribe and practice the relation to the unconscious of the other; it was also thanks to him that the superego took shape.

Eckermann had no "subjectivity"; no possible subject position could seriously account for him: he belonged to the Goethean apparatus and effaced himself when he needed to. He always knew, with Freudian precision, how to protect Goethe from his own potentially murderous movements. For example, Eckermann reports their argument over the doctrine of colors that Goethe had developed. There is a struggle over the paternity of this doctrine, and the matter becomes very dangerous for the couple they form. Who has the right to sign and to present himself as the author of a text that was so important to Goethe? Why does Eckermann insist so much, when the theory of colors is one of the texts Goethe cares about most? Goethe wants to be seen as scientific above all else, and Eckermann wants the credit for some of the observations made in the work. In this very delicate moment for the Eckermann-Goethe couple, the disciple, the friend, finds a rather lovely strategy; he distances himself and says: you see, Goethe was a very protective mother toward his child, the *Farbenlehre* (the theory of colors). The economy of the narrative is quite effective: Eckermann remains the father, he can keep the paternity of the *Farbenlehre*, he doesn't have to eliminate Goethe, because Goethe has become the mother and therefore ineligible for a patricidal attack on the part of little doctor Eckermann. This maneuver is almost too Freudian, but Eckermann has found a way to protect

Goethe at the very moment when they are taking each other down. There is a kind of honesty and marvelous rhetoric at work in this episode, which has been noted by historians. At the same time, if this book, the *Conversations*, was to be conceived as the "best product of the German language" (Nietzsche) and the best text by Goethe himself, Eckermann had to be sacrificed. He has become the excrement—there are fairly explicit passages on this theme . . . there is a point where I call him "dreckermann" (*Dreck* means refuse, crud, smut). Moreover, this is one of the major themes in my research: I am interested in leftovers, in waste and remains in thought, literature, poetry, and in political manifestations like Valerie Solanas's, for example: hers is organized around the smeared figure of scum. Eckermann is the refuse that guarantees the purity and the propriety, the "properness," of Goethe's work and signature.

> In many respects, philosophy maintains a phobic relationship with "purity"; it wonders how it can avoid being "contaminated" (by opinion, doxa, and so on).

Yes, a sort of obsessional neurosis on philosophy's part tries to keep what is "proper" to itself intact within its own discursive realm. In a way, Derrida is the one who gave us the access code enabling us to decipher this obsession. I don't know whether he would have appreciated being designated as the one who opened up all the trashcans of literature for me, but in English "litter" means "trash," and that's the *littérature* I work on. Eckermann was thus the refuse and the price to be paid so that Goethe's glory could traverse the ages. As if Eckermann were a deformed, shameful creature that an entire culture had to hide. Even the professors who manage the institution that has been built from Goethe's writings have taken part in this great plot aimed at keeping Eckermann out of the way, out of our sight. It was Nietzsche who wrote: "'I am ugly' created the beautiful"—in other words, I-as-ugliness create beauty; the same thing can be said of the Goethe-Eckermann couple. I don't know whether or not everyone has an "Eckermann." I myself have "symptom-friends" who are not presentable but for whom I feel responsible and who themselves may feel responsible, from time to time, for my work. Levinas cites Dostoevsky in speaking about the relation that makes us responsible for others, those toward whom I assume an immense and nonreciprocal responsibility. However, unlike Dostoevsky, Levinas does not single out a few exceptional individuals, symptom-friends or disciples, or a pathos-based court made up of fanatics! At another level, while I owe a lot to Eckermann and his lessons on responsible passivity, he made me aware of something else as well. I think there are people who have or produce trash-bodies. In *Crack Wars,* my book on addiction and mania, I tried to work on the body of Emma Bovary as trash, a dependent body subject to a lethal addiction. I studied *Madame Bovary* as the first representation of a body under the effects of addiction. There are trash-bodies, symptom-bodies, beings-in-the-world that nevertheless inspire a certain grandeur, a certain magnificence. To what extent was Goethe dependent on precisely such a trash-body for the measure of his grandeur? In a sense, the price a culture pays for Goethe is Eckermann, who takes on the disavowed trash part of himself, does the dirty work and signs off on it, even though (and perhaps because) he had been persecuted, mistreated, and poorly remunerated by Goethe—and later by the Goethe Society in Weimar.

The relation between Goethe and Eckermann had many disturbing aspects. One of these emerged in the pathological relation between life and death that hounded each of them in different but ultimately compatible senses. Eckermann was in a way a living dead man. He had a brother presumed dead, that is, half dead half alive, with whom he secretly identified. His father was a desperately poor peddler who resorted to begging at times. Goethe himself is known for his mortal anxieties—he was haunted by the fear of death, and his commentators have often stressed the importance of his "death neurosis." He must have chosen that particular living dead man, the undead little Johann Peter Eckermann, to assure himself of something, and must have kept him close at hand to conjure away a mortal catastrophe. In the book I wrote about Goethe and Eckermann, I also tried to show the extent to which Eckermann was a rival of Goethe's son, and I almost came to believe him responsible for the son's death. Sometimes one has to turn philosophy into a crime story. August von Goethe went to Italy in Eckermann's company. He died there; we don't know how. One would have to investigate the Goethe family archives and go back through the chronology step by step. I've made the accusation, but I have no tangible, court-ready proof. I've read and seen that Eckermann was unquestionably jubilant over the death of Goethe's son; he knew and said that from then on he would be alone at the great man's side. There would be just the two of them, and he himself would occupy all the positions, father, mother, son; there would be no more rivals (Goethe's women apparently didn't count, and his many friends did not bother Eckermann much—they were filtered through another narcissistic loop). August's disappearance during the trip to Italy is very mysterious, and the way Eckermann deals with the son's death is fascinating. He ends the chapter in *Conversations* by noting that Goethe uttered not one word on the subject.

I want to stress that these *Conversations* make up a book of great honesty and unparalleled beauty. Eckermann is a creature of writing, a sort of rundown tramp whom Goethe kept close by his side because he needed his discreet presence and his eerie intelligence. The fact that Eckermann was deviant and schizoid and that he lived in a sort of self-made crypt full of birds is certainly intriguing, but this isn't the only direction in which we need to look. The essential point is that he remained undead, a remnant: no one wanted to bury him, no one wanted to see him, to acknowledge him, the phantom at Goethe's side. As Eckermann himself had become a symptom, no one questioned the need that the work had for Eckermann—for whom perhaps every work has a need. I try to use my imaging scanners to see the moments when the Eckermanns appear—inside us and a work or outside. Maybe my partiality to deviants offers an allegory for my relation to philosophy, where I often feel like a squatter or a homeless person, like someone in Werner Herzog's documentaries, for example, in the land of darkness and silence, as well as in the company of the category of particularly intense writers, artists, and thinkers. In any case, I don't necessarily take the major highways (even if, as in the case in point, a giant like Goethe is in question); I'm interested in the back roads, the little byways that aren't well marked. But the fate of the small, the perverse, the purportedly deformed isn't just a function of my own curiosity or predilections; everything always happens in back alleys, I believe in philosophy in action. When we think about Socrates, about his impasses, his vanishing points, the way he practiced dialectics in back alleys, it is easy to imagine that he was a punk, and I'm still very fond of punks, or certain schools of miscreants.

Eckermann was both a parasite and someone, or even something, who guaranteed the construction of a body of work as such. He was always at the master's side in a way that is invisible even today, and he remains the unacknowledged and imperceptible refuse—the debris—from that work. When I began to study the Goethe archives, I was very impressed to find at every step of the way the figure of that abandoned, forsaken being, literally persecuted by Goethe, and so substantially tied to his work. Inside what is called Goethe's biography, or thanatography—if one can speak of an "inside"—there was a "spot" called Eckermann, in the form of a dangerous and threatening insinuation or presence yet one that at the same time ensured the lasting quality of the work signed by Goethe. Eckermann was thus the "witness to the poet in his solitude," in Blanchot's formula. Goethe's survival depended on Eckerman's "will without will." Eckermann manifested a kind of implacable passivity. It is he who constitutes the remainder and the unavowable refuse of the great work that is established as "Goethe."

The interpretation of a work presupposes taking into account this continual displacement of boundaries—but especially Goethe's, for they never cease to shift in a mystifying fashion. What belongs to his signature and corpus? What should be rejected, removed to an outside, viewed as a supplement or fateful accident? Goethe's texts are also capable of programming accidents and diverting destinations. For example, many of Goethe's own texts are what I would call "killer texts," and in more than one respect.

# III

# Killer Texts

What do you call killer texts?

Freud's relation to Goethe, enormously rich and complex, marks the place of a weeping wound for the doctor and puts into place a kind of trauma center for his oeuvre. Freud rushes to Goethe on highly invested occasions, when things are going wrong or cannot be accounted for. Sometimes the emergency involves the birth of a new theory, the launch of a new concept that is about to burst out. Goethe's work was there from the start, as if meant to shake up the young Sigi. Freud feels invaded by it primally, as the force that brought about the sudden inception of his own work. He focuses on a text that he experiences as traumatizing, a text that gave birth to psycho-analysis, he claims. One day, when he was eighteen (and eighteen is a highly significant number for Freud, as for the Kabala, where it signifies "life"), he heard someone read one of Goethe's texts aloud. This reading disturbed him so greatly that psychoanalysis was violently inseminated in him then and there. I did some research to find out what this was all about. I discovered that the text Freud had associated with Goethe was not in fact by Goethe; it was a spurious text, a pretext. It so happens that the "real" text that had just appeared—and here we're edging into hermeneutic science fiction, it's one of my specialties—is a text that was very important for Goethe himself, the one in which he presented his discovery of a tiny bone in the jaw. Now the jaw was precisely where Freud's cancer was to be located. Is there a connection here? Or am I just overreading a medicohermeneutic dossier? Goethe had produced a remarkable scientific text, setting forth a discovery he was proud of, because until then that little bone, the intermaxillary or *Zwischenkiefer* now on display in Jena, had been invisible; nobody had found it or named it. Goethe liked to use his discovery to demonstrate, among other things, that nature does not tolerate voids, and erases discontinuities. Well, in just that spot in the jaw there had been a missing element, one that scientific studies had previously overlooked. So why was this text hidden behind the one that Freud remembered? What can be said about the substitution, which evokes an unspeakable trauma? In this sense, Freud and Goethe are both talking about binding and specifying a wounded body, mapping it out. Up to what point can a text provoke a pathological state in the very matter of what is called the body?

Is there such thing as a subtle body, as the alchemists supposed, or several bodily fields, as Asian philosophies propose, or only a fleshly body? Or is it the unconscious that begins to "ex-scribe" itself, as Jean-Luc Nancy would say, in this place of the body where the still latent trauma finds itself awakened at the encounter with the text? Psychoanalysis was the first to bring explicitly to light the question of the destination of each word in the symptom-body. On the basis of his reading of Freud's Rat Man study, Lacan says that every word is itself a body that inserts itself into the body. Every time the analyst speaks, must we not ask how the word takes on body? Where does the analyst's interpretation arrive, if it arrives at all? In "The Rat Man," there is a remarkable moment when Freud shows that the subject could not utter "the thing"—the fantasy of a rat invasion; it was too horrifying for him. So Freud helped him out: "into his anus, I helped him out," he writes. The patient had Freud's words inseminated in him through his anus—one might think here of Lou Salomé's work on anal zones and the transitioning of sexual markings. Edward Glover also wrote a remarkable essay on the problem, stressing the efficacity of this or, rather, *any* imprecise interpretation. It's very important for the analyst to be capable of doctoring a symptom, even violently, and it doesn't necessarily have to be real or testable.

I often wonder about the incorporation of language into the body. Since Freud's day, it has been legitimate to ask oneself how and in what site certain statements arrive, where they are posited and deposited. . . . I say this so I can send Goethe back to his "killer texts." Not only did these mark the place where Freud was going to suffer, but Freud himself found a screen-text, as it were, to mark the origin of the trauma. By no means merely a cipher for a classical work, "Goethe" remains a traumatic event for all of us, in this sense, in the history of the German language. *The Sorrows of Young Werther* was a text that assisted in the birth of modern literature: it set off a form of hysterical mimicry as soon as it appeared. It was not only fashionable to dress like Werther; it was also fashionable to commit suicide. Well, not entirely . . . Goethe backed off on implementing his own destruction, after all! Moreover, the question comes up over and over, from Kleist to Blanchot: how did Goethe survive his own suicidal drive? *Werther* was a text that programmed suicides, even right here in the Seine. Shortly after *Werther's* arrival in 1774, several drowning victims were found with Goethe's text in their pockets. This was a scenography of suicide by insemination, with the book as the program. Thematically, *Werther* gave Goethe the means to invent the idea of *Krankheit zum Tode,* sickness unto death, which interested Kierkegaard and others. It was the first time in modernity, I think, that someone had conceptualized the sovereignty of the subject to the last outpost of self-determination as including the right to kill oneself. In the process, Goethe took the question of suicide away from the precincts of morality and religion.

*Werther* was initially published anonymously. Denounced and forbidden from the outset, it was already trafficked as an illicit, clandestine drug. Not only were there discursive moments in the book that supported one's right to put an end to one's life, but *Werther* was in a sense the first stealth bomber: the book really caused a lot of damage in its wake, and this result was to a large degree calculated, programmed. The effects of "killer texts" aren't limited to the field of literary or philosophical criticism; they're infinitely more corrosive.

Did *Werther* have a real posterity? Or was this book rather just a moment in history that announced a new era, a different relation to the world?

It seems to me that the book functioned like a virus, that is, by poisoning and programming disasters that continued to mimic the text. Napoleon is said to have read it six to eight times! He had taken it with him to the campaign in Egypt; later, when he met Goethe, he made the famous remark: "Voilà un homme" (here's a true man). Goethe complained to Eckermann that Napoleon had reproached him for *Werther's* exaltation of suicide and held him responsible for mass deaths. Napoleon thought that his own impact on history was less catastrophic than Goethe's! He even indicated that there was a sort of *militerary* strategy in the text that acted along subterranean pathways, whereas he himself, Napoleon, as a "killer text," was more or less readable! Perhaps *Werther* worked like a vaccine, poisoning first so as to "cure" afterward.

Then things calmed down. As I see it, Goethe created a poison that has had its moments of latency and its moments of uncontrollable emergence. As a text, *The Sorrows of Young Werther* (and, semantically, *Werther* means "value," even "surplus value") is really a machine for producing and destroying values; this no doubt enchanted Nietzsche, even though *Werther* falls on the side of sickness. Still, the work was anti- or un-Christian on many of its points, especially the ending, so it may have evaded the charge of pessimism, fatigue, or general creepiness—qualities to which Nietzsche was sensitive. Let us not forget that for Nietzsche there are also good illnesses and the matter or promise of convalescence, which he underscores for instance at the conclusion of *Zarathustra*. We need to think the Nietzschean promise from the perspective he opens on the ailing being. Goethe, for his part, wielded spiritual illness in a decisive way. As text and machine, Goethe sowed the seeds of a virus against Enlightenment notions of progress. Of course, we would have to try to answer the question "Was ist Aufklärung?"—what is enlightenment?—to see what this unique meeting between literature and philosophy signifies. With *Werther,* Goethe was able to insinuate a critique into blockbuster Enlightenment tenets despite the absolutely nonreciprocal coupling of literature and philosophy. By way of *Werther,* though by other routes as well, his work has scattered obstacles along the path of that meeting, obstacles to which the philosophers have tried to respond, positively or negatively, explicitly or covertly. We can understand why Freud was swayed and even subjugated by Goethe, for Goethe is one of the few who maintained that there is a weakness, a fissure in the psyche and particularly in the possibility of mourning that cannot be resolved, not even by the bright lights of the Enlightenment. In *Werther* there is something like a mourning disorder played out and an inclination toward what is called melancholy. Goethe did not restrict the motif of illness to a theoretically manageable condition or to a recognizable set of consequences. Something that Goethe calls a "sickness" operates like a pathology, something beyond all pleasure that, during the Enlightenment, navigates among the mores, the historical movements, and the question of *Bildung*—of education and upbringing. A spot of incurable melancholy that cannot be educated out of you, a path or pathology that already points beyond the pleasure principle.

It was a psychic sickness that spread against the current and was not embraced by philosophy. In Kant's storehouse one found lists of illnesses, intoxications, aberrations, but here we are talking about something else. Because what interested Goethe was not only some sort of speculative malady. Goethe launched *Werther* right in the middle of the Enlightenment. He gave the floor to someone who could not be saved, a hopeless case par excellence, and that existential impossibility of being saved shocked and also satisfied the world. *Werther* attracted a world of unbearably close readers. We really have to raise the question of close reading, texts "closely read" as one would say "closely guarded"—or those that trigger a "close call." Heidegger put it differently when he said that certain texts or statements can destroy you or undermine you for years, or for centuries. I would love to see someone armed by *Werther* and by Goethe address Kant, the Enlightenment, the complex and still latent itineraries of rationalism, and call all this into question, cause it some more trouble. There's something here that has not found an echo in our works of philosophy.

# IV

# Ambivalent Stances
## Philosophy in Anger and Meditation

You're a thinker who's always searching. How do the philosophical "attacks of nerves" you've talked about get inscribed in your own work?

To tell the truth, what lies behind my acute sensibility for deviant structures, mutations, as well as marginal blips and textual irritation, is what Walter Benjamin called the "rights of nerves." He articulated this with regard to Karl Kraus against hermeneutics. I refer to this nervous nub because scholars sometimes have to justify themselves and make it clear why they have chosen a particular area to study, why they have come up with a distinctly circumscribed argument; that's when I invoke the right to nerves. One's approach to problem areas is often motored by exasperation and not at all by enchantment or the ideology of "have a nice text." My textual decisions often point up issues related to an indefinitely postponed justice, to indignities that burn me up and are well stated or surprisingly elided by philosophical and other texts. Certain things unhinge, attack, terrorize, enrage, and for me certain more-or-less invasive philosophemes, common or undetected, provide an adequate interpretative guide—they get me going.

Nerves are located somewhere between the soma, the psyche, and thought. Heidegger, for example, can be said to have taken sedatives all his life. He even injected Nietzsche with sedatives; he tried to calm down the Nietzschean corpus, its historical agitation and often out-of-control cries. However, he was despite it all an understanding and altogether brilliant diagnostician, and Nietzsche's work possibly needed to be calmed in order to make it through some considerable blockades, some of which still exist. In Germany, Nietzsche often enough remains guilty by association, and a left-wing Nietzschean probe still seems improbable. But let us stick with the impetus to thought provided by frazzled nerves. Heidegger asserted that certain thinkers needed to scream. Nietzsche, who was according to Heidegger the most timid of philosophers, the gentlest, the least ballistic, if one may say so (and this isn't always the case), needed to *scream*. He writes and screams. So we too could try to evaluate writers' *Schreiben/Schrei* or *écrit/crit*—their writings and screams—according to the volume of their exasperation, the way they steam up and fog the writing space (there are fog banks in Nietzsche). Works and their philosophical conductors are in various states of agitation and react differently to the shocks that they register. There are those who fall asleep while driving their ideas and those who are in a punctual state of rage, for the most part more or less concealed. The approach that tries to mark this (would you call it mood, *Grundstimmung*, tone, inflection, attitude or *Einstellung*, fictive stance, narrative pout, etc.?— it's hard to say) would be difficult according to existing norms to justify or circumscribe with precision, but at the same time pretty convincing, I think, especially if a text emerges from a palpable kind of neglect or rather from chronic fatigue, an exhaustion of being, a disposition of crankiness. The stress of a text can also be measured in terms of its sense of depletion, its reactivity or resentful intonations. All of this, I know, is a matter of interpretation, but one should not hold back or restrict the scope of the probe. To come back to Nietzsche, he put his body on the line, and it was also he who tried to measure the quality of a thought or a text by the degree of excitation or prostration experienced by the body. Goethe, with his multiple and interminable attacks of nerves, Goethe, as a weapon, was a permanent threat lodged in the insomnias and dreams of almost every *Dasein* in the German language.

> Can we hear these exasperations in the texts, or are there overpowering effects of effacement?

That's a very good question, and we have to ask with what apparatus one going to measure the effects of overstimulation or not enough tremor—the whole range of excitability—because there is not really any place or taxonomy that would allow us to read some registers of effacement or exasperation with much confidence. Even if a text vomits (Nietzsche was an exemplary "vomiter"), even if it overturns dialectics, it sometimes points toward something else that's happening to it or to an entire referential system; it has a destination beyond its own anger alone. It's like the birth of the stars: it may be that, as soon as one perceives the attack of nerves, its drama has already taken place and been eliminated, and that there is a huge lag between the signal's reception and its origin. The text will have calmed down in the interim, and it may even be dead, as it were.

There are texts that are allergic to their purported object, exasperated, hysterical, phobic, and one cannot perceive this at the level of thematization alone; this is really what is hardest to register, you need very subtle detectors to capture the signals. We hear exasperation in Thomas Bernhardt's work at once in the themes he deals with, in the different levels of rhetoric he uses, and even in his syntax, for example when he uses and abuses anacoluthons—that is, when he provokes ruptures within what he is expressing.

In this connection, I've allowed myself to write about an indefensible text by Valerie Solanas, the woman Norman Mailer called the "Robespierre of feminism." She ended up unforgivably shooting Andy Warhol and writing the *SCUM Manifesto*. She belongs to the category of female figures that have existed since Medea and Antigone, legendary killer women who suddenly snap, shooting off their mouths and any other handy weapons—often ID'd as lesbos, sados, and so on—like the one portrayed in the film *Monster* (2003). There are a lot of texts by exasperated women, or by men who pass into and as them, but this doesn't necessarily mean much or stagnate around thematically stable gender issues in that there has always been an element of becoming-woman or becoming-minority in the act of writing. And that act implicates those who claim to be men as well as those who sign their works as women. In Valerie Solanas's text, there may be some typically American elements, that is, Solanas opens up the plight of revolutionary figures who have no disciples, so to speak, who are all alone and are consumed by a sort of psychotically pitched solitude. There are those who carry out their revolution with a typewriter, and then it passes. Friedrich Kittler, the German techno-critic, reminds us that the Remington typewriter and the machine gun were produced by the same company, and that in a certain way they make the same sound and share a similar history. No one would want to generalize Valerie's positions, and I try very carefully to track her practices and stances in my work on her explosive yields. Nonetheless, she is a writer to the core, even in the most banal sense of what it means to pound out a text, to close oneself off and to duck into often-dangerous bouts of seclusion in order to get it done. We have a tendency to forget that writing is manual labor: a writer has to be pretty sturdy and pretty angry to bring it off.

Anger is in some sense the site of thought. One can be in states other than anger, but if there is no anger I don't see how one can think.

25

Restoring anger to thinking constitutes a highly unusual move, I must say. Let's reflect on this move, noting that Heidegger may well take a stand against polemics, without trying to be polemical—and he makes us sensitive to the war (*polemos*) that polemics implies, which he says has little to do with thinking. He does not necessarily brush aside anger when cordoning off polemics. Though he would shudder and get angry with us if we were to start psychologizing here. So let us consider for future reflection the place or mood of anger, an area from which philosophers have certainly stepped away in their writings. Even Freud, as Lacan has reminded us, has no place for anger. Writing certainly requires stamina, and it may be fueled by some modality of anger, a natural fossil fuel for getting thoughts down on paper or up on the screen. I am not an angry person, but I may have centuries of revenge coiled up in me; I am often clenched, but up to now I have read that as despair rather than anger—are these always dissociable, I wonder? There is also a form of repetition in the face of impotence when someone begins to write, like the one boxers experience. When I was writing my thesis, impelled by the paranoia that I needed to feel in order to pump up and get myself to write, I remember that I often compared myself ego-ideally to Muhammad Ali, because I had the impression I was boxing the text. I grabbed hold of it and fought. For me, boxing and dancing are the same gestures, as they are for Ali, the same ones Nietzsche instructs us or entices us to perform (especially when you're on the wrong end of trying to rope a dope).

> I'm going to make a big leap here. In the progression of your thought, how do you move from this front of refusal, or reflection on hostile territories, to Buddhism, to meditation? Are these the two facets of a single reality, or on the contrary is this a very paradoxical evolution of your personality?

I'm going to tell you something, even though it makes me wince. One day, when I was still young, an intellectual teenager, I went to a philosophy colloquium in Heidelberg. During a break, I went for a walk with Hans Georg Gadamer, "Mr. Hermeneutics," whom I knew from two other colloquia. He was marvelous, and already old, he'd been old for fifty years. We drank a lot together, we emptied three bottles of wine, and at the time I myself was something of a rogue, a young punk critical philosopher and litcrit type. The *Herren Professoren,* the serious colleagues and students around him, the well-known and well-established Heideggerians, gave me the impression that they couldn't stand me (I admit that I get that sort of impression often, even very often). They wondered what a young Jewish woman—and punked out to boot!—was doing there. In the evening, I would sit next to Gadamer, and we were really I thought scandalous, at least according to a certain idea about how one is supposed to behave. We said impossible things, we almost danced on the tables, and the disciples didn't dare say anything. One morning when I went walking with him (we were still sober), Gadamer asked me why I hadn't gone back to Germany, since my parents were German Jews. He didn't realize what he was saying, I thought to myself, "Why did he ask me that question?" as if there had not been an absolute interruption—the most serious of breaks, the Shoah—in History. He told me that I was essentially German, that I ought to go back. This identification startled me. I answered that it wasn't possible, it was even almost impossible to spend time there, I somatized, I was nauseous, so "to go back" . . . It was unthinkable. We kept on walking, and he said: "You know, Avital, to be a real thinker one day, you have to find a master. There is no other way, no other possible route. You have to attach yourself to a master and do the painful work of apprenticeship. To go on otherwise is an illusion, and it isn't real philosophic work." I was twenty-five at the time, I was revolted by all known forms of authority, and he was telling me to go look for a master! I almost heard fascist overtones in what he was saying . . . For my part, I thought one had to be indecent, that it was better to go striding along the blackened pathways of philosophy and history and grubbing around in forbidden sites than to look for a model and turn oneself into some sort of bonsai disciple! But I was both horrified and fascinated by what he had said to me, and as I'm an obsessional neurotic, let me admit this right away, his words quickly became an injunction. I had no choice—that's what *Zwangsneurose* means, that you are *compelled, forced* to do it; OK, also that you are neurotic. I had to find a master, I had to submit to others—or at least pretend to submit. At the same time, the battle raged internally. If grappling with history was now a matter of wandering about in libraries and archives, I wanted to decide for myself, with phantom-friends at my side and a reliable transcendental switchboard that directed my calls. What would I do with a living in-your-face dictator/director telling me what to think—someone I would maybe have to relate to like a real human being, probably a narcissist? I didn't know if Hans G. Gadamer, when he laid down the law of true philosophic learning, was going to offer himself as a master. In any case, I rebelled, I shot back that what he was proposing was so intolerable, so authoritarian . . . I told him that I wasn't ready and that I didn't give a damn about the authority of masters. At home they had wanted to control me and I had protested, I had seceded, and I was certainly not about to become the puny disciple of anybody at all! I was furious, but affected, because Gadamer's words became law for me. I accepted his verdict and eventually I joined up. I did my training in the "Derrida camp." I went toward Derrida to make myself suffer and to train myself the way one signs up for the worst military service imaginable. I signed up for the philosophical marine boot camp because I had to have at least that much. Besides, becoming "Derridean" was comparable, at the time, to the situation of the early Christians. We were thrown into the pit with the lions, before the institutional gladiators, and I really did suffer a lot. At the beginning, I came to France with the idea of doing my "internship," and I have to say that when I went back to the States, after two years of intensive work and training, I found myself pretty much alone in the arena, probably because of the kinds of places I ended up temping as a lecturer or assistant professor. I was fired twice from universities where I was teaching.

When I was fired from the University of Virginia, it was not only as a Derridean (there were others who invoked Derrida, but they weren't part of my fairly solitary circle and didn't deal me in), but also because I came from the Germanist world, having studied German and Continental writings and thought in depth, and the others didn't have that literary baggage. I had been hired, I was told, because they found me exotic, and because I was venturing onto still-unexplored ground. But they didn't trust me, for the same reasons. I am sure that this sort of suspicious surveillance was practiced with respect to Derrida, and Foucault, and Deleuze—with respect to every philosophical prophet, really—and thus also with respect to those who committed themselves to work alongside them. I hope I'm not giving the impression that I'm a certified visionary, but as soon as someone has a little magnetism with students, as soon as the "children" start to listen, one sets out on the road to crucifixion.

Socrates was accused of corrupting the young . . .

And let's not forget that in telling philosophical stories I find myself trapped by a hyperbolic, mythifying rhetoric. For philosophy has to be made captivating, especially in America. You have to turn it into a detective story—which means that philosophy has always been a Hitchcock movie, and Hitchcock, as everyone knows, like Columbo, has always been a philosopher. It is true that my classes were crowded. My way of teaching is very committed: I prepare the way boxers prepare for a match, with the same urgency, tension, revolt. This brings us back to the question of Zen and the philosophical wisdom that isn't limited to spiritual asceticism, to noncorporeal thinking, and that finally isn't really so "wise." There has always been a form of "athleticism" in philosophy that we tend to forget about today, so

28

we can reduce the critical pursuit to a bookish, academic discipline. Thinking has been dissociated from exercise and physical force, and yet force is necessary to be a philosopher. Heidegger took a veritable—OK, maybe it was figural, but not solely figural—leap. Certain philosophers leap, others swim. We examine the leaps and we reflect on what leaping is in Heidegger's work. The Platonists used to organize wrestling tournaments, Olympiads. At the time, sports, the display of athleticism, weren't divorced from philosophy. I mentioned Muhammad Ali earlier, because I consider him a hero in the same way that Socrates was a hero in his fight against the sophists. Ali insisted on the fact that he was black, that he was a dancer, a thinker in training. In philosophy there is a sports rhetoric that is, for whatever overdetermined reason, too often overlooked. For example, in Rousseau's thought, *Les rêveries du promeneur solitaire* describes a veritable decathlon. We witness trials of all sorts, self-testing sprints, the fierce disposition of the competitive drive that consists in overcoming and positing, walking and sprinting. A lot of floating, too.

Is philosophy an athletic trial? I actually think so. Let's look back at the history of academic knowledge and how it was constructed: when was physical education adopted by universities in Germany and America as just as essential a component as laboratory experiments, especially in America? Another reason given for firing me at UVa was that I went to the gym on a regular basis: my colleagues were shocked by this—it didn't correspond to their image of an academic woman! At the time, it was simply unacceptable. I began to work out when I was a student at Princeton. I was the only woman lifting weights and exercising like that, and I remember that, two years later, when two other women showed up in the gym to do some very hard work, the trainer said: "Oh no, there aren't any women here," whereas in fact I was there. I was afraid, at the beginning, but I quickly realized that the men who work out in these weight rooms are so narcissistic that they don't see anything but themselves in the mirror. They don't look at the women; in the mirror they only see a little muscle that's just popping up, and they're delighted. No one was interested in me there, even though at the time I have to say I was pretty well put together. At the university I wasn't obsessive about physical exercise, but it was part of my daily discipline; without it I got sick, and I had to be strong. If I hadn't worked out, I would have had to start seeing doctors. Exercising was also a way of keeping anxiety at bay. So, in Virginia, one of their arguments, beyond the fact that I did what would soon become known as French theory, was the fact that I went to the gym as if I were a guy. That didn't stop me from going, but today it's no longer a deal-breaker to work out, or to work your way out of certain thought-sports, as Musil says. I am not unaware of the mechanicity or despair of staying in place. One might say that my philosophic trajectory has been constituted by a sort of stationary mobility. The Zen tradition includes, besides a certain skill for stillness, the arts of war, the martial arts. These entail an incredible discipline, a relation to a master whom one never surpasses. They don't involve any recognizable economy of parricide—that's what interests me in Zen. In the Western traditions, this frenzy of *Überwindung* is perceptible everywhere, the will to rise above oneself, the self-competing delirium of outdoing oneself as well as the revered other, whereas the cohabitation of modesty and the possibility of affirming oneself without one's "self" is the distinguishing feature of the Oriental traditions. I practice the humble warrior pose.

Ultimately, you've always insisted on this close relation between body and mind; the work of the body cannot be detached from that of the mind . . .

This has come about involuntarily; it probably betrays a trace of feminism, or of an anticipatory postfeminism. First of all, taking care of my body by following programs or doing exercises allowed me to progress, or at least to hold onto the illusion that something—my own body—was occasionally under my own control. I didn't get to "play" sports—there weren't many ladies' dream teams in my day, but only solitary drills. In certain respects, getting the body into good athletic shape reflects and reproduces the efforts of thought, whereas the two processes seem to be antithetical. I hope I don't sound like Leni Riefenstahl! Jacques Derrida, too, in his early days, would have liked to be a soccer player. He even wanted to play for a real national team! As for me, I've provoked minor disgraces without meaning to. Once, for example, the comprehensive examinations were scheduled for a day when I knew I'd have my period. Well, my period was always painful, and it kept me from being in possession of all my faculties, so to speak— which probably means that that was my most authentic state, closest to the ground of my finitude. In any case, it was a matter of three days during which life was really hard for me and I suffered a lot. In all innocence, but at the same time gathering all my courage, because I was one of the only women in my class at Princeton, I went to see the department chair who supervised the examinations and asked him: "Can the dates of my exam be changed? They're completely arbitrary, anyway." He answered that it was out of the question, but he wanted to know why I had made the request. "For medical reasons," I answered. "And how do you already know, two months ahead of time, that you'll be unable to sit your exams for medical reasons?" he retorted. I said I had a calendar and that I knew my own body pretty well. He then responded that he did not accept such reasons and that it was infamy to make such a request (that's how they talked at Princeton, whether they came from the Deep South or Brooklyn, all covered over with pseudo-Oxfordian accents and matching diction). But since I was probably the only woman in his department who was not completely self-effacing and intimidated, he was distrustful and nevertheless went on to ask: "May I know what these medical reasons are?" I opened my calendar where I had noted the dates of my period and showed that it would fall on those dates. He turned beet red and threw me out. He thought that I was being gratuitously provocative, that it was monstrous to have dared speak to him about my . . . He couldn't even say the word. I remember telling a colleague about it later. "But you're not going to organize your life around your period, are you?" he asked, astonished. "But I am!" I answered. "On those days, I feel extremely anxious and everything becomes impossible; I'm in despair. At least I'm aware of this, even if I'm ambushed by it every time."

Much later, when I was teaching at Berkeley, I had a young man as my assistant, and I wasn't aware that he too was keeping a calendar. One day I went into my office and blasted him with an endless string of complaints. He calmly looked at the calendar and remarked that we were in the fateful days, so he closed his books and said he'd come back in three days. I was stunned! But I was grateful to him. All right, Berkeley was "politically correct," but I hadn't suspected that it was part of my assistant's job to know at what point it was best to avoid me! Zen—meditation—is also part of my trajectory, and no doubt revolt, too. Derrida had pointed out to me that, for him, meditation had more to do with Descartes than with the Zen masters. And yet, especially in the last stages of his illness, when he was consumed by pain, he opened up to other approaches, and even, with me, to meditation. In any event, meditation isn't the adversary of work but the precondition for it, for carrying it to provisional completion. I believe that meditation belongs to a discipline of thought, that it's indispensable to the exercise of thought, just as it's indispensable to the creation of a necessary void.

An indispensable airlock for nonthought, as it were?

The emptying that is created, called forth, by meditation is perhaps what Heidegger would have called *Gelassenheit,* lassitude, an "inner" space that is at once controlled and not mastered, not masterable. There are obviously mediations and adaptations in the Western tradition, even in its appropriation of Zen. In the Zen tradition, violence is not proscribed, on the contrary. Some masters compliment their students by striking them. Violence marks certain Zen practices; even meditation can't be opposed to violence. If one is in a sitting position for hours, one has to maintain correct posture; this is a form of violence exercised against the body, against the relaxed attitude that is purportedly more natural to the body. One can't simply apply to that tradition the categories and axioms that are familiar to us. In the act of "creating the void" there arise moments when traces of thoughts become enigmatic, almost unreadable. We encounter these paradoxes in certain passages of Nietzsche, Blanchot, and the later Heidegger. What interests me in Zen, from the standpoint of my own work, is the destiny of what is called the koan, this koan being a sort of trial or test, a vibrant puzzle. At the end of *Was heisst Denken?* (*What Is Called Thinking?*), the idea of the trial is posited in a quite radical way. The French translation of this text is problematic, moreover, because the *on* of *Qu'appelle-t-on penser?* doesn't show up in the German title. Now, in Heidegger's work, as you know, the equivalent for the French *on, das Man* (conventionally rendered in English as "the They"), is anything but neutral, despite appearances. In the English title, as in the German, there is no subject, nor any substitute for the subjectivities that flourish in our day. The French have dragged in the *on* to domesticate or neutralize this sort of question. Or else it hasn't been given any thought, whether called for or uncalled for.

And for you, this question is something like a koan?

Yes. At the end of *Was heisst Denken?* Heidegger writes: now we're going to shed everything to come back to Aristotle, you're going to study Aristotle for ten years. Among other effects, this pronouncement resembles that of the koan master: one lives with one's koan, it remains a question that is sometimes tested throughout one's whole existence. In the first place, every question falls back in on itself: it is not in fact just a question, but rather a question about questions—it calls all questioning into question. We should ask ourselves what philosophy would be without questions. Could we still philosophize? This is the question the koan puts to us, because it's a question without question, not very far from Blanchot's "relation without relation." To go back to the theme we've been pursuing up to now, it seems to me that the bodies of philosophers and thinkers are often codified like bodies lacking envelopes: flayed neurasthenics, hyperreactive bodies that betray, if I dare say so, a certain disposition for thought, suicide, morbidity, the attraction of extremes. Not always. Obviously, Nietzsche was the first to have signed his writings with his body. Since then, in the exercise of thought there are forms of limit-states of the body; dissociation is no longer strictly possible. Now, a certain critical thought in the West has always sought to disconnect the uncontaminable site of thought from the body from which thought emanates. Think Socrates: famously ugly, shriveled, and withered as he spoke the living logos.

We are in an era that stigmatizes this distrust of unfashionable or untimely reactions (in the sense of Nietzsche's unfashionable observations, his Untimely Meditations); I'll call it a war between the limit-states of the body and those of the soul. Today what is required is a healthy, calm, docile body. Everything that is plunged into anxiety must be absolutely domesticated and restored to calm by all available means.

Yes, there is a marked intolerance concerning the uncontrolled body, the irritation it can provoke. Nevertheless, there is a relation to the body (if there is *a* body) that is a bit more complicated than that as well, even if it is somewhat sublimated, as for example in some of the exquisite passages of Levinas. He has some fine, well-known pages on the caress: what he describes there is rather the opposite of the agitation we have been talking about. Jean-Luc Nancy, recently, and Derrida, before his passing, had written, and had written to each other, about touch and tactility, without becoming agitated, it seems to me. Moreover, they themselves are quite gentle.

I've written a good deal about the incommensurable encounter between the texts of Zen and the philosophical texts we're familiar with. Even in Nietzsche, there is a sort of war of nerves, he pushes off what he relates to Christian pessimism or nihilism onto Oriental thinkers. I don't know whether one can still speak of "Oriental thinkers" in France, but in America this is not "politically correct"; one has to say "Asian." I don't see why this would be better, but in English, I've just committed a linguistic crime—but for now let's not go into the ethics of ethnicity!

In the part of the Zen tradition that attracts me, one finds differing and differentiated trajectories, schools, and topoi, but what is at stake is almost always a matter of knowing how to respond to hostile forces, situations, and conditions. There is the practice of tai chi, which allows one to think about the fundamental structures of the displacement of forces and meanings, no matter how subtle. For example, in tai chi, instead of facing the other person, instead of entering into direct opposition with hostile forces, the idea is to shift one's position so that the hostile force dissipates on its own—this is another syntax of action, which also suspends the presumed difference between activity and passivity on which part of Nietzsche's work rests, as Rousseau already knew. Rousseau was badly interpreted by Schiller, as Paul de Man pointed out, for *far niente*, passivity, presupposes great efforts of ingathering; even in Rousseau's most passive moments, he is exerting himself and constructing nothing less than the modern subject, a subject founded on still waters. Certain moments in the fifth reverie resonate astonishingly with some Zen sketches, when the narrator tries to pin down a present that can only be sensed, and Rousseau himself makes a Zen gesture by withdrawing—he purposefully retreats to the shade, where the oppressive forces have been slightly repositioned. The way Rousseau recedes from the burning excess of the sun becomes an important motif for Hölderlin's understanding of history. Heidegger then develops his thought of the *Entzug*, withdrawal, building on this lineage of recession.

In Rousseau and Hölderlin there is already movement here that consists in meeting lethal force, but with different strategies that have been somewhat forgotten or that can be reread from an Eastern standpoint. At the same time, even when the koan and Rousseau's reveries prove capable of disclosure, truth is not what is at stake. There is no crucial ideology that could be reduced to a goal, a result. It is not a question of having won something, or of having known how to—or even having been able to—sketch out an alias, some absolute knowledge. The efforts and difficulties are the same, but they do not seek to delimit themselves by a kind of closure; the relation to the limit is not the same. Nor is it a question of the Western logos rushing to find its limits in order to come to an end at last, to conclude. The frenzied haste to conclude is not at work in Western thought alone; it can also be seen corrupting, as it were, a whole gamut of political actions.

I try to read the two Gulf wars, for example, as impelled by the West's desire to get things over with as quickly as possible, by the impatience, the frenetic hurry to conclude that, for Flaubert, fell under the definition of stupidity. Logos rushes us—to judgment, to action, to conclusion and shutdown. All sorts of distinctions, historical expanses, and tensional qualities snap or are collapsed as a result. In order to launch this war against Saddam Hussein, which was to become a drawn-out war against Iraq, the instigators needed on the one hand to resuscitate Hitler symbolically, and on the other hand to represent the war as a crusade that had to be brought to a successful conclusion. There is obviously no tolerance here for ambiguity, for the hesitation that is linked to an avowed lack of knowledge, for the anxiety of unreadability.

Following a path traced largely by Jean-Luc Nancy, I have tried to show that contemporary crusades are led by the impatience of the logos which seeks to conclude, to come quickly to an end, and thus to dominate the adversary. Today we go to war and we say at the outset: "There, it's almost over," and we have professed to believe, if only for a moment, a long one,

34

that over there, in Iraq, there will be a democracy "like ours," with all the irony that implies. The other aspect that interests me in this process, starting from my own studies of Zen and Buddhism, bears on what I have called the "test drive," the nearly unquenchable need to test oneself. Nietzsche is the one who discovered, let's say, our *experimental disposition,* our need to test ourselves, but according to a structure that leads to failure nearly every time. That "nearly" keeps us hanging in there, betting on the exception that testing holds open.

Failure in order to be able to pursue this same logic?

I wonder to what extent the koan corresponds to the "test" as we define it in the West. In other words, does the koan correspond to our idea of the test, or does it lie rather beyond the test? Is it another type of trial without result? Because in Zen there are many stories of people who have lived with their koan, people to whom their masters have said, when they presented a response: no, that's not it. And yet that does not invalidate their relation to the koan, to the "progress" of their "research," which is empty but as demanding as any that comes from a culture of dossiers and material proofs. In both instances, we're dealing with a culture of the permanently hypothetical.

How would you define a koan?

Perhaps, to begin with, as an enigma, a puzzle, that is given to someone for safekeeping. And that requires the recipient both to answer to it and to let it go. A koan is an enigma with which one has to contend, almost existentially but without the ontological question mark. What interests me also in this tradition are the cultivated rough edges on which the texts on the ten thousand and one doubts are based. Certain scenes really trigger nervous breakdowns. Cohabitation with a koan must also provoke a crisis, an experience at the limit of conceivable tolerance on the part of body and mind. Doubts have to invade the one who has agreed to live with this koan, for the riddle is never certain to be resolved. The koan is your intimate persecutor.

Someone told me a story in India that makes me think of your koans. It's the story of a man who had come to see a master for a teaching. The master gave him a riddle to solve. The man came back two or three years later and said: This is how far I've gotten: I've thought of this and that, I've found this and that . . . The master says to him: "All that is very well," and takes him for a walk along the river bank. There, he asks him to go into the water, and suddenly he grabs the man and holds his head under water to the point of near-drowning. Then he asks him: "Now you are going to reflect for nine more years with as much energy as you devoted to trying to breathe, and afterward you come back and see me." He comes back nine years later and announces: "Here I am, master, I have reached the limit of my strength, I have changed." The master replies: "But that's very good. Well, now, for nine years, you forget it." Then the other man went away, despairing. He came back nine years later, but he arrived two days after the master's death. He saw a disciple who had been close to the master, a child, and he said to him: "I am in despair, all that for nothing, and I was so sure I was on the verge of finding . . ." And these were the child's words: "Perhaps you had found it from the beginning, it was the path . . . the path you followed to come see him, the trajectory you didn't even see, preoccupied as you were with getting there on time."

Some passages in Heidegger resemble koans, resonating with *Off the Beaten Track* (*Holzwege*); these are aspects of the method, that is, of the path (*methodos*) that must be traveled for thought actually to occur—and this path is in no way constituted by the weight of knowledge or by some notion of scientific method. That is why I am drawn to questions of athleticism/inathleticism, because for a long time people have been walking in the company of Nietzsche and Heidegger while writing, erasing, tracing, experiencing a certain relation to time that is very important in all these displacements.

Even so, are there any zones of possible intersection between the experience offered by the reading of certain philosophical texts and the experience of a Japanese koan?

That is one of the questions I raise in my most recent book, *The Test Drive*, in which I wonder whether one can imagine a *Dasein*, a being-in-the-world, without a test, in other words, a relation to existence without testing. If I raise the question based on a reading of Nietzsche, I see clearly that the test, or the trial, provokes, among other things, a displacement of the question of truth. I'm trying to discern our relation to truth. Here again we have to go back to the Greeks. We can't question our relation to trials or to truth without turning to the Greek texts. In Greece, there was the notion of *basanos*, which means trial, both as torture and as test. There are fascinating texts on this subject, in Aristotle, for example. He reminds us that people used to torture slaves to obtain the truth. In a judgment, to know the truth about the events, one was supposed to torture the witness, even if he was prepared to sing like a canary. Truth depended on torture.

I work this into the contemporary inclination in some sectors of our government toward torture—the justification for torture as an instrument of telling what you know has a very clear metaphysical basis and relies on inherited economies tying up truth and subject.

In French they say: "Put to the question"...

... and because the masters couldn't be tortured, the slaves had to be put to the question, thus becoming, somewhat like Eckermann, as it were, the masters' truth and body. Attached to and detachable from the master who could tell the truth. Even Aristophanes, who made fun of it to some extent, supported this form of torture witnessing. Not until Aristotle did a philosopher rise up against that practice by showing that one might say anything at all under torture, so truth could not necessarily be obtained that way. This was new and bizarre for the Ancients. What I zoom in on is the forgotten, repressed logic of torture that comes back in what I call the *test drive,* the passion for trials, and persists underground in the need to put oneself as well as the enemy other (sometimes hard to tell apart) to the test and the question. In Zen thought (especially in the test of the koan), torture is presented as a relation to a truth that is presented differently. I also try, in that study, to conceptualize the koan in relation to Perceval and the quest for the Holy Grail, because this represents the conjunction of a difficult question and an original quest. Perceval had to ask a question from the realm of compassion; he faced a king who was suffering, but he didn't know how to ask the question, and then this inquiry and this quest—that is, the trial to which he was subjected—began. Can we read these traditions of the question and the trial together, without suspending the differences, or not? What are we looking for? Does the path itself contain the answer? According to Heidegger, as soon as a response is advanced, the question is eradicated. Consequently, could we conceive of the question outside the horizon of a response? One of the questions that I open up in my last book is this: Why has torture marked our relation to truth, in the West? It is the slave (as it is also in some measure each one of us) who is exposed to the trial and even to philosophical introspection. In Greece, certain slaves were marked in their very bodies: for example, they conveyed messages tattooed on their scalp, like secret military codes, indicating at what moment a battle should begin. The slaves arrived as postcards, as it were, and the person who received them shaved their heads to have access to the information. This interests me inasmuch as the slave is the bearer of a message that is inscribed on his skin but that he can't read; he himself thus becomes a letter, an aggravation of destination that Derrida discusses in *The Post Card.*

37

# V

## Valerie Solanas
### For a Radical, Politically Incorrect, and Morally Indefensible Feminism

So I was asked by Amy Scholder, a well-known editor with Verso Press at the time, to present a text—by some measures truly indefensible—titled *SCUM Manifesto*, which was reissued twenty-five years after its initial publication. I prepared a long introduction to this radical, in some senses delirious, feminist text, written by the woman who tried to kill Andy Warhol: Valerie Solanas. She gunned him down one day, and he remained in a coma for five weeks. He never fully recovered.

Why Warhol? He isn't the man one would see as the primary target of a feminism in revolt...

One of the reproaches addressed to Valerie Solanas was precisely that she chose to attack him and not one of the frankly stupid, vulgar, macho figures that are so prevalent—if not a major and destructive leader, at least some really powerful adversary. But for her, no, it had to be Warhol, precisely because he represented "art," and she had worshipped him for a long time. In her eyes, he had betrayed a sacred cause. One might almost call it a permutation of the relation between Nietzsche and Wagner, or Brutus and Caesar. By her act, she stigmatized the moment when someone is transformed into an icon, swells up with pride, and poses as a Philosopher, an Artist, or a Caesar. In her eyes, Warhol had betrayed the frayed movement, the ceaseless transgression that he was supposed to represent and embody. He was supposed to represent precisely nothing, only to know how to designate that "nothing" produced by the culture; but now he was beginning to represent Art, that is, the power and money-guzzling capacity of art. In addition, a war of technologies was emerging between Warhol and Solanas: she was always a writer bound to her typewriter, and she was an editor as well. Warhol, for his part, was into images. This was the beginning of unedited films, serializations, uncut footage. Warhol was starting to manifest a desire for a break, calling on writing to become something else. He no longer needed scripts for his films, and that was her job description. Beyond that, Warhol couldn't bear butch women. The women around him were his "glamour girls," that is, mostly transvestites—obviously very sexy ones—and drag queens. Valerie Solanas adored the drag queens, because they transgressed the social order, the conventions, they were "quotations of women," neither man nor woman but part of the staging of a fantasy. As I mentioned in the previous chapter, Norman Mailer called her the "Robespierre of feminism." Her text, *SCUM Manifesto,* appeared at the same time as Derrida's "Les fins de l'homme"—"the ends of man." I try to show, with many precautions, the extent to which she targeted the classical unity of man, deconstructed its myth, and also attacked what, among "classical" women, maintained man in his posture as man. And Andy Warhol became the locus in which this was serialized, because there was nonetheless a sort of machismo in his persona. Yet he was neither an avant-garde homosexual transgressor nor a macho man, any more than Michael Jackson is; neither one thing nor the other, he was instead a white zombie, pale and deliberate, but at the same time he poked fun at her, and so did his entourage. This did not sit well with our Valerie.

> At the time of the attack, was Valerie Solanas already a well-known artist and feminist?

No, not yet. This was when Warhol had lost the manuscript she'd given him to read, *Up Your Ass.* He had liked the title, but he'd lost the manuscript. She was indignant at the thought that he could have thrown it in the trash. At the same time, she thought that he had appropriated it for himself, that he was plagiarizing from her. His carelessness was a sign of hideous indifference and he plagiarized it because he loved it so well. The manuscript, a work lost and wasted, became a stolen part of her of which she was deprived. Today, reviewing the particulars of the case, people would say that Andy Warhol was her symptom. She owed him a lot, moreover: he had brought her into existence as a writer, he had encouraged and celebrated her. He had invited her to appear in movies such as *I, a Man,* in which she got to play the lesbian with shock value, but she was also featured in *Women in Revolt,* a film in which he was making fun of feminists and where he really did make her look ridiculous as a member of a group he called P.I.G., "Politically Involved Girls." In that film he dealt with several war fronts, including the war between the sexes, whereas neither he nor Solanas could be saddled with a traditional sexuality. I try to show how, in him, through him, she pursued the signifier "man," because she was nonetheless targeting Andy Warhol the man. She was an androphobe, and she had fantasies about the hole around which women are built. War-hol(e): it may sound abrupt and rather ridiculous to run after the signifier like this, but, when the interpretive grid doesn't work and analytical prototypes fall apart, I often venture out to where normal sense stops, into this zone of the seemingly ridiculous; Kant and Proust both affirmed that it was sometimes necessary to do this, so who am I to hesitate? Plus, there is nothing too offbeat as far as the itinerary of the signifier is concerned. Many things were at stake in that period—it was 1968, after all! I don't need to remind the French of what that represented in terms of political takedowns and attacks on the culture industry—and that was why I found myself confronting the enigma of Valerie Solanas. It was about arranging a meeting with the Zeitgeist, making an appointment with the spirit of the times; at that juncture mentalities were changing, people were rebelling, trying to find themselves, dismantling values and tutelary figures. Against a background of assassinations: Robert Kennedy, Malcolm X, Martin Luther King Jr. We often forget the intensity of what was being played out then, the "up against the wall" fervor that has left an important if often barely detectable residue. Valerie Solanas—I find it symptomatic, too, that her book is coming out again around now and is being retranslated in France—muddled the codes somewhat, because she wanted to kill the president, and because she turned against Andy Warhol, a fact that, despite all her explanations, remains disturbing. At the same time, at certain moments, something comes into view, and this eruption or filiation may be related to the moment when a Medea figure or an Antigone figure appears: all those figures of women who can no longer stand the stranglehold of a forcibly phallocentric language, and who are suffocating in an extreme paleonymy—stuck and stifled by language wielded by men and power, an inherited language that cuts no slack for women. I have tried to trace these frenzied, agitated movements of a radical feminism that may no longer exist as such, but whose interrogations persist.

> How can one account for the apparently blank space between 1968 and 2004, when *SCUM Manifesto* was republished with your introduction? The fact that Solanas herself remained silent all those years?

I have the impression that, when she fired her gun, a silencer was placed on her weapon. A silencer in every sense: she was imprisoned, interned, declared mad.

I am sensitive to people like her who against all odds have an acute sense of justice and injustice. They are outlaws of socially uttered, permitted thought. Her intensities and derangement make me wonder if we don't need to think more with Nietzsche's hammer. I'd put this in touch with Heidegger's saying that sometimes we need to scream. He showed that there is a very marginal and provocative moment in writing, a moment of constitutive but very dangerous externality that crosses over frameworks and domestications. That moment can be identified with the madness into which Nietzsche fell, or with the moments of irrationality that can be read in Rousseau or in others I hardly need name: Hölderlin, Lenz, Artaud . . . very fragile thinkers who passed over to the other side of their own writing, an always neutral, disembodied, disappropriating writing.

> Except that in the case of Valerie Solanas we would have thinking done "with a hammer" but anchored in the radical feminism that had declared a war from which there may be no way out.

Yes, and that is what caught my attention, the way she took herself out of the loop, put herself in lockdown without recourse or appeal. I don't know whether France is as misogynist as the rest of the world where linguistic usage is concerned [laugh track], or whether people can understand that struggle in France the way it is understood in the United States, but Solanas also attacked a kind of typology or taxonomy of feminine utterances that degrades, undermines, and sabotages those who have accepted or constructed themselves as women. I mean that she began by attacking a brand of women. Women who chatter or gossip or are scatterbrained with language—the stereotype of women's demeaned relation to language. There are a number of words in English (a fact that already arouses suspicion) to describe this: chatting, nagging, bitching, moaning; in other words, complaints as acts of utterance, as linguistic acts that are as annoyingly inessential as they are inevitable. They are not even utterances, moreover, but a sort of sideline of language, impoverished and enervating. And stupid. Stupid but insistent, and dangerous, and in the face of which men must always wear bulletproof vests. A language against which men and children always have to protect themselves. In the case of Antigone, when she prefers to be buried alive in the crypt, it is speech itself that is being rejected.

I try to reflect on these landmine-strewn grounds inhabited by certain slightly "deranged," disturbed women, adjacent to a prestigious, very "upper-class" milieu, where "feminine" maladies, or maladies depicted as such (for example, in the precincts of hysteria) are very much in fashion, respected, because they harbor perfectly honorable transgressions, entirely

41

accepted subversions. There is Anna O, Dora, even the Marquise of O; there are psychic (I hesitate to call them "mental") maladies or disorders that do very well and that garner a good deal of social value and approval up to a point, the uptown hysteric, for example.

But other zones of marginal utterance that have not yet been domesticated or assimilated to our discourse do not belong to this norm-governed acceptance. And Valerie Solanas—who was a squatter in the house of language—belongs to these more forlorn zones of articulation and brutish despair. What captivated me were the deviant linguistic acts—real acts, for nothing can be more real, according to Carl Schmitt, than being able to cause someone's death. The way she shot off her mouth and her weapon effected a troubling coincidence. She belongs to the ranks of those who unpack language with savage intensity, ever closing in on those unsheltered quasi-discourses that are sometimes labeled madness. For they are linked to psychotic acts or breaks to which Valerie Solanas relentlessly testifies. The fact that she produced a cult-text that retains that status today is interesting—even if the term is not an adequate one. Texts that are delirious, that are often dangerous precisely where they cease to be delirious, have led me to think about typically American revolutionaries—if we may call them that—such as the Unabomber, who wrote in isolation, writing to and attacking the targeted State and its corrosive practices. In their delirium and their phantasms, technologies or techniques are always at stake.

Valerie Solanas thought that men had appropriated technology to turn it into a war machine that would devastate the Earth; unlike the Unabomber, she was not against technology, but she wanted it to be feminized, as it were; she wanted it to return to its essential roots in order to guarantee a sort of uchrony, utopia, that is, in order to prolong life, to render brutalizing and alienating work obsolete. As she saw it, men played the role of Prometheus, they stole a power that was a gift and systematically transformed it into killing machines. And she couldn't bear it. She worked with animals in a laboratory, and she spoke with great lucidity about the advent of animals' rights, about relations between science and the lie of biology, about biology as thanatology, the science of death. She was on good days a sort of female Nietzsche, but Nietzsche also identified himself with Eve—the first figure of the scientific method, the one who was inspired by knowledge and got punished for it. She thus saw herself as a new Eve, because Eve's "gay science" opened onto a catastrophe.

We have to wonder why Valerie Solanas found herself in a state close to psychosis: after all, psychosis is driven by something in reality, it is not completely dissociated from a sort of injury or shock. One of my first books,

42

*The Telephone Book,* pursued a different pathological track and questioned the relation of schizophrenics to technology or, to put it differently, considered our necessarily schizophrenic relation to technology.

> I am more and more convinced that psychotics are reacting to the presence of death-dealing factors. I often think that madness, in this sense, is the ultimate refuge against perversion. There are psychotics who "choose" to become psychotic in order not to enter into perversion. Don Quixote illustrates this magnificently.

The economy of "decision" that you indicate is fascinating. I thought about some of these substitutive moves when I was asked to present Solanas's text: so controversial, unpresentable, but at the same time a key text that is at once symptomatic of the underground culture and unique in that culture: everyone of a certain generation and milieu knows it, everyone has read it, a fact that astonished me, moreover. I think she wrote it to struggle against the forces of death, of eradication, of forgetting. She had an irrepressible sense of needing to put out a piece of writing that was also a lethal action. She was always carrying a piece. In 1968, her book was distributed just the way some of Rousseau's texts were passed around surreptitiously, in her case through the circulation of photocopies. At the end of her life, she was alone and fairly demolished and living in poverty in San Francisco; her mother, on the other hand, claims that she had lots of friends, that she was happy to the end. We lack information about her childhood; she used to say that her father had beaten her and she talked about her mother's constant intrusions. I mention this because we need to locate where the State picks up the relay of such abusive paterno-maternal machines. In general I also try not to bracket out the autobiographical triggers of those who enact an extreme relation to justice. Let us remember that the first cry for justice is an infantile one that most children share when they yell or pout or sob, "It's not fair!" Some get used to that fact growing up and out of it, others carry the injury into adult states of responsible or wounded concern, sometimes both (at times woundedness lays the groundwork for responsibility, so I am not putting these qualities in conflict here—and as for adulthood, it is always pockmarked by a childhood that returns incessantly to stifle voice and reason). I try to show that it is very important, and problematic, that Valerie wanted to turn her text into the form of a manifesto. What is the history of the manifesto? Why did she avail herself of its embedded intentions and stamp? Within the history of the manifesto she is both breaking and aligning herself with the implications of a manifesto as she puts one out there. When prodded and pushed heuristically, this futurist manifesto

43

written by an "ultrafeminist" is, from a certain perspective, absolutely antifeminist and "antiwomen." The first futurist *Manifesto* was notoriously antifeminist. How can one declare war against a war, or write a manifesto against any possibility of manifesto? It's a warlike act, and this form of combat is also a fight against the entire history of the sort of empty positing, the peculiar type of promising and enactment that we associate with manifestos. Is such a manifestation of the manifesto still possible in our day? In part because the very possibility of *manifestation* was to be destroyed, Valerie Solanas sought to bring down Warhol. He is the one who showed that there was nothing more to manifest.

Do you think that today's world has been feminized since May '68?

I think so, and that is why absolutely unbelievable macho convulsions are erupting here and there, and we are in some ways reentering archaic dimensions of virility as if to bring back a failed and mythic empire. However, we are living the failure close to its ground, because no one believes anymore in the culture of virility, even if some sectors of humanity are faking it, hyperbolically asserting values and poses of relentless machismo as it is fading out in terms of transcendental credibility. The same goes for extreme Christian cultures—the leaders often turn out or seem to be faking it, taking a series of poses that barely cover up a sheer will-to-power, what I call "W2P." When some leaders are photographed in the pious pose of praying their eyes are often squeezed shut like children when they are pretend-praying or trying very hard to mimic the prayerful bow. Let us return to the question of a feminized world, now that so many male props have been pointed out. Has the world been feminized? If I answer that lovely and provocative question in the affirmative, I am situating myself in Kafka's parabolic world: yes, but not for us. Or else, with a Heideggerian accent: yes, but there is no more world. Still, something has shifted, and we find ourselves before a "masculinist" reactivity that is nonetheless rather disturbing. What I wanted to show in the case of Valerie Solanas was that, just when she says all men have to be killed (which, let's agree, indicates a very radical stance), she also shows the inanity of the proposition, the impossibility of turning against men in a way that would be unique or the least bit competent. There is nothing that one can do against men that they are not doing against themselves, for men desire death and kill one another for pleasure and out of obedience. She says that the majority of men are destined to become homosexual. Consequently, as in an autoimmune laboratory, men don't need an external instance to effect their encroaching destruction: there is no need to intervene, since they'll bring about their own disappearance. Thus it isn't really necessary or even interesting to kill them. However, because she's impatient, she claims, it would be good to kill a few from time to time. But it isn't worth it, she adds, because the Zeitgeist, the spirit of the times, is on our side. Her real targets, and this is what I feel obligated to stress in my reflections, are the women who, according to her, support the phantasms of the sturdy, courageous, competent, powerful man.

Solanas shows that women, but also especially mothers, fabricate and operate a machine that produces mythologies and mystifications that they themselves control and perpetuate. As for men, she says, it is already settled: soon we won't even need them as sperm donors. She anticipated cloning and glimpsed the dematerialization of exchanges and of money. We won't need money as a thing any longer, this device invented by men, who are always attached to their own excrement and who transform the world into shit. (In psychoanalysis money and shit are primal correlatives, so crises in economy always imply anality, and can be traced to a calamity due to a heightened level of activity in anal-erotic zones of aggression.) She also said that the docile women who pretend to need fathers, presidents, and leaders are the only real problem, because they are very powerful; they glorify the supposed power of men and act against their own camp.

> It's the game played between the master and the hysteric, Freud tells us: there's no master without a hysteric to support him in his semblance of power and knowledge.

That's exactly right. Women are the ones who, out of perversity and their often unanalyzed hysterical assaults, play against themselves, undoing their own legitimate bid for mastery. Men are stronger than women solely because of their projections onto them, projections that stick and sting. And because men detest passivity and mimeticism, they project their own lacks and weaknesses onto women, and women take these on with astonishing complicity. The projections that women pick up, accept, and perpetuate are the only realm in which men are more powerful than they are. Men are powerful only insofar as their projections are made to rule—and in this case they rule out women's strength of being. Valerie Solanas is furious at women who hold back in these political and ontological contests, who are not sufficiently arrogant or violent, women who are not troublemakers. Women who are so powerful that they finally rise up against themselves and their sisters. Women who in the end, and by all sorts of conditioning that they accept, detest and weaken one another. Men don't dominate them; instead, women do the dirty work themselves. They too are in a sort of

45

autoimmune laboratory, but a much wilder and more implacable one, one that is enmeshed in an outpouring of destructive pleasure.

The provocative, irreverent aspect of my presentation of Valerie Solanas's *Manifesto* probably lies in the fact that in it I brought to light this critique of women, which some feminists have found very hard to tolerate. I convoked Nietzsche, Derrida, Kofman, Cixous, and their weapons of interpretive warfare, and I recognized that the figure I saw in Solanas's viewfinder was woman. Men, for her, were only poor suckers who were no longer even worth attacking. But when she affirmed that men desire death and derive orgasmic pleasure from it, by giving them death she allowed herself to be caught in turn by her own logic—she was still serving the man, unable to extricate herself from giving pleasure and going beyond the pleasure principle on an irreversible death drive.

In thinking about Valerie Solanas I evoke her youth and her evolution, everything that was inassimilable in her life. I investigate how she had to prostitute herself to pay for her studies, and I imply that many, many others, supposedly above suspicion, have done the same thing—I mean, who hasn't? She came out and said so. It has become politically correct to speak of "sex workers"; we no longer say "prostitute." "Neither whores nor slaves," as they say in France, but what about those who work in the field of sex? The debate in the United States is quite raucous, led by figures such as Catharine MacKinnon, who often suggests that pornography is at the root of it all. Her position is interesting, however, because she denounces the omnipresence of pornography but not solely from a moral standpoint. She is gripping, sometimes in terms of insight even a bit like Valerie Solanas, but more academic and even refined—she could come across as a puritan, but that's not what she is. Most intellectuals on the Left object to the conclusions she draws. And yet she embodies an interesting dissident path. Recently, she carried out a study on the fear of rape in war. In it she says that, even though it is undeniable that women are raped during wars, in contrast no one ever mentions the extent to which men rape one another, performing rituals of mutual or hierarchized debasement that remain hidden from discourse or view.

# VI

# On Television
## The Feminization of World

Can you say more about the feminization of the world and maybe connect this to your work on media technology?

This requires a bit of maneuvering, some conceptual ad-
justment. I don't want to respond as if we know what
"feminization" means and implies (I even dispute "world,"
which Heidegger showed quite a while ago was shattered
as concept and entity. We can no longer speak, for instance,
without considerable backtracking, of *Weltanschauung*, worldview). I do
not want to proceed from a misogynist base and inadvertently equate the
feminine with some downgrades. To get back to the very relevant question
about the hypothetical feminization of the world, then, I'm inclined to say
that war itself has been feminized, or at least its means of justification. War
has often been triggered by the feminine symbolic, whether it be concen-
trated on Helen of Troy or Delacroix's *La Liberté guidant le people* (*Liberty
Leading the People*). But I am talking about another shift, another type of
cartography where feminine attributes and markers prevail. Almost every
war now, including the current war against the Taliban, is waged at some
essential level in the name of women. Hannah Arendt showed that having to justify a war, or having to find a way to justify war, was a relatively
new phenomenon in history. We can also see how the justificatory drive
introduces a form of feminization of war, pulling away from the more
masculinist aesthetic evident in, say, Native American war dances and body
painting. Until late Roman Antiquity, no one and nothing needed to justify
the pulse of war, which belonged to a repertory of high creativity and an
inescapable social libido. Things have since turned around, downshifted. I
can only speak in shorthand here of an enormous set of implications and

consequences for a culture or nation-state at war, declared or covert, wanted or denounced, legitimate or entirely illicit. What happens when war—which used to measure (up to and in Hegel) historical becoming, introducing a new era and horizon of law, as we see at the end of *Hamlet* with the arrival of Fortinbras, "strong arm"—what happens when war loses solid footing in our more-or-less collective sense of what constitutes a justifiable practice of sovereignty? Not that long ago we saw the degradation of war into poses of what Jean Baudrillard, in *Libération*, called "war pornography," that is, American soldiers who showed themselves in pictures, openly smiling, in the posture of rapists. We had already had the experience of "feminizing" the enemy in the first Gulf War. At that time I wrote about the porn films the fighter pilots watched before going off to drop bombs. They amped up on drugs, watched pornographic videos, and listened to rock music as they headed out to bomb a highly symbolized "Mother Earth," feminized and rendered rapable. In the first phase of the Gulf War, given the way the first George Bush pronounces his vowels, in English we heard an amalgam between Saddam, Saddamization, and sodomy. He pronounced the enemy's name as an act of sodomy. At the time, I described the unthematized thematization of the pictures themselves, the technological "take" with which war is henceforth associated.

I have tried to read and analyze wars, the contemporary eruptions of violence that are becoming more and more "literally" embedded. At this time, I was coming across all my favorite themes: drugs, technology, violence, music (war or military music seems understudied to me), deviance, all-out mobilization, the vapid orientation of libidinal aggression—the anal-erotic war zone that Freud has designated.

> How far can one take this literality, this "pornographization," not in the moral sense but in the sense in which everything is put on display?

I've written extensively about the rhetorical unconscious in the context of national decision and policy, but every time a war intervenes, or every time there's an aggression on our part against another country, the repercussions are observed, it seems, in acts of everyday micropolitics. There are more battered women, for example; the percentage of acts of violence against women rises. Something is let loose in the symbolic realm. In my own very limited but no doubt telling case, as soon as the second Bush started bombing Baghdad, I almost got run over several times while I was crossing the street. Men rolled down their car windows and, instead of apologizing, called me a f'ing bitch—this was not the urban norm, even though we're talking about New York f'ing City! You could feel the tension in the city, and I told myself that, as soon as serious aggressions get the green light, the death drive goes into high gear and spreads everywhere. Like a contagious disease, like an aggression compulsion, even in the workplace, the war between the sexes rockets back to the surface in what are seemingly the most anodyne negotiations or discussions of daily existence. As I've just mentioned, I myself, a sort of little gangster-type whom few would mess with, more or less well-armored (even though I probably have several subpersonalities that are by turns hysterical, unhappy, and fragile), was insulted with unprecedented brutality right after we started the bombing assault. Moreover, racial battlefields are coming back to center stage. Many more racist acts are evident in everyday life when war gears up, which does not contradict the advent of Obama but is part of that field of tensions and unresolved conflicts that simultaneously say "yes" and "no" to new conceptual or street arrivals.

Indeed, nobody talks about the consequences of a conflict in the country that initiates a punitive expedition—as if declaring a war in a remote land, at the other end of the world, had no consequences here, in our own social and personal realms.

An opening comes about, as with ritual: people let out much of the aggression that was once contained and constrained by all sorts of social bonds, even by politically correct ones. I'd like to add that I'm not against the idea of political correctness, which we've made so much fun of, especially in France, because it was so exaggerated. Important advances and undeniable protections have been accomplished thanks to the persistent claims of political correctness. Even on television. In France and in Germany, the person in charge, much of the time, is a white man, after all. In the United States, we mustn't exaggerate the scope of this phenomenon, but there isn't a single television series without a judge who is a person of color: Indian, Puerto Rican, Mexican, African American or something nondominant. OK, maybe I'm dreaming. But color is coming in, if gradually and according to minimal gradations, and even the White House is newly blended.

In France, Élisabeth Badinter has led a struggle against the legalization of parity; she thought it was better not to legislate, because parity should come about naturally. Only, since we aren't there yet, it would be better to legislate in the meantime; otherwise, nothing will happen.

Has anything ever come about "naturally"? The law or even fictional representations of law can produce astonishing shifts in the way things are run—or obsolesced. In any case, the relation to law has become the business of specialists; it is so difficult and so serious that we can no longer claim to know what is happening when legislation is passed, or by the time it is passed. The legal arsenal has become so complex that no one can master it any longer. This complexity constantly produces effects that we don't control. At the same time, legal recourse in America sometimes functions as the place where resistance can be marked and outrages can be brought to light, if often without coming to a successful conclusion. There are other channels and systems of transmission, sometimes unexpected or barely capable of registering material effects in our world of obdurate transaction. I am thinking of the turnabouts that TV is in part responsible for, even and certainly unintentionally. How do liberal politics settle in, quietly colonize some aspects of the technological grid? I am not even talking about the overtly activist zones of internet noncompliance. If we have to watch what is produced on television every day by the epigones of Benetton, that's the culture that will end up taking over. Fundamentalist Christians don't allow their children to watch television because the programs are deemed too liberal, too "leftist," too "Jewish." They're afraid the children will be contaminated by cultural alternatives, even though the vast majority of programs tend to be, in terms of overt themes and values, conservative. But let's set aside these empirical aspects, which I find too sociological for my taste. Looping and repetitive, always on rerun even when it's fresh, television comes across as a continuous program, a sort of uninterrupted discourse. Whereas, in reality, in the televisual phenomenon there is something that breaks radically with the continuous flow of images, and this is what attracts my attention, a kind of invisible channel on which television depends and by which it is haunted. Something is happening to it, to us, that it cannot tell us about but that hitches a ride on every program, no matter how inane or laugh-tracked up. What interrupts continuity in a radical way is trauma. A historical and structural trauma that television repeats. But can trauma be *shown,* much less televised? In trauma, we're dealing with images that return without interiority and at the same time are endlessly repeated as flashbacks. What is shown—or not shown—on television is structured like the return of what doesn't get successfully repressed. There are invisible networks, as it were, cables to which we don't yet have access and that tell a different story, the one that doesn't allow itself to be told, or shown, or archived. If our history is a history of trauma, this puts us in a very difficult situation, because memory is affected by trauma—some even consider that memory *depends* on trauma, a tight paradoxical knot—and what is forged, at that moment, is a history without memory. Television announces nothing else. It asks us to consider a history without memory—is this at all possible? Is this what we're left with?—the plunges into reruns that cannot be interiorized, maybe only vaguely remembered or memorized like an alien body of quasi-facts? Are we condemned to channel-surf our own histories, in search of substance and ground?

In what sense is television traumatic?

I was prompted to study television in terms of trauma first of all because of the unprecedented on-screen proliferation of dead bodies. Television produces corpses. What relation to history is involved? And to what history? At what point in material history did television emerge as part of a family setting? When did the national addiction begin, following what fatal prompters or set of conditions? Television came on the scene, and became the scene, installed the screen (and codified screen memories) directly after World War II. I started exploring some of these links in an effort to construct a genealogy of its ascendancy. When the State knuckles under to technology and decides to deploy an economy of death—death deprived of all its symbolic structure, and industrialized on a large scale by technological means—it's called Nazism. Maybe I should spill the fact that in my so-called life, the Nazis mark the beginning of everything, that is, the end of everything from the get-go: the beginning of the catastrophe that keeps on repeating itself. As the daughter of German Jews, I was confronted with that burdensome reality when I first started to talk—or started to listen, which was earlier; the word "Nazi" was part of my initiation to language, among my first phrases in Hebrew. To come back to the more-or-less domesticated forms of technology, I believe that the economy of death bound up with Nazi arrangements continues to operate, even if through subterranean networks. The relation of our world to technology is not foreign to what was set up under the Nazis. Please forgive this abrupt series of descriptions, all of which are more carefully discussed, and with scholarly pacing, elsewhere in my published work. So don't jump on me for something that may sound like a drive-by, warped and off balance. On the other hand, I am told that my writing is often difficult and in some instances bars access, so I am trying to distill and simplify, which goes against my nature—in fact, it's killing me!

Let me suggest a seemingly anodyne example to get us off the ground. Two everyday technologies: radio and television. To philosophize is also to conceptualize the means of technology and its relationships with everyday reason.

The Nazis voted—their only "vote"—against television and for radio, because at a certain point they had to choose their weapons, that is, choose the technology for the *Volk* that would secure a reliable and controllable form of transference; thus they chose telephone and radio. The Germans were simultaneously hooked on Hitler's voice alternating with Wagner's music, and they developed, we could say, a dependency on the radio. They can even be described as hypnotized by that technology, transferring something like the collective libido onto it   their ears were trained on the radio. I have written about this addiction via the ear of the German population—because everything came through the ear, a nationalized ear—but it was a captive ear, already technologized. "Addiction via the ear," the addicted ear, is a major motif, one already present in *Hamlet* (not to mention the Virgin and Ernst Jones's article on her ear, or Hélène Cixous or Nietzsche, where the ear's *jouissance* is also at stake). Derrida wrote the *otobiographie* of Nietzsche, which I translated. But to cut off the ear, let's go back to what was competing with radio. After the war, the television became a parasite in every family, every household. And another system of transference was introduced little by little into the social body. One day, at the Guggenheim, at an installation featuring many television sets embedded one alongside the other, one of my friends pointed out that in the early days when television had just been standardized the sets were very small, and families—that is, human beings—were huge, all clustered around the little box, while now the family has been miniaturized, and the TV screen has become enormous, monstrous, proteiform—it swallows up, devours, the family space that it also often constitutes. We mustn't forget that television came on the scene after a quite specific historical trauma, the Shoah, and I think that break in and of historical representation is installed in what marks the enigma of television. The small screen, in that sense, shows that it is impossible to show what has happened, but it produces narratives that are substituted for the unrepresentable. Endlessly. Television, when it tells stories, favors crime scenes and the work of detectives. It regularly goes to court, stages hearings, makes earnest statements about the rendering of justice. It is bound to the law to the point of astonishing hyperbole and in the mode of repetition compulsion. It cannot repeal its incessant petitions to the law. Television narratives seem stuck on making justice present. But justice cannot present itself as such; it is not presence. This is what keeps television frustrated, frustrated by the endless postponement of justice—but the nonpresentability of justice also keeps it going, as if pursuing its elusive object with passionate conviction. This would be part of its unconscious programming, the way it runs after an infinitely deferred justice. Some of the runs are foolish or stupefying, of course, but television is replete with juries, even on the level of style and fashion, filled with acts of judgment and backed by the legal idiom.

Television colonized all sorts of crime stories. The enigma of survival—a term used by Cathy Caruth—is presented over and over, hour after hour, but this time with the help of narratives populated by policemen, commissioners, judges, evaluators, and Superman. On TV, the police are everywhere, that is, the police as figures and as television (in the United States, television recruits viewers to help look for criminals, fugitives, pedophiles, and so on). Walter Benjamin characterized this best in his critique of violence: he showed that the police are a phantom body. This body is everywhere, it looks, keeps watch, but is only a formless body (or, as Derrida says, a "figureless figure") that is found in an obsessive and compulsive form on television.

I raised the question of police action in relation to television, the incessant recourse to crime time. When Rodney King, a black man, was beaten by white Los Angeles police officers, the event captured live on video intruded on screen in its excess during the early phase of the war in Iraq at a time when no war footage was being shown; this void was what Blanchot would call a "neutral" space. Concerning the war, there was a sort of blindness at play, television signifying simply that it could show nothing at a time when images were really needed; television was turning back into radio. After World War II, television had come on the scene and produced stories that were deemed completely digestible, consumable. There were even TV dinners; we were shown things that we could swallow. In almost every story on TV, there is a murder, but one that is solved. Things fall back into place; the scandal is wiped out. In a sense, the coherence of the world is restored.

Simultaneously, a discourse of effacement accompanies this scenario: even when, thematically, it is a matter of seeing inexplicable murders on television, the puzzle requires a solution, and that requirement will be met. Viewers' inability to comprehend the murder that is substituted for a genocide is masked, because, while many people are eliminated, there still remains the enigma of those who survive these tenderized and domesticated murders. Invasive, familiar and familial, television creates a supplementary space inside—if one can localize this exteriority as interior—every home. From this point on, are we still at home? Or is it the case, as Heidegger said, that the house of being is destroyed by the technologies that have redefined it and turned it into a new decor of a stripped-down ontological cast? It is a question of houses, too, of homes and *l'homme,* of what still holds something like humanity all together, and these calmly erased murders serve as allegories for a collective screen memory.

Television is a screen that simultaneously wipes out genocide and shows other stories that are metonymic substitutes for murder, the inexplicable murder that, even in our day, does not allow itself to be seen, that continues as a specter in its spectrality, unable to be forgotten. There are corpses that no longer need to be wept over, for which no more mourning is needed. I could put this differently, somewhat dialectically, and say that this is all we do in front of the TV, in the very fact that we find ourselves as somewhat damaged trash-bodies in front of the tube; on both sides of the screen, basically, we, wasted bodies, encounter a sort of exhaustion, anguish, and sleepiness. Hitchcock himself watched television while he was filming *Psycho,* because it was an effective soporific for him, a necessary antipsychotic drug. Television has also become, after all, a place for witnessing—even if the testamentary temper is a sleepy one (as, by the way, in Kafka). One is called to dim one's consciousness and witness, to watch in the dark. Besides the atrocities that have been put up for display, we have seen Lacan on television making statements about racism, and even Heidegger said that television was like his thought, the essence of his thought—I don't know what drug he had taken when he said that, but he did say it!

> Is television still an ambivalent tool, for you, or is it in the end wholly destructive?

Whether we like it or not, and to put it in outmoded terms, the essential questions today have this thing at their center: television and its derivatives or its satellites. I think Aristotle would have been interested in television. He would probably have had to revise his thinking about terror and catharsis to some extent; at the same time, he would have seen television as a modulation of our relation to the world, an unprecedented mutation. But it is a difficult thing for philosophy to conceptualize; we are on unstable ground inasmuch as television raises, among other questions, the question of violence and force. Force eludes philosophy, since it is neither a concept nor, well, anything that can be grasped by our huge apparatus and voracious knowledge-pump.

This is why I try to analyze the striking force not only of the police but also of the essential texts that in some ways continue to legislate our existence, to determine parameters and crucial boundaries that we can't easily skip over or simply drop. Violence is something else again, and critical philosophers have had a lot to say about it. So has everyone else. What I mean is that in so-called everyday life people always begin, in America (I don't know if this is true in France), by claiming that television is the source of violent impulses in children, that it incites a pernicious mimeticism.

Television is no different from other drugs; like all drugs, it produces two contradictory effects—and everything depends on the dosage. Either it is said to be the source of the problem because it favors a certain form of violence and makes that violence less real, or it is thought to absorb violence by symbolizing it and thus to act fundamentally as a calming agent. Very well-supported contradictions are brought to the surface in the debates over television.

The question of violence, the persistent question of street violence, comes up in this context; this is why it seems to me that one must absolutely attempt to "think" television, this formidable little packed-up think tank, in all its ambivalence, with all the degrees of resistance that this implies. I have tried to bring to light what I call the *Gewissensruf* of television, the appeal to the conscience of the witness who sometimes bursts forth inside television, like the call of conscience according to Heidegger. This is why I've tried to analyze the phenomenology of television through my reading of Derrida, Levinas, and a few other regulars.

> This is the paradox, which Derrida pointed out, of a civilization that was haunted, after World War II, by the archive, in which everything is destined to be categorized, archived, museumized, but which is no longer anywhere in memory, no longer a reflection captured by memory. As if the fact of archiving took the place of the work of memory.

It is absolutely necessary to recall the dual movement of hypertropic conservation and forgetfulness in which we find ourselves today. At the same time, what interests me in television (as futile and uninteresting as it can be), is that it makes no pretense of archiving anything at all, and all the while it proliferates documentaries, appeals to memory and to archival fervor; it reinterrogates the past and tends the networks devoted to history. These documentaries show us precisely what history cannot show live or prerecorded, or rather they reveal the fact that history has nothing to "show." There is a compulsion, now, to show everything; we have intrusive phenomena, reductive repetitions of everyday life, a tele-reality that denies story and brackets history. It has neither the pretension nor the scope nor the ambitious intentions of a "real" historical archive, but it always brings us back, as does trauma, to flashbacks that feature glints of wars, genocides, all those things that we cannot see, that we have not known how to see.

Trauma is something that cannot be assimilated or communicated, as if it were always stammering in a remote field. Television evokes Oedipus's trauma, the trauma of someone who blinds himself in the face of his own crime. Oedipus runs, in a way, or limps, through the networks and programs like an eye that has seen too much and that has blinded itself. Hölderlin wrote about that eye that had seen too much, the third eye of a sort of transcendental television. I am concerned with the "two eyes" of television, the other one being the encapsulated video, but these are henceforth blinded eyes because the knowledge hidden behind them is too heavy to bear. People watch a huge number of crime movies; in my opinion, these constitute the central "body" of television. Because what is in question, as we saw earlier, is the phantom body of the police, the one that fascinates and obsesses us. This is something that TV tries, blindly, to express; the police and murders are involved, but informed by a very normative and ultimately reassuring logic. At the same time, we witness a headlong flight forward, because we cannot control, even remotely, the content of the programs—those other registers of inscribing disaster that television highlights.

In sum, there are things that remain unsaid and unseen, but there are also eidetic movements that point, like hunting dogs, to the invisible prey, off range. We do not know what they are trying to show us, metonymically or allegorically, or even ironically; they show what they cannot show, posting negative hallucinations: we see only what is no longer there (Heidegger distinguished between positive and negative hallucinations). This is a characteristic feature of a drug, and it is for that reason, too, that I have been keeping a close eye on the harmful, euphorizing, and anxiety-producing effects of television, and on our need for this round-the-clock drug.

> There is also a dimension of sorcery. The world is too difficult, too stressful; we turn on the TV and we forget the rest. Subsequently, the television set becomes a member of the family.

Yes, it becomes a necessary, reassuring presence for many, a supportive mother or a benevolent father: we recognize people on the screen. This probably has something to do with the atomization of society and families, the fast-paced velocities that keep us apart while we're striving to be together. The family bond is displaced in practical terms from the genealogical to the visual. The visual dimension is surely primordial, and in the meantime we start to talk about bodies that are on television and at which we stare. It's a form of seeing without seeing . . . There's a sort of stupor that descends upon the viewer, no longer utterly alone; we don't know where it comes from, the tranquilizing sensation, if indeed it actually happens. There is always something else; that's why I think that this colloquy among stupefied persons invites phantoms. Today, people often turn on the TV without looking at it; my neighbors do this as soon as they get home every evening. It's a presence without presence, and this is what interests me and plagues me every night. But even when looking at it, there is a way of not looking, of turning oneself off—of splitting off in a supplementary and introjected version of a split-screen.

Then there is the additional way television has appropriated the police, in a reciprocal reflection: television acts on the world of the police, which watches everything, sees everything, keeps everything, we sense, under surveillance. Earlier, when I was responding to the question about power relations, I specifically evoked the beating of Rodney King; this corresponded to the very moment when we were being given nothing to look at concerning the war in Iraq.

Whereas, in the attack on this man, everything had been filmed . . .

Yes, by an amateur with a video camera, but it was especially the gaze of a witness who had grasped everything. (This was challenged during the trial of the policemen who attacked Rodney King, moreover: can a video camera testify, or is it not preferable to rely on the memory, even the defective memory, of a nontechnological witness?) As I've noted, this happened at a time when the war in Iraq was more or less wiped off our screens. Here is a metonymy, a displacement of the eradicated scene by a different one: we see policemen beating a brown or black person, we even see the police chief who was fired and says at the end of the interview: "Shit, they've treated this incident like it's more important than the war in Iraq!" When images of the war were taboo, the camera shot another scene of violence being visited on a body of color, more local-color, before roving elsewhere, to another channel of concern to us, a weather channel.

But we have to recognize that at certain points television has done its work. Where Vietnam is concerned, for example, the images retransmitted were a factor in ending the war. The fact of showing turned out to be crucial. At the time, American hippies and GIs alike were asserting that "the whole world is watching." America itself took on the transparency of a television set that was constantly turned on and that the "whole world" was watching. When something happened, people told themselves: "The whole world has its eye on us." Now we have proof that, when video cameras are authorized to film, as they are for this war in Iraq that in 2003 started revving up again (well, they were authorized in a limited way for about five minutes), they still don't show very much. There were no pictures of torture in Iraq, before the sensational revelations of which the greater part was missing. I don't know whether these pictures can accelerate the American withdrawal, given that the status of the photo has shifted. A certain media logic had led me to believe, until very recently, that, as soon as an injustice was revealed on television, it would, in principle, be stopped. But television is pulling back from its ethical watch, from the mandate of an implicit round-the-clock assignment. The question that arises for me is this: in what way has television been able to become the topos, or rather the atopos, of a contemporary ethics?

This type of concern is why I study the various levels of the relation between law and television within the televisual field, that is, the relation of television to itself, but also the interaction between the law and television. Legal decisions were made after videos appeared showing without any ambiguity that the police had used illegal force against Rodney King. The court said that the videos could not be taken into account, that it was necessary to rely only on the memory, and the gaps in memory, of witnesses, which means that a story cannot be reduced to a sort of filmed truth, for there is no interiority, and its attendant defaults, in the visual report of a video. From a juridical standpoint, the living, imperfect witness always takes precedence. Even when someone says something and a video contradicts the statement, the judge rejects the video account because justice must not become explicitly based in technology, and the witnesses' testimony must not be stripped of its credibility by purely technical speech, that is, by death as opposed to living speech and its embodiment. And this invites reflection, because starting from the point where it became possible to archivize the crime and the site of the crime, it was decided that this type of visual archive was not valid as testimony, no doubt also because of our metaphysical prejudices about interiority: we are not ready or willing to give up the presumed presence of a human being who can always lie or not remember. The fact that this presence is fallible creates the basis for truth.

When there are gaps in memory, lacunae, hesitant recollections, a representation is much more true, more "real," than the more-or-less faithful visual restitution by a video camera that can only go as far as verisimilitude. I am not even touching the problem of framing or other narrative manipulations at this point—that is for a sidebar. The law is forced to make choices and to take up metaphysical decisions. This is understandable. The phenomenon is not new. Already among the pre-Socratics, and especially in Plato's wake, we find great mistrust of the technology and technicity of testimony, and a recourse to accounts elicited under torture, which must have seemed more dependable and firmly grounded. This is part of our legacy.

# VII

# On Drugs, Polydependencies, and the Drama of Immunodeficiency

I have tried to develop the notion of "narcossism" and also, from the standpoint of literature or art, the notion of "hallucinogenre." I realized not long ago that in French, as compared to English, there really is no lexical field that designates, for example, sudden abstinence from a drug, that is, withdrawal. In English, in contrast, this lexicon is omnipresent, disseminated in all imaginable linguistic registers.

"To withdraw," in French, is *décrocher*, "to unhook," from a drug or from alcohol.

But in English at least four words spring to mind to designate the bodily state provoked by the sudden and total deprivation of a drug, accompanied by trembling, sweating, extreme cravings. In English, this way of designating lack comes into play even in the very relation to the act of writing. One can say, for example, "Oh, I haven't written anything for a month, and I feel like I'm crashing, f'd up, really f'd." There is the expression "cold turkey": I used it to describe what happened to the body of the drug-addicted woman Flaubert invented, that is, Emma Bovary's body; toward the end of the novel we learn that she is involved not only with poison but with a whole pharmacopoeia. Today we would speak of addiction to prescription drugs. I try to show, in my essay *Crack Wars,* that Emma is structured around a lack, that she takes serial lovers and smokes/consumes them like crack. To come back to "cold turkey," in *Madame Bovary* we find a kind of circulation of the turkey that Emma Bovary's father offers to her husband, Charles. I can imagine another interpretation of this episode showing that Emma is in the addict's state of acute and painful withdrawal, and I can open this theme up by following the text very closely.

In English there is also the word "jonesing," which means that one is experiencing a desire to smoke, consume, or shoot up drugs. But one can also say "craving." How is this translated in French?—not that I want to limit our discussion to building vocabulary lists. But this will get us going.

> *Crever d'envie*—dying of an intense desire to have or do something. But it's true that the vocabulary specific to addiction is still fairly limited in French.

Starting from this lexicon of deprivation and unsatisfied or even insatiable desire, I have tried to establish a critique and—this is perhaps a little presumptuous—I have had the nerve to call into question the structure of this desire as described by Lacan and psychoanalysis.

Lacan, the somewhat Hegelian Lacan, tried to inhabit the interval or the difference between need and desire. But thanks to drugs, if I can put it this way, other modalities and mutations are at work in desire or "irrepressible urges," and these sometimes provoke rather Kleinian articulations. Thus I have dealt with the difference Lacan establishes between need and desire as a luxury theory, that is, a theory that did not take into account the drugged or scarcely conscious subject in the truly abject precincts of being. Somehow psychoanalysis relies on a propped-up subject, more or less ready to speak (or remain meaningfully silent), despite entire symptomatologies that stall and block the subject's access to language. A certain level of being-present is a prerequisite—quite understandably, by the way, but this remains a problem. Why does psychoanalysis shy away from the addicted subject and the peculiar absences with which addiction is associated? Where does addiction begin? In fact, as Edward Glover has shown, anything can serve as a drug, and moreover Lacan was very explicit when he excluded drug addicts from the psychoanalytic scene, perhaps wrongly, given Freud's impressive though officially discarded texts on cocaine. But Glover showed that anything could serve as a drug, including, we could add, work, the "workaholic" syndrome, or athletic training, or piano practice, and anything that involves repetition, need, lack. I don't mean that a new characteristic of drugs as drugs is emerging—on the contrary, drugs respond to an internal appeal that is probably already present in all of us. One of my questions is: why are we equipped with receptors, as if built for drugs? In other words, we are all potentially subject to addiction, constructed as we are according to addictive qualities of attachment and need. What I find interesting are not only the abyssal nuances of desire, urges, or destructive *jouissance*, but also those of the seductiveness of technology and the often crushing ethos of work.

60

I'd like us to talk about AIDS here since, as it happens, I have been writing about it ever since it made its appearance. I'd also like to come back to this subject because AIDS belongs to our technological era. But first, because of what impresses itself upon us as headline news, let me offer some reflections on the rhetoric of national security that, perhaps surprisingly, is not unrelated to this nexus. A philosophical vocabulary of security has been developing ever since Hobbes. Today, questions of security turn up everywhere. According to well-known discourses, security appears to be a necessary response from the viewpoint of the "State" (still a useful shorthand term for what deserves to be unpacked if not dismantled) to the irreducible fear of the people or subjects gathered together in the State. Everyone talks about it, and since September 11, 2001, security has been a topic of tireless national discussion. Moreover, it is impossible to deny that today, in all spheres known as democratic, a questionable policing invasion is taking place in the name of "national security." What is troubling is the way in which this new imperative of security reinforces the very idea of the nation—national security also means security of the national as concept and substance.

Perhaps art can teach us how to read and analyze these lugubrious issues that have been rigidly imposed on us and that rightfully call on us to offer reflections in their direction. I'm thinking of the work of a performance artist who puts surveillance equipment on stage, makes screens and monitors disclose their idioms in provocative ways. Julia Scher, who often wears the uniform of a security guard, is interested in lesbosadomasochistic acts—not just any acts, but those that inform us about the attitudes and micropractices of the State. Her work is inscribed within a psychoanalytic prediction, I would say. She hones in on a masochistic politics that psychoanalysis was hinting at all along and whose logic would produce an unprecedented docility on the part of a highly technologized subject. This politics of submission no longer belongs to any recognizable lexicon of oppression, poverty, or class determination. For his part, Giorgio Agamben writes about a proliferation of surveillance, which is threatening democracy. I am not saying this claim is false, or simply true, but what compels my attention here may be all the more worrying, even more disturbing than the installation of these arrangements, namely the *desire* to be tagged, to be penetrated, so to speak, or the *need* somehow to be squeezed by invasive technologies that are never in remission. What form of seduction is proper to this intrusion that "subjects" invite of their own will? In the phenomenon of tele-reality—reality TV—people derive pleasure from the fact that they are watched, observed in their most intimate and thus "extimate" moments.

61

In fact, the problem of security is no longer what it was for Hobbes, the problem of the imposition of the State on the individual, the State being clearly designated as the aggressor, but the individual's own request to be under the sway of the panoptic gaze of the State, "seen through" in the privacy of his own body by medical interventions. A person who attempts suicide isn't yet thrown into prison, but we could reach that point . . . We may well reach the point, even if it's still science fiction right now, when individuals, in the name of security, will go so far as to ask the State to classify as outlaws people who want to kill themselves; we will no longer even have the right to dispose of our own lives.

I wonder about this Schreberian desire to be invaded by the spreading clinch of the State and to have ultrasound scans prescribed that will reveal the states of the soul and the body. Certain bodies open themselves up of their own accord to technological invasion and probing. It seems to me that by speaking of the problem of national security, by developing a critique of the problem, instead of being content to drag out the old myths or slogans and protests fired out on automatic, one would already have to try to understand the furtive desire that has put those technologies in place, that in some senses welcomes the breach of encroaching techno-talons.

I've gotten into the philosophical habit—if one can call it a habit—of asking myself, when confronted by a phenomenon—or even by an object that is not self-evidently appropriable for philosophy—what it corresponds to, since it responds necessarily, after all, to some appeal, to a crucial instigation and call. At Washington Square Park in New York, where I live, there are surveillance cameras everywhere, and certain people dance around with the idea that their own image is seizing the gaze of a hypothetical witness. When you walk by the window of a department store with such installations, you see your own image. There is a narcissistic flare-up that reflects back this image captured by the camera, and you respond to it by inclining the body/the "soul" toward the technology, which is there, after all, for the purpose of capturing your image or perhaps, as Native Americans thought, to steal something more intimate, or to conjure away the sacred.

To persist in thinking that the State is the intruder—I don't deny this—is not entirely honest, philosophically, in the sense that one is not getting at the foundation of what is happening at this moment in our dominant cultures. We find ourselves face-to-face with this often unavowable desire to be technologically devoured, to be restrained, confined by a technological apparatus or something of the sort. Here the Heideggerian question of the dwelling comes up again: where is that shelter, that house of being, located now? Freud said, and for him it was an important phenomenon, that to understand America one might observe the complete houses that were moved on trucks. Freud tried to explain the displacement of symptoms by this remarkable movement that seeks to show, via these prefab houses on trucks, an effect of contingency, the fact that ultimately there are no substantial roots. (Werner Herzog also uses this figure to track the fate of Bruno S. when he leaves Berlin and immigrates to America; Bruno S. and his little alternative family soon lose their mobile home and we see it carted off.) According to that figure, the house of being is already uprooted, displaceable; it traverses a sort of arbitrariness before settling down on some plot of land. The way in which American houses no longer contain ghosts, or ancestors, or any discernible traces of the past, remains a problem for Rilke and Heidegger. Nevertheless, phantomless places disturb Europe as well—why should only Europe host the ghost?

There are no longer any haunted houses, but there are haunted beings.

One can affirm that the phantoms have been displaced: they no longer inhabit the places they have occupied "forever," they're no longer sheltered, under cover. It's rather a question of displacement without phantoms.

To return to this strange demand for intrusions or unconscious invitations extended to policing institutions, what interests me are the secret complicities and the unavowable concessions that allow for technological control. There are "posthuman" bodies that need these intrusions and that need to leave medial traces. We have to understand the extent to which technological mutations are also structuring, prompting true adaptations. For Freud, from this standpoint, the telephone was highly invested, as a new structural element in the psyche. He used to say that the unconscious had everything to do with a telephone. He showed that the relation between the analyst and the analysand resembled a telephonic communication: there is the one who speaks and the one who listens. The same apparatus both marks and provokes distance, because one connects only to the absent, the departed. (For Alexander Graham Bell, this was a literal impetus—to connect to his deceased brother; he knew nothing of electricity, which is where Thomas Watson came in, himself a practicing medium who was also a professional electrician.) Every technology designates and surmounts something that is deficient, that does not work, that is definitively lost and that must be recognized as absent or defective. The typewriter was first invented for the blind, and the telephone, as a synecdoche for technology, was created to supplement ears that could not hear anything, those of Alexander Graham Bell's mother and wife, both deaf. I have worked on this directly, on the techno-hermeneutics of mourning, on the fact that in every technological arrangement there is a way of mourning some lost thing or faculty, someone or something that is lost but has nevertheless left traces, if not a number.

I think that technology creates a certain type of body, and I find this fascinating, worthy of study. Of course, we are in agreement that there has never been any question of a natural body, even though people and theories subscribed to that belief for a long time. Elsewhere I have spoken of the installed *Gestell,* in the technology of bodies, and what interests me is the way technology reinscribes the body for itself, the ever-posthuman body, that is, the already-technologized body, not only a body to which prostheses are added but also a body that harbors the intrusion of disruptive and foreign elements—even if they are quite at home and part of a larger irritation that affirms life—within itself.

> But doesn't this desire for intrusion necessarily lead toward greater alienation?

Not necessarily. I am considering the angles of a politics that would perhaps be masochistic, led and controlled, or remote controlled, by technologies. Heidegger noted that our era would see the domination of technology, but he didn't give enough thought to technology's demands, its increasingly insistent and transformative demands. This is probably where one would need to look for his weakness, the vulnerability in his thought of technique and technology. Let us not forget that, for Heidegger, the "discovery" of the *revelation* for which technology is responsible was of unparalleled importance. He made himself vulnerable in this respect. He thought of technology as "other" inasmuch as its advent implies a hostile, implacable force that is uprooting and altogether destructive. He predicted that it would impose itself with all its crushing negativity, and he has surprising moments of naïveté when he describes that technological incursion. He is not alone: there are very few places, or sites, where one can find thinking about technology that tries to interrogate with great frankness, and great indecency—because in this area one has to take risks—the always Promethean seduction, the desire to submit oneself to a technology that is also tied to a certain transcendence. Heidegger set us up to look for these qualities, but he himself for the most part desisted, and would have considered further interpretation no doubt trivial. Yet technology is in some sense the god of our time; if there is a key to a promise of eternal survival or indefinite prolongation of life, it is found here, and people are ready to fall on their knees before this promise and the reach of salvation on which it's pivoted—in other words, technology comes with its own brand of redemption and it would be interesting to pursue the way monotheism has steadily drained off into the technological articulation. Even Almighty God was already a sort of supreme technician, because he listened in, he heard everything; he represented, already, an instance of generalized surveillance.

We maintain an essentially ambivalent relation with technology; this may be a way of assuming our castration by knowing that we are in a world that has been split apart and reformatted by technology. Genuinely political thought would need to take the essence of technology into account, its sway and the ethics of decision that it impels. Technology is really what wins out and in many senses makes the decisive moves. It may be via television, candidates' self-presentations—whatever the case, the State constitutes itself technologically first of all; politics are secondary, it seems to me. By the way, I'd like to emphasize again that the logical conclusion to all this is that the "State" has faced its own dissolution as a metaphysically subsidized entity. I prop up this term, the "State," out of deference for its obsolesced grandness. With or without the State's participation, I don't know whether alienation has increased since technology began to dominate. I don't know whether I would affirm that, especially if the gods have taken refuge in technology. One might say that, for women, this is not always the case.

> I think that what remains transgressive, finally, is Freud's second model of the psyche, that is, the metaphorical affirmation that the hysteric does not always tell the truth when she claims to have been abused by the other, but that she is in that situation through her desire. And this is such a revolution! Even a child can be the place of desires, mad, perverse desires, and so on, and he grows up with that, but one can invite a desire in order to become alienated, and that does not always go down well today, I think. For example, the fact that what children say is now taken into account in all cases of sexual aggression is so important that it cannot be said to be a step backward, that would be truly criminal, but at the same time it participates in the victimization of society that means we are once again caught up in the phenomenon of designating the aggressor without taking note of what we all have in ourselves.

In America, the brunt of Freud's relation to hysteria is still contested, I mean morally contested and held suspect. Even if a woman or a child initiates some perverse behavior, the weak person cannot bear full responsibility for it in the eyes of the law. At the same time, in human relations surely there is to some extent a need for a violation by the other—a prod, or what Heidegger calls in another context a *Stoss*. Levinas and Derrida suggest our openness to such a prod or the awakenings that can be traced to similar traumatism. On a different but not unrelated level, we have to try to understand the shared responsibilities, from the very beginning, for acts that escalate to extreme aggression. We must reexamine these new cartographies and conducts, hysterical or otherwise, that are proposed, remodeled, by the evolution of technology. There is the regime of the new teletopias, reorganizations of our relation to the body; there is the way technology breaks with figures of autonomy, of sovereignty, of the whole gamut of humanistic values that try in spite of everything to keep intact things like the State, the body, the psyche—even if it is divided, after Freud (although Freud was particularly sensitive to these syntagmas, for he was open to technologies). I've pondered the extent to which the terms of his lexicon were borrowed from electricity in its infancy, for example, his concept of investment or cathexis (*Besetzung*). What is linked to the principal notions according to which the always-too-human being is constructed is the body without transcendence that nourishes technology, but this is not new. Dostoevsky, for example, remained flabbergasted before Holbein's *Descent from the Cross,* in Basel. It was a shock for Dostoevsky, a real trauma, because he saw in the depiction of pure corpse something that promised no resurrection, a body presented wholly without transcendence. Moreover, the fascination and horror he experienced before this painting organized his novel *The Idiot,* where he stages the return of a sort of flashback he cannot shake. I have the impression that there is something tending toward fascination and horror in that body that gives itself over to technology, that allows itself to be penetrated and invaded before being recuperated and upgraded by meaning.

We can note, in the problem raised by technology, that there is no specific point of origin. Drugs, television, the obsession with national security, and the effects disseminated by technology are "things" that are uprooting and uprooted as soon as they appear. They do not have a specific origin that could be readily isolated and analyzed. In this regard, I began to think about AIDS, which was, as I saw it, a crucial figure of technological revelation (I am quoting Heidegger), not only because it arose to a large extent in the technosphere of large cities.

At issue here is something that man has done to man, or to himself. At the beginning of the disease, it was known that the mutant virus had been passed along through monkeys, but it was not known at the outset that this was a manipulation. In any case, it is no longer possible to think of this epidemic as a punishment coming from elsewhere, as Jean-Luc Nancy also says; a technological immanence is involved. We are dealing in the first place with systems of urban transmission that function as movements, objects, structures, or technological topoi.

Furthermore, the problem of illness was under censorship, subject to a political and social taboo. No one remembers this any longer, but at the White House, in the 1980s, AIDS was a forbidden word or acronym. At the time, Reagan was president and AIDS, officially, did not exist. The word wasn't uttered; the subject was taboo. As was the case in China, even quite recently. I followed the political effort that amounts to believing that one can eradicate a problem by withdrawing the word that names it from circulation or by eliminating it from all official discourse.

In addition, I did a lot of work on polemology—the way in which war and disease tend to be constituted and organized around rumors. In what stirs up and gives birth to a rumor, there is terror in the face of something that cannot always be named, something that is going to spread uncontrollably. Even in Daniel Defoe's texts on the plague, the origin of the one or the other—rumor or disease—cannot be named: which came first? Which hits hardest? Do we really have a rumor about a disease that spreads horrific anxiety, or do we have, rather, a disease that spreads like a rumor? But the disease or rumor often comes up again in very dramatic moments or in big organizations like the one behind the Olympic Games: the games' organizers, for example, establish "rumor control centers," as if everything would be at risk of breaking down if rumors were allowed to spread everywhere like an epidemic or like Olympic relays. During the Second World War, there were reminders on Allied posters everywhere that "loose lips sink ships," rumors destroy or kill. This stems from what I see as a ballistic theory of language.

I've studied the connections established between rumors that circulate and disease (or the terror of disease) that spreads, starting with Rousseau, who complained about being persecuted almost to death by rumors—to the extent that he saw his own obituary in newspapers. He is taken down by the rumor of his death, a mighty weapon against his fragile constitution. I don't know whether or not this is the source of the prejudices philosophers entertain toward journalists. The latter are treated like leprosy that is spreading; Heidegger calls this *Gerede,* that is, linguistic parasitism, the sly inflation of a malicious rumor, gossip. He tries to save Nietzsche from *Gerede*; he is very fearful that Nietzsche may fall into the notorious inauthenticity of journalism. On the other side, there is Blanchot, who turns writing into a sort of murmur without an author. And rumors that can be valued positively—perhaps the dream of all writing, and of any text, is to be able to circulate—why not?—like newspapers, as quickly as a rumor, with the unstoppable velocities of an epidemic. When he arrived in the United States, Freud made a remark that has remained famous: "They don't know it yet, but I'm bringing them the plague." And let's not even mention deconstruction, which was disseminated throughout the United States in record time and has been charged with a destructive run that any cultural epidemiologist would want to investigate closely.

Keeping everything in perspective, these things that propagate themselves, these utterances that are disseminated and that contaminate are minority utterances, exiles, and philosophy has always been suspicious of them when it has not tried to suppress them outright. Heidegger, for his part, does this deliberately, openly. He seems to think that Nietzsche's text has to be locked down, cleaned up, saved from the attempt, or rather the temptation, to become a sort of epidemic and to provoke historic allergies. Whereas Nietzsche himself was very interested in the spread of symptoms. He used to say about his own writings that they were books for no one and for everyone, thus opening himself up to a politics of contamination that Heidegger tries to attenuate, the way firefighters try to stop flames from spreading.

I try to detect the immunocompetence of certain texts, that is, the way they deal with threats from the designated "enemy": these are texts that are afraid to catch something, afraid of being infected. It is even a matter, explicitly, of the way in which they simulate their own immunological deficiency, and this particular pathology is what I explore. These texts stand in opposition to others that, for their part, open up to contaminations and "diseases" from elsewhere, and recognize them. These are two contrasting ways of dealing with borders, limits, the self . . . Certain texts resemble the more phobic stances of the United States, and develop the type of obsessional neurosis that consists in wanting to defend their borders at any price, with a whole system of customs outposts. As we know, such strategies cannot succeed and serve only to stoke exclusionary hysteria.

> As far as AIDS is concerned, it must be said that in the beginning it was thought to be a shameful disease reserved for the homosexual community, then for that of drug addicts, "depraved" communities in which the idea of contamination as you explain it was omnipresent.

In the beginning there wasn't even any conceptual apparatus to make the nature of the disease comprehensible, whether it was a sin or an infraction or an affliction or a punishment or a short-term crisis or an aberration or even an unprecedented practical joke, and so forth. I remember Hervé

Guibert when he wrote about having AIDS himself. I met him in Rome thanks to Pierre Alferi and Suzanne Doppelt. At the time, he said that one of the first times he crossed paths with Foucault on the stairs—they lived in the same building—Guibert said to him: "Have you heard the rumor? There's supposed to be a disease that affects only homosexuals!" And Foucault apparently replied, laughing: "Ah, that's the latest, now there's supposed to be a disease for us, just to do us in. Ah, that's unbelievable!" In the effort to make AIDS understandable in the United States, we saw the reappearance of a huge moralistic regression. The lexicon of social infection, depravity, had immediately been grafted onto AIDS. And philosophy, or the philosophical language adopted by everyone went right along—one should not hesitate to examine street philosophy and its lexical choices. (In France, as in America, I think, people say "my philosophy of life," which induces the assumption that we all have our own philosophy that we use to contain, or to defend ourselves against, the unthinkable—or the thinkable.) I have tried to show, as I did for drugs, that AIDS had already infected Nietzsche's writing and thinking and compromised the always-too-young Mozart, whose death is ever untimely and to this day still cloaked in diagnostic mystery. At the end of *Thus Spoke Zarathustra*, Nietzsche praises the possibility of convalescence; certain diseases follow different structures of development and include phases of latency. We have to take into account, as Nietzsche did, the complexity of the immune system, for an organism that defends itself can turn against itself, by aggressively secreting antibodies. Nietzsche had anticipated and worked on this onto-medical network. I have been attentive to Nietzsche's antibodies, antibodies that misinterpret the other, the enemy, that let the enemy enter like a friend, that haven't read the texts on friendship of Aristotle, Aubenque, Blanchot, Tiberghien, and Derrida. Antibodies that let themselves be governed by another system of pairing. There is an almost technological intervention that changes the signals, because it is a matter of signals, a docket of plans, a relentless program. It is also a matter of a hermeneutic adaptation or misadaptation: the antibodies interpret the signals they obey, and they go off to pursue their war where they believe they are summoned.

In America, and perhaps especially elsewhere, a taboo was placed on the word "AIDS" for a long time, but then when people began to say it out loud, they refused to understand what it was and how it had been able to provoke a mutation in our very possibilities of thinking, of perceiving, of self-policing and especially of analyzing the AIDS phenomenon as being not only the effect of a great technological mutation that, like any trauma, was as structuring as it was upsetting. Since the advent of AIDS and the somatic September 11, the password for understanding language and social behaviors has changed. Each of us has been affected, and any vestige of innocence has become obsolete. Adolescents have had to grow up very quickly, or turn to virtual or telephonic sex. We have witnessed the emergence of a new form of police surveillance internalized by everyone, forms of self-surveillance, new tests for detection, in short, the pervasive idea of a latent harmful invasion, one not yet visible . . .

Which presupposes a state of generalized suspicion . . .

Certainly, and I would say that surveillance begins when everyone asks everyone else if he or she has been tested. On this basis, I have tried to consider how AIDS, repressed, moved elsewhere; for example, in the war undertaken by the first George Bush against Iraq. The conflict was organized around a vocabulary that was unconsciously centered on AIDS. It was a "bloodless" war, that is, highly technological, and "safe," the president repeated that word over and over, it was "safe sex" grafted onto politics, as if this were now possible. In the first phase of the war against Saddam, people spoke of phantasms of sodomy, of "saddamy"; the war was run with a remote-control vocabulary of immunocompetence and the Iraqis were represented as diseased, dysfunctional, and warped figures—there was fear of being infected by the enemy. But, when that first phase ended, they hadn't managed to liquidate Saddam. Bush 41 said things that corroborated the idea that this was a national test, and they were able to bring that phase of the war to an end knowing that they had tested negative, that is, there had been no infection, no contamination of the national body (we still have to look into the phantasm of a national body that has to be kept intact—by what means? by whom?). In contrast, GIs were falling ill. By displacement, repressed AIDS invaded the bodies of men presumed to be heterosexual, for at the very same time, starting under Clinton, people were talking about opening up military service to gays and lesbians. There were soldiers with autoimmune diseases, but this became once again a taboo subject that has been brought to light only quite recently and after legal intervention.

Except that the very thing they tried to repress, to displace and void, came back by way of the language used to describe the war, and it came back, too, in the bodies of infected soldiers. There had thus been contamination after all, with the problem of autoimmunity that reverses the stakes. The national body subjected itself as a whole to a form of test to find out if it was contaminated or not. We know very well that American officials are seriously phobic in their discursive and policing habits. Marguerite Derrida told me that once when she was entering the United States the customs officer asked her: "Do you have any snails with you?" This may sound amusing, but it is always a question of suspecting microbes, foreign (lit.) critters or bodies that are going to infiltrate. Discrimination against snails is not the worst of it. There are corresponding movements in the United States that consist in attacking the weak. Some political scientists invited me to speak about the rhetoric of the national unconscious; it is sometimes disturbing to observe someone like me who practices institutional contamination, because almost everyone in the academy tries to reinforce the boundaries of his or her discipline. There are customs outposts, borders everywhere, even if people say that the most important thing now is interdisciplinarity. This proves only that there are disciplines and that it may be possible to have antimicrobial bubbles and bridges.

> What do you think of what are called "gender studies," and of Judith Butler's work, for example? Do you think this work is inscribed within the neurotic defense of borders, or on the contrary that people are trying to put a little virus into the machine?

I would tend to choose the second option. Judith Butler is interested in the artificial, constructed aspect of gender, and she is situated, without seeking to be, I think, on the side of the virus. When she speaks of drag queens as citations and contaminations by a sort of image or iconic character of the artificial woman, I think she is developing something philosophically important. I know that many people appreciate what she has done, what she is continuing to do and undo. In one of her latest books, on prisons, she is interested in what happens to detainees. She worries, as we all do, about the renewed extension of poverty—something I link in turn with the AIDS phenomenon. Starting with the emergence of AIDS, we have gotten the green light to blame and severely culpabilize minorities, the weak, homosexuals, the poor, and the list goes on . . . I believe that the field of gender studies pays a lot of attention to the status of minorities and the disabled, foregrounding those who practice, intentionally or not, a kind of micropolitics. There is no longer sexuality itself, unquestioned, but a staging of the distinctive mark of gender with all its opacity and consequence. Butler talks about "gender trouble" (her book by this title has become famous recently in France), because people are troubled, disturbed, by these questions about sexuality in relation to gender. Here and there Judith Butler is attacked, and in a certain sense this is the fault of the French, because they wonder how it is possible that gender studies don't exist in France, implying that the field can't be interesting if it doesn't exist in France! The absence of the word "gender" in French is presumed in certain limited quarters to disqualify

71

what she does ("What about *Gestell*," I counter, "what about *différance*," and then you can't shut me up). She simply laughed when someone told her this. As for me, I would note that her book is in fact titled *Gender Trouble*, which means, according to her, that she is troubled by a disturbance she did not originate. The question of gender and the question of biological sex are often confused; people ask "what is the sex of your child?" whereas "gender," in English at least, means that this question lacks all stability, that it is stated as a question precisely because there is no surefire, categorical way of naming what one thinks one knows about the sexual determinations of the other, even of Being, as Derrida showed in his texts on Heidegger's *Geschlecht*, which introduced another relentless version of gender trouble. I know that some of what I've been saying here is Gender Theory 101, but that's because the French, in a strangely willed or unconscious way, are just not getting it—yet.

> In France, I think the common mistake is to take gender studies from the standpoint of a defense of a natural state, as if it were a matter at the outset of defending the fate of minorities (homosexual, transsexual, or other, "queer," for example), as precisely a sort of natural state to which they are thought to have a right and of which they are thought to have been deprived.

Indeed, gender studies can be perverted in that direction. But Judith Butler is a philosopher; what she does is rather difficult, sometimes very dense, and in any case, even if my appropriation has a tendency to go a bit fast or far, it seems to me that she would be more or less in agreement with my basic—if in this context simplistic—reading, that is, that gender is precisely something that is constructed, that is not at all stable or natural, on the contrary. The more a man shows off as macho, the more he looks like a drag queen; this is well known. For example, in May 2003 Bush 43 staged a theatrical coup, the famous "Mission Accomplished" episode: he landed on a warship wearing a pilot's uniform and everyone could see a prominent bulge between his legs. This may have been something that aviators wear to protect themselves, I don't know, but Bush showed up in supermacho form, walking with his arms a little out in front; you would have said he was mentally defective. He had a prosthesis—enormous genitals—and this was so exaggerated that it was funny. The very presentation of the body disrupts and disturbs gender. For example, in the gym I go to in Greenwich Village, a fairly gay neighborhood, the guys in particular tend to have very athletic bodies. Here again, since AIDS, the image of the homosexual body has changed: gays used to be seen as vulnerable, with more or less fragile bodies, and all at once the image of a really macho homosexual is that of a healthy body, a body codified as handsome. And it is de rigueur among gays in my neighborhood to associate the Greco-Roman heritage with leather.

Since the advent of AIDS, there are bodies that collapse, break down, deteriorate according to a new logic; and then there is this new stereotyped body, very strong; it's an evolution a little like that of the body of Israeli Jews. I am taking risks by moving too quickly, here, but the machine won't let itself slow down. In my imaginary field of projection, and not only in mine, the Jew is always someone who has a very vulnerable body, who looks like a victim, who gets picked up by the police, who allows himself to be deported, so to speak, who has a docile body, ready to let itself be crushed, eviscerated. Now we see the muscular, often bionic bodies of Israeli soldiers, killer bodies: these bodies appear to be redesigned, altered, and the whole profile constitutes a technologized body, artificially created. Those who were the most vulnerable are walking around now with bodies and buns of steel. I wonder what Roland Barthes would have made of this, because when he describes boys' bodies they are sleek, quivering delicate bodies that he would like to "wrap up."

In my analyses (for instance, in "Queens of the Night: Nietzshe's Antibodies" [*Finitude's Score*, 1994]), I wanted to show that AIDS existed prior to its phenomenal emergence, and I needed Nietzsche to denounce what I call the "medicine of *ressentiment*," which tries to track down only reactive threats and which does not have the honesty to speak and to insist, to struggle against what I still call, for want of a better term, the State. I find that, in some quarters and wards, medicine has become more reactionary and more reactive than ever. There are obviously several schools and several practices of medicine. I am talking about the dominant tendencies of contemporary medicine as practiced in hospitals and teaching institutions. It is devoted— and this is why I deployed a Nietzschean interpretation—to destroying any threatening reactivity whatsoever, but it is not interested in the entire set of political and cultural procedures involved in the evolution of a disease. It does not raise fundamental questions, and this is understandable, moreover. A whole history of vaccinations is profiled here. On the one hand, philosophy depends on a certain medical vocabulary to do its own work; it is interested in prescriptions, in health, in the vital being and becoming, thus in the animate. It borrows an entire symbolic system from medicine, in particular the idea of health and recuperation, of the reasonable, of the nonalienation of being, and, to become somewhat classical, of harmony. On the other hand, medicine goes to war, it leads attacks, prepares for battle, but for the most part it does not have sufficiently complex relations with disease or with health, it seems to me. To be sure, there are different kinds of medicine, and I don't want to simplify things or indulge in piling on caricatures, but decisions have been made, there are empty fields that have not been explored: until very recently there was not enough research on women's bodies, for example, before women themselves and some feminist men became gynecologists, research focused almost exclusively on men's bodies, and the imbalance continues even today. For the most part, only men's bodies are tested and universalized. In the twenty-first century, this is quite troubling. In the face of the increase in infectious and tumoral diseases, there are places of socially willed ignorance about which medicine has nothing to say, and, by the same token, a kind of silence, an unsaid, minimal interest in alternative zones of care and intervention.

You don't think that this is an effect of both philosophy and medicine? Medicine locks itself away in its deafness to any other discourse.

It's also because medicine conducts wars. Some strategies, tactics, maneuvers are not questioned, and, even without being a doctor, I can ask myself questions about the prejudices and presuppositions that are constantly manifested in the lexicon, the tendencies, the preferences of the discourse, praxis, and idioms of medicine. And even about the fact that funds are awarded to certain research projects and not to others. Some investigations are not considered important and necessary, others are compromised by shameless collaborations with the major pharmaceutical companies, groups, and lobbies underwritten against homeopathy. An immense amount of investigative work remains to be done on the theoretical motivation for such shutdowns—something beyond the perks and bribes offered by the pharmaceutical and insurance interests.

One wonders, for example, whether the constant increase in cancers, about which very little is said, might not be due to pollution, to the use of pesticides, or to other factors. But the pharmaceutical industries, which do spend enormous sums on anticancer research, also have dealings with the major chemical industries. One has a strong sense that there are unregulated zones that one cannot enter except by making dazzling speeches that have nothing to do with the logic of the economy.

In France, are there doctors who denounce the State, or industries that invite philosophers to work with them? We need to open the doors now and allow questions to be raised about their blind spots. Obviously I don't think that a person who carries out this type of research will raise fundamental questions: that's our job. Still, some people have begun to shake up the scene of academic-medical writing, most notably Hans-Jörg Rheinberger, in Germany, who produced a description of the culture of the laboratory according to a rigorous grammatology. Heidegger, for his part, went quite far when he said that science doesn't think: *Die Wissenschaft denkt nicht,* it needs thought to launch a necessary, deeper reflection. There are all sorts of things like this that I have tried to uncover and also to work on, very cautiously: one cannot simply stroll about in a highly complex laboratory that has its own history, its own necessity, its way of censoring, and toss about unfounded accusations. Plus, we still need to come to terms with what Heidegger may have meant when indicating his scruples and protesting the scientific impasse. One would have to take up Husserl's work on scientific crisis, the embargo on thinking that he sees announced, the questions he raises concerning the way science conducts its research. We are all getting sucked into an objectivist scientific warp, he warns, and, correspondingly, our values are being severely imprinted in truly worrisome ways—everything is being taken down to the level of objectivist criteria, everything.

# Nietzsche

## Symptom and Virus

So you work on the science of virology applied to philosophical questioning?

Let's start with some nano-thoughts on the AIDS virus (the strictly virological interpretation is being questioned in some research). It seems to me that it's important to reflect on the structure of latency according to which a virus can be dormant in an organism and suddenly awaken several years later. But we also need to reflect on what constitutes a break with the medico-philosophical diagnoses, if it's true, as Plato said, and Kant as well, in different terms, that part of philosophy's vocation is to be medicine for the living being.

Many of my strategies or tactics are perhaps paradoxical insofar as they are conservative, in a sense, while at the same time they are at the service of an idea or a force that may cause a given system to implode. They're little philosophical smart bombs. To advance, if it is a matter of advancing, I start, as others do, with canonical texts, and I try to show the subversive power that they already possessed in their own day, but also the way in which they have been or are being left dormant in the philosophical corpus or in the social body such as we experience it. I seek out and bring together topoi, places, traditional sites, or texts in order to be able to say "you see, the poison was already there, latent" . . . In other words, I try to see what happens when a text suddenly collapses (or awakens) under the effect of this corrosive "thing" that was not legible before and then abruptly emerges or is provoked out of its hiding place. Wordsworth's texts on idiocy are a perfect example. In his time, these were marginal texts that distressed his friend Coleridge, the eminent drug addict. The latter, the great philosophical *erectus,* tried to convince Wordsworth not to write such indigestible texts; he said that such writing was pure regression, and he was sincerely horrified by poems like "Idiot Boy," the one of which Wordsworth was fondest and which those around him found altogether disgraceful.

This exchange occurred in the mid-eighteenth century. Since then, commentators on Wordsworth, among them the revered scholar Geoffrey Hartmann, have not deemed these poems readable either. The texts are not understood, and their fate seems sealed for all time. However, one day, something in them is going to become readable, for all sorts of reasons and historical availabilities. And Wordsworth for his part adored his own poem on idiocy, though we don't know why. He could never let it go; he never regretted having written it. Worse still, he chose to publish it.

I try to show that idiocy, for Wordsworth, for Rilke, for Wallace Stevens and others, is poetry itself. It is the place of extreme nonknowing, or rather the site of an absence of relation to knowledge, a place of pure reflection that nevertheless has nothing to do with philosophy or cognition.

Wordsworth gives birth to a little idiot boy who becomes the central figure in the poem. With Hölderlin, the poem that describes the task of the poet is called *Blödigkeit* (stupidity), but no one has found it appropriate to translate as "stupidity." Translators have chosen "timidity," "deference," "openness to being," and other detours around its dismaying title. So how does it happen that this poem, and the one he wrote at the same time, *Dichtermut* (the poet's courage)—each mirroring the other and together describing the poet's task, disposition, and vocation—cannot simply be read together and translated more literally? Even Walter Benjamin couldn't bear the idea that *Blödigkeit* meant stupidity. It was completely blurred, scandalous. Even in Benjamin, who had worked on idiocy in Dostoevsky, after all, a certain allergy and blindness to the relation between poetry and idiocy can be observed. And yet these poets assert it. They say, in these poems, that there is something that resists all signification, all complicity of meaning, something that every great poet encounters and says often, precisely, without being able to say so.

Something essential is being stated here with respect to the sayable and the unsayable, but it has nothing to do with the cognitive registers of thought as we have appropriated them for ourselves. These poets confront us with the radical disappropriation, the dispossession, of the poet, with a lassitude or weakness of spirit that is virtually quasi-constitutive of what makes the figure of the poet capable of receiving the poetic word. In this sense, poems are opposed without being opposed to philosophic thought because they are the approximation of pure thought. Sometimes Heidegger, when he becomes more contemplative, fearlessly approaches a sort of stupidity or idiocy—a form of the Hölderlinian *Blödigkeit*—and he gets very close and goes very far along this unheard-of, unprecedented, untraversable path.

There are sometimes shadowy deposits in texts that we cannot really read, that have no arrival date or landing permit. They have not yet been stamped; the address is also missing; the communications are lost. As for me, I have set myself up as a sort of operator who is waiting for calls. It is a different relationship to *aletheia*, to truth, that appears here. I am not saying that I am the chosen one, although . . . why not! No, it is a matter of a certain relation to "truth" or to the unveiling of something that could be in hiding or could be resisting its own exhibition, or revelation, or manifestation. One no longer believes in manifestation, today; nothing manifests itself any longer, in our time, but there is surely a way to install oneself as the telephone operator by taking the calls that come in and light up the switchboard.

I have wondered, in connection with AIDS, whether other cases of illnesses in the archives resembled this enigma. For, at the outset, it was an enigma, owing to the very fact that one could get infected without knowing it for a very long time. And everything about the way this virus worked was unreadable. I fell back on the figure of Mozart, who died young and in an inexplicable way. I was interested not only in his mysterious illness, but in the way in which his last complete work spelled out the conditions of deterioration, that is, not the *Requiem* but the opera (or the operation) he called *Die Zauberflöte* (*The Magic Flute*). This opera is an absolutely improbable object for doing theoretical research on AIDS, but at the same time I think that reflection must precisely approach bizarre or resistant objects when it is thinking with or against the body. I proceeded with Mozart the way I did with Freud and Goethe, because I wanted to understand how the traumatic illness or traumatism of a bodily rupture is expressed and written in the body or enfolded bodies, in the corpus. And I wanted to understand the relations among these three networks—trauma, writing, thought—when they come into contact and interpenetrate one another.

I thought about *The Magic Flute* for several reasons. First, it is a violent and improbable encounter because, as Nietzsche says, Mozart is so *zärtlich*, adorable, sweet . . . And then, it turns out that thematically, in the opera, the flute is at once a threatening and an immunizing object, but this was also true in reality for Mozart, who detested the flute, by the way: something had to happen to that instrument, because the one who possesses the flute is redeemed. This opera turns out to be hospitable to invasions on several levels, multiplying the powers at work and the microbelike forces that insinuate themselves. There is Tamino: I call him Contamino, because he introduces this contamination. It all starts with the appearance of a sort of monster that has to be attacked and conquered, and Tamino is afraid. He doesn't have the immunizing powers needed to fight this monster that is protecting the space of the night. Tamino attacks the intruder in the realm of the queen of the night. But the queen sends him the three antibodies (the lady magicians) to do this in his stead. I wondered about the status of the flute, which is subjected to a cleansing process: *Sauber* and *Zauber*, almost the same word in German, *Sauber* means "pure, cleansing," implying a purification of the body, while *Zauber* means "magic." I have been interested in the status of this type of object in psychoanalysis, in this thing we take along to defend ourselves, somewhat like a talisman; Freud used the word "apotropaic" to designate an object that helps us defend ourselves and that is often poisoned. We follow the logic of vaccines or the inoculation of a poison that permits a cure, or rather, let's say, the phantasm of a cure—which is also very possibly a remedy.

> ... the way that repeating the trauma in the transferential space of analysis makes it possible to open up the trauma in the patient's life, in order to neutralize its deadly power and its repetition.

Yes, in a way. And I've been considering the way this flute circulates not only to help Tamino/Contamino and his allies win the day, first because we are in the realm of the queen of the night, but also to allow that object, that metonymy of strength, of immunizing power, to carry out a "Nietzschean" destruction. What wins out in the opera is Enlightenment. As we see in his correspondence, Mozart identifies with the queen of the night in her defeat, her loss of power, of strength, because it is she who gives the phallus-flute to the other, to the one who is going to defeat her and take away her daughter as well as her occult powers.

Among other things, this is about the feminine realm of the queen of the night, about the power of the lunar sphere henceforth dominated by the Enlightenment, a sphere whose paternal figure would be Zarastro, a sort of anti-Zarathustra who has the same name, the same face, but who would be, instead, in the service of Enlightenment and of the destruction of the feminine and of nonknowledge, of the mystico-matricial and uterine powers of the realm of the night. From a Nietzschean perspective, we can say that the domination of the queen of the night marks the triumph of the weak. Moreover, for Nietzsche, opera is the very genre of contamination, it is pessimism, Christianity . . . In addition to its manifest themes, opera stages a sort of battle, a kind of reciprocal infection between words and music;

music in its Dionysian purity is already contaminated by words. There is a transferential frenzy: music wants to *say*, while language dreams of becoming pure song. At the limits of the death drive music and language are kept apart—a predicament that no marriage of Figaro can resolve. The Enlightenment tries to erase some of these dark edges, against which the raging queen hurls her pained arias. Driven to despair by Enlightenment, she sings of *Tod und Verzweiflung* underscoring the vantage point of "death and despair." In his late correspondence, Mozart describes himself as weakened. And his lexicon is the same as the queen's: he speaks of *Tod und Verzweiflung,* of a nocturnal power that arrives and contaminates. We find this contamination again, besides the incredible name of Tamino/Contamino, in the character of Papageno, who is afraid of all sorts of invasions and encroachments—he's the only one who explicitly hangs onto life and vitality ("Das Leben ist mir lieb"—I ♥ life). In any event, everything starts with contamination; the opera is rooted in this originary and always problematic *master mix.* Perhaps this is also why the opera, like most operas, deals compulsively with impossible marriages.

I try to show the layers of latency, of mysterious relationships to illness, to theories of other illnesses, illnesses of the other, logics of contamination and the spectral fear contamination represents. I think that for Nietzsche the fatality that represents the realm of the night is the catastrophe on the basis of which the figure of the superman arises. But I would first like to stress the catastrophic translation of *Übermensch, surhomme,* in French.

How should it have been translated?

Differently. In a way that leaves room for the feminine, let's say. In English, I can allow myself a play on words: Nietzsche was an "overman," like us, he was "over it," that is, it was "all over," he had had enough of man—it's done with, "over." Heidegger thought that *Übermensch* should be translated, or understood, as the transhuman, because *über* does not necessarily mean superior; it can also mean beyond, in motion. In the prefix "trans-," there is transition. In any case, we should say "human" rather than "man." But, en route to *Dasein*, Heidegger doesn't care to see if there is something else, a micropolitics of the *Mensch.*

Recently I have worked a lot on the figure of woman in the work of Heidegger, Kleist, and Nietzsche. *Mensch* is different from *Mann,* moreover; Nietzsche doesn't say *Übermann.* But we haven't translated *Übermensch* by "transhuman" in either French or English; we've resisted this. We've produced lots of caricatures of the "superman," a term that mainly brings to mind a comic book character, today. The way the Nazis cannibalized Nietzsche, thanks to his sister's manipulations, is stupefying. Thanks to a program that fed this possibility no matter what, Superman was quickly transmuted into the Nazi idiom. However, Musil called this the only historical revolution that took no interest whatsoever in books, in texts, in any form of intellectual backing or life. It was a truly mindless political project, characterized by enormous stupidity, according to him. So how did they bag Nietzsche? There are a number of important hypotheses to consider, but we can leave that question on the shelf for now.

I am thinking about the failure of the realm of the queen of the night, which leads us, so to speak, toward the culture of the *Versuch,* that is, to tests, trials, proving grounds, in Nietzsche. The figure of the trial coincides with the theme of becoming or with the other themes raised around leaps and metamorphoses with a great deal of lucidity in the philosopher's work. What interests me is what opens up to feminine figures in Nietzsche. He himself identifies with a radical, audacious femininity, which is linked at every step to science and which sabotages its own essence, as Derrida shows.

In *The Gay Science* and in *Human, All Too Human,* Nietzsche writes about the philosophers of the future; I use this a great deal in my book *The Test Drive.* It is indeed a matter of tests, of trials, of a provisional logic of the trial, for trials or tests have a lot to do with the calibration of failure. Nietzsche creates a different logic with respect to failure, destruction; he introduces an absolutely new approach to these themes. The way he announces the arrival of the philosophers of the future (and they are always in the plural—this may also have been forgotten) allows him to introduce a new variable and allows us to elaborate a new political repertoire in Nietzsche. He calls these figures to come a *neue Gattung von Philosophen,* which has been translated as "a new species of philosophers." But *Gattung* is more stimulating than "species," to the extent that it implies gender as much as sex, the two sorts of gender, and new generational affiliations, some of which have been addressed by Derrida in his essay "La loi du genre."

Nietzsche does not settle the question, here, of the gender of the philosopher of the future, a question that motivates in part his pluralization of the philosopher. The pluralization of the philosopher-to-come destabilizes all sorts of philosophical customs and hierarchies, including those that honor the singular nomination to the function of philosopher-king, because it is a question here also of the queen, of the feminine/masculine cleavages in this function. As far as we know at this stage, future philosophers could well be a brigade or group of women, or perhaps they prefigure, in the approximating manner of a sketch or a laboratory test, the "transhuman," which in no way effaces the feminine.

The *Übermensch* is not an *Übermann*, not a superman; it has renounced the classical unity of the *anthropos*, given up on man, but at what price? The text is recalcitrant on this point. It offers a set of irresistible arguments for retaining the feminine as a trace of the future, even if it considerably complicates the Nietzschean heritage. It nevertheless stems from the experimental work that Nietzsche is setting up, even though in this text he eliminates one type of feminine force to the benefit of another.

There are at least two feminine types competing for the scientific legacy that Nietzsche is interrogating. Nietzsche attempts to get rid of the first one, which is accusatory and fatiguing. The other type for which he projects a future, as well as a name, has passed the test and has transvalued ordeals such as the exorbitant duty of submission that prepares one to be accepted as a philosopher. This new species, which can be named, in harmony with the Nietzschean notion of the *über* (which I continue to translate by the prefix "trans-"), transfeminism, will have brought the philosopher's curriculum vitae up to date. Transfeminists have understood and put up with the trial period during which they had to lay low, hold back, even hide; they share in the double bind, the double constraint that Nietzsche evokes in preparing the necessary testing grounds. They seem to cancel the match even as they play it, affirming its irrevocable character at the same time that they reject and dismiss its foundations. Veiled, self-contained, the philosophers of the future will perhaps refuse to let themselves be found out, as Nietzsche says. They communicate secretly with the figure who opens *Beyond Good and Evil*: "Suppose that truth is a woman—and why not? Aren't there reasons for suspecting that all philosophers, to the extent that they have been dogmatists, have not really understood women?" (trans. Judith Norman). There is thus a residue that philosophy has not known how to read, for which it has not been able to account. When matters become urgent or when truth is at stake, Nietzsche gives this residue a name: woman.

The "woman" hypothesis launches an appeal, it magnetizes the philosopher. Abundantly interrogated, it questions him as well, inasmuch as it is operating as a mere hypothesis, it grabs the philosopher by the balls. But let's not be too indiscreet or excessively anthropomorphic: woman, in putting truth into play, shares in this thought that skips the refrain of metaphysics. It is a dangerous "maybe" that Nietzsche establishes in order to put the philosophers of the future on the right track.

Try to imagine a philosophy that would subject itself rigorously to the "maybe" of life. The leap beyond signifies, among other things, that Nietzsche is not simply proposing woman as an outgrowth or a surpassing of the one who has been lording it over us for so long. Such a project would not be radical enough for him, would amount rather to a relapse. He is not seeking to reverse philosophical values or to change direction by means of a simple inversion of values. Woman in the place of man, one horizon for another: the horizon that would tolerate the self-importance of such a maneuver is perforated by Nietzsche's style. When Nietzsche opens up a space of complication for gender, he is not seeking to introduce a surreptitious dialogue or a rescue operation; in other words, he is not marking an end or doing an about-face only to fall back on one of the options that have been inanely imposed in the house of metaphysics.

One of these strange alliances and conceptual disgraces affirms that only misogynists and feminists know for sure what a woman is. For his part, Nietzsche invites the reader, in a performative style, to conceptualize this new gender, the one so badly translated as superman, the *Übermensch*. He creates a new species that contains some recycled components and other evolved structures, to be sure, but it is impossible genuinely to know or to say what that species is—this uncertainty belongs to its hypothetical character and marks the relation to a future that we cannot yet make out (if we could, it would not be the future).

We cannot say, since we are dealing with what was for Nietzsche a radical and still incomplete experiment, how the plural aspect of transfeminism binds, replicates, dissects, or levels woman. For example, to go further, Nietzsche would hesitate, before letting his thought prefigure these aspects, to subscribe to the projections of Richard Rorty, the presumptive heir who has produced woman as the response to an existential crisis proper to philosophy. Rorty names Catharine MacKinnon as the future of philosophy.

Catharine MacKinnon is a fairly important and controversial theorist or antitheorist whose pronouncements are, so to speak, conservative-radical, on the question of women and sex. She has railed against pornography; she has hard-hitting theories that could pass as conservative if she were not so interesting herself. She often makes war on so-called feminist writers such as Judith Butler, whom she deems too rhetorically honed. Many progressive, left-wing women find her positions inadmissible. At the same time, if we succeed in reflecting beyond political parties, she represents the sober counterpart of Valerie Solanas, the properly philosophical counterpart who worries about the constant humiliation and the equally symptomatic rape to which women are continually subjected.

Richard Rorty takes MacKinnon as an exemplar of the woman who is going to save philosophy. He himself defends an ethical, pragmatic feminism, apprehensive and impressive, but once again we have to suppose that we know what is involved in the transfeminism announced by Nietzsche and leased out in part to Rorty, beyond the regimes of lack, appendix, extension, reflection, and repetition that are ascribed to it. This new figure, proposed by Nietzsche, is a way of naming what is continually put to the test, and it takes on the language of viability without being able nevertheless to resolve anything at all, or to satisfy any condition, reason, afterthought, or primal memory. In this sense, it designates rather the requirement of the test, revving up the "test drive."

If woman appears as a hypothetical but imposing being in the opening lines of *Beyond Good and Evil*, Nietzsche introduces a hormone injection into the female body—toward the end of the text, he talks about the philosopher as "perhaps a storm himself, pregnant with new lightning": Nietzsche is "pregnant." Nietzsche, once again, is expecting. And, on the other side, there is Eve, it's all about Eve . . . Eve is the one leading the fight to know what was forbidden, and it is owing to her that Nietzsche can say that God vetoed science. God is terrorized by science, and no less by Eve: it is because of this troublemaker, a scientist before (her) time, that things are going so badly. Nietzsche thanks her for having introduced the viability of evil, life which is henceforth hypothetical, scientifically driven.

The hatred directed against women that comes out of the Judeo-Christian tradition is hatred directed against the impulse to know, Nietzsche more or less says in *The Gay Science*. *The Gay Science* itself poses a problem of translation, since in English and German it is a question of exemplary science and not of knowledge or of what is understood under the regime of knowledge—the French translation may not catch this drift with *Le gai savoir*. Now exemplary science has gotten itself mutilated and punished by man, who was servile and docile toward his God. And science is Eve's abandoned kingdom. Obviously, Nietzsche needs Eve, because she went "beyond good and evil," because she knew very well what was presented as evil and that she was the first to have gone beyond it; she is the scientist, and if religions detest women, if cultures say that women are led by vulgar curiosity, it is primarily because they condemn and repress Eve's scientific impulse. This symptom is what survives the brutal repression: by nature or by naturalization, women are curious. Curiosity remains a somewhat negative idiom; a case in point is Heidegger's hatred for the *Gerede*, that is, everything connected with curiosity, in *Sein und Zeit*.

Nietzsche as a symptomatologist is interesting.

Nietzsche has a lot to teach us on this point, as everyone knows. He should have fascinated Freud. But Freud had a difficult relationship with Nietzsche, formulated according to the logic of the borrowed kettle: Freud says that he has never read Nietzsche because Nietzsche expresses the same thing he, Freud, expresses, and moreover Nietzsche is wrong because he says the same thing as Freud. What persistent abnegation on Freud's part! There are two detectors of concurrent symptoms, here, two doctors of the soul and the body, as it were, and there is a great deal to be said about their relationship—starting with a dossier of complaints opened up by Derrida.

What has become clear to me in Nietzsche's work is his aptitude for detecting viruses. He is not simply a genealogist of morals, he is also an expert in cultural virology. I would not want to betray his work by dialecticizing it artificially, but I would like to return to the way in which he communicates his admiration for strength and power—because this loyalty, expressed in all his work against the strong, has often been very poorly interpreted by the powerful.

> This has often been read, in the wake of his sister Elizabeth, as something that, in this philosophy, could pave the way for burgeoning fascism. It is not said often enough that strength, for Nietzsche, is not the strength of the "blond beast," it is even the antithesis of that strength; it is rather the decadence of the last man. The strong are not the ones who dominate and who exercise power; these latter would be, rather, the "last men," the decadents.

And the strong ones whom Nietzsche praises are also the weakest, the most exposed—because they are risking everything, they have everything to lose—and they are the most apt to get infected by pessimism and other types of lies with respect to the crucial vitality. There is a massive "non-reading" of Nietzsche which leads to all sorts of a priori assumptions and misunderstandings about his work on this topic. Of course, something in Nietzsche has allowed for these perversions. What I want to suggest is that, when Nietzsche tries to develop the destiny and fate of the structures of the strongest, he has to go into his autoimmunitary laboratory, where we see that the strongest are often the most vulnerable. But there are also those who are strong and who tolerate parasites; these figures put themselves in jeopardy, however. Heralds of radical hospitality, they invite parasites and foreign bodies to dwell in them. Being so great and so confident, they run the risk of being poisoned by destructive forces, even by bacterial or microbial organisms. Nietzsche's work is of course replete with medical obsessions, but the question of reabsorption of semen that he practiced or preached, for example, has particularly piqued my curiosity.

> Let's come back to idiocy, which continues to constitute a blind spot for philosophy today and at the same time may be its hidden driving force. How is it different from vulgarity or stupidity? The stupidity of the media, for example—is this different from what you're talking about?

If one doesn't know what idiocy or imbecility are, one doesn't know what knowledge is; idiocy and imbecility cannot be simply opposed to thought. If we had to talk about stupidity on the part of the media, we would have to start by interrogating a transcendental stupidity. This is perhaps a projection, or a hallucination, but I have the impression that most thinkers and philosophers in France are left in peace, or else left to carry on inter-necine, thus autoimmunitary, wars. In America, we witness not only the wars declared on the poor, on drugs, on education, on the weak and the abandoned, but we also see an avowed and pernicious anti-intellectualism, of which the dominant culture is actually proud. This is a stupidity that is openly espoused and from which part of the culture benefits.

This no doubt is one of my phantasms concerning France, and perhaps Germany, and it is a way to experience things hyperbolically, but I believe that in France one would never be proud to be stupid, as people sometimes are in the American homeland. But, once again, these things cannot be set in a relation of simple opposition. The idiomatically American forms of stupidity give rise to unsuspected structures and knowledge, and even to quite astonishing media, with a remarkable use of language. In contrast, when President Bush declared time and again: "You see, I got bad grades and I'm the president anyway," he doesn't add: "And I'm destroying the planet anyway." There is not always a guilty conscience in the United States with respect to this crushing vulgarity, this generalized lack of discrimination. It is surely a complicated matter, because people are at the same time more open, they allow themselves to be "infected," happily, they allow themselves to be devoured, they submit to others, that is, to the seduction of foreign thought, and very important movements counter the manifestations and hold of the dominant stupidity. But once again we encounter theoretical problems. What can be opposed to stupidity? What would it look like?

If I were in France, I don't know whether I would have wanted—or been able, philosophically and theoretically—to work on the theoretical intricacies of AIDS and drugs. Or even on telephones, weaponry, or other philosophemes from the street. When I come to France, I wrap myself entirely in a cocoon in a doubtless artificial way. Away from home, one necessarily becomes a conformist, because one is so grateful to the host country, and it's harder to perceive the difficulties or the unacceptable things that go on there. Whereas in America I succumb to insomniac anxiety all the time; this is surely my way of remaining vigilant—I'm hyperlucid in the sense of PTSD'd to the max. In France, I don't judge as much; I'm more taken in by what I see and hear, and I'm not in the state of irritation that I reserve for the United States, where it is part of my civic duty to practice skepticism and invent forms of critical alert.

When I started working on AIDS, in relation to the circuits that Nietzsche and Mozart set up, it was first of all for ethico-political reasons, because no one wanted to touch that problem, as if the subject itself were as dangerous as an infection—or crack cocaine, for that matter. When I gave my first seminar on drugs at Berkeley, some students' parents called the university to complain, because there are things one isn't supposed to teach, or say. In their eyes, I had become a de facto dealer. They thought: "But who is that person who's dealing drugs to our children?" Or else: "What is that woman doing, talking about AIDS? That's going to infect us all!"

What's at issue here is the coconstitutive status of rumor—speech that spreads—and infectious disease. As soon as someone announces a theme, including sexuality, it's already perverse, even if nothing has yet been said, no content filled. When I teach in America, I often make a point of scandalizing my students, because there is a sanctioned refusal to reflect on these objects of thought, or on themes like addiction that are not at all theorized. My students know what they're in for at this point, so we work on things together without a sense of scandal or provocation beyond what the work provides. Still, there is a sense of crossing a line or brushing up against a censored area of thought. In France, censorship probably traces a different cartography, I don't know. But I don't see any departments of pharmaco-philosophical thought anywhere . . .

> Elsewhere, there might not even be anyone to speak out against you or contradict you.

Idiocy may be intruding into new spaces at the moment, but it isn't the stupidity I was talking about earlier. As a good Nietzschean, I'm always thinking about how to detect the transvaluations and mutations that are underway. In a certain form of idiocy, we find the conditions of radical innocence. Joan of Arc, for example, was illiterate, and yet she was able to receive orders from elsewhere, from above. There are figures in our history who have opened themselves up to an appeal or call, and the response to that call presupposes a stupidity that would be the same thing as a maximal opening to the other, that is, access to an emptiness that would not (it's a dream, a fantasy) have been corrupted by writing, by learning, by the material aspects of thought. The way George Bush thinks he is open to the call of God! Bush, for his part, governed in a state of extreme paranoia, claiming that God's will is accomplished through him. Sometimes the heavens manifest their choice by organizing quasi-transcendental trials.

On the subject of trials and tests, I wanted to say something, too, about the way George Bush reacted to September 11. Throughout the day he was in hiding, absent. When he finally appeared, that evening, he said among other things that we were undergoing a trial: "Our nation is being tested." For me, spotting the idiom of testing is a very important task. It cuts across all sectors of politics, ethics, and aesthetics. Joe Biden disturbed his party's campaign in 2008 when he stated that Obama would be tested. We can also follow the red thread of testing in the realm of interactions between medicine, moral values, and the social body. In work on AIDS, we are constantly confronted with the "test" (for HIV), with the trial of this test and the way in which people are being tested now; these are concepts or quasi-concepts that interest me greatly.

There is a politics of contamination of idioms, words we use every day that have come to designate our relation to the world. Now, in the circulation of these idioms, what is qualifiable, or, on the contrary, what is disqualified, is no longer so much the relation to truth. The way the vocabulary of testing has entered language modifies the status of truth and of certainty. There is a whole network of changed, transformed relationships that could be conflated with—without being consciously reduced to—the problematics of testing, the truth serum, the necessity of which was first marked by Nietzsche, I believe. And it was Nietzsche who identified America as the site of "aggravated experimentation." He even predicted—I mention this because Reagan has his undead way of returning and Schwarzenegger keeps on being reborn—that America would be the place where actors would become politicians.

For Nietzsche, this had its good and bad sides, that is, what he called role-playing, the ease of putting on masks. This whole register is very provocative. He sees it as the American dream, saying that in America everyone can realize their dreams (and their nightmares)—you're a plumber one day, a musician the next: only in America can you change rhythms, styles, masks with incredible facility. But Nietzsche also says to watch out, because actors are going to dominate in America. In contrast, he himself, who knew how to appreciate the values of masks and fictions, shows the good side of all that, as well, saying that the best masters of role-playing are the Jews, for example, because they are obliged to play roles; they have neither the choice nor the right to be, as people say wrongly, authentic. They need to master roles in order to survive. Nietzsche, as a Jew by adoption, because he wandered as a Jew through some key passages in his work, often says that Jews are more gifted than others for role-playing, that they master roles well—which means that they are perhaps like those women or men who know that there is no essence, essence being always dangerous, and no substance of being, but only a necessary and unpredictable becoming. Nevertheless, any mastery attributed to Jews or to women signals a problem, and indicates a certain disturbing manipulation, even if it is Nietzsche who says this, in admiration before the fiction asserted.

> When one is operating within a logic of autoimmunity and contamina-
> tion, doesn't the culture of testing become more and more predominant,
> since even so-called nature becomes suspect?

Let us give the logic of autoimmunity its historical place at the table of critical discussion. It is no doubt necessary to observe in a new light how things collapse on themselves. They are disabled, not by some outside force, but by a misreading of what constitutes friendly or hostile arrivals, intruders, guests, or crashers. Henceforth we have to contend with the way "autodestruct" prevails over events and historical narrative, informing suprapersonal and private encounters—this logic supplies one of several triggers that deserve our attention. I wanted to situate the culture of testing and self-testing within the history of Protestantism, insofar as Protestant culture was constructed against all dogmatism, in a respect for doubt, for hypotheses. Nietzsche sees those lies that constitute racism as the absence of tests, because there is no proof for the racist phantasm. I study the notion of retraction in Nietzsche: thanks to tests, caesuras, the culture of caesuras, one must be able to retract oneself (even at the price of an intimate tearing-apart), because it seems to me that from now on that idea belongs to contemporary thought and to physics and to philosophy. What Nietzsche shows admirably is that with tests, examinations, trials, one works up to the limits of failure, up to its orgiastic enjoyment. A test implies failure; the two take shape together. As far as Nietzschean rhetoric is concerned, tests and the way they are fueled by failure are related to the structure of promising. For Nietzsche, man is defined as the promising animal. But keeping a promise becomes a vertiginous adventure, bordering on the impossible. Owing to his finitude, man is not in a position, finally, to keep his word. At the same time, one can only promise to promise, can only (*sich*) *versprechen*, which also means, in German, to make a slip of the tongue. Thus man tirelessly betrays the promise of his essence. Henceforth one will no longer get oneself whipped by his lordship if there are no results, one will go looking in the trial itself for the validity of a thought or its invalidity, which would also be important, because we are still getting burned by a culture of results.

Nietzsche's thinking about promises and oaths shows that we are not in a position to promise anything at all, because, among other considerations, in order to promise, we must first be in a state of inebriation and illusion, as it were, allowing us to think that we can project and conquer eternity. We say: "I'll love you forever," yet as finite beings we are not in a position to make such a promise or to carry out that speech act. This shows that we are constantly in suspense. The acknowledgment of the weak hinges of promising may seem to open a Pandora's box of immoral allowances. In fact, this offers the conditions for hyper-responsibility, an offshoot of Hölderlinian sobriety. The tendency to promise is great and inerasable; it happens every time you open your mouth. So we need to give this primal impulse some serious thought and not shy away from looking straight into its downside.

# IX

# On Trial

*The Test Drive*

Can you give us a sense of the stakes and essential direction of your recent work, which promotes an unusual critique and philosophical appraisal of science?

The double-edged title of my latest book, *The Test Drive*, signifies both the drive and the desire for a trial. But "test drive" is also the expression used when someone is trying out a new car, in the space before saying "yes" or rejecting a purchase—this moment links testing to the problem of decision. I invited Suzanne Doppelt, a photographer and writer, to participate in the construction of my book. The book includes some quite experimental photos: ghostly, difficult to make out, and at the same time very powerful. These photographs are there to set us on the path toward complicity in this modulation of the relation between *technê* and *episteme,* technology and knowledge. My hypothesis is that the culture of the *Versuch,* that is, of the trial and what belongs to the whole field—semantic, theoretical, and material—of testing, is one moment in the deployment of technology in which we find ourselves. It involves the need for, and almost the invention of, a new instinct: the instinct that leads us to test our mettle, so to speak (with Shakespeare), and to get through trials, to put everything to the test, including ourselves and those close to us, and their particular form of relation to us. I think that this new instinct, this passion for tests, in fact entails a major displacement in our relation to truth.

The omnipresence of testing, of the examinable and the testable, which has been emerging for several decades, is nevertheless not new. The God of the Old Testament was already quite addicted to testing and contestation, to ordeals and trials! In the Bible, even souls are tried, put to the test. We can see the Devil, the figure of the tempter par excellence, as an apparatus that tests without pause, setting traps and tests meant to trip you up—or upward, heaven-bound, if you pass them. Goethe made this a major theme in *Faust*. Mephistopheles is engaged by God to put the most faithful mortal to the test. At the beginning of the trial, he is a dealer: he supplies Faust with ecstasy prepared by witches, a special blend of witches' brew that opens our hero to all sorts of temptations.

For Nietzsche, temptation, that is, *Versuchung,* is an experience bound up with a *Versuch,* a trial. Nietzsche is tracking the fate of tempters and attempters.

How can this help us read modernity, if it has always been there?

Everything depends on how our way of being in the world, our "being-there," is announced—according to what modality, what requirement. According to Heidegger, we haven't entered the age of machines or technology; rather, there are machines and technologies because it is the age of technology. It may be that there have always been "machines"; *technê* has always exerted pressure, at least, starting in Antiquity and even earlier. It may be that nothing is absolutely new, but we see that mutations of structures or marks are leaving their places of latency and showing up, imposing themselves in broad daylight. In addition, there are "appeals" that bring to light particular articulations of *technê*—an entire calling system that I tap. I am trying to pursue the mutations, the caesuras and alterations that are scarcely legible, but at the same time my attention is drawn to what Heidegger was able to designate as the *essence* of technology.

With reference to some of Heidegger's texts, the initial question, in relation to these mutations, would be: what is the source of this need we have to submit everything to proofs, to examine, to test everything? If testing is an integral part of technological domination, to what necessity does it correspond? How does it get articulated in unexpected places, in different and persistent ways? Since the appearance of AIDS—a considerable mutation in the history of technology that we have been discussing—when two people go out on a date a particular question is now part of the amorous discourse: have you been tested? It is the start-up question in the relation to another being. I even ask my lipstick if it's been (animal) tested.

Here I am sliding toward a popular or everyday use of the test drive. In general, I proceed in circles around everyday phenomenological habits, between the gutter of *Gerede* and high philosophy. Or even, sticking to low-flying philosophy, Carl Schmitt, who had so much to say about enemy relations. So, Carl Schmitt, have you been tested? One offers the test to the other, as a token of sincerity: there's no hostility here, no one wants to kill you (yet). In the will to seduce, it's still necessary to demonstrate good faith, that is, to have a kind of certificate in the form of test results. This is the empirico-Schmittian side of things.

Then there are at least two forms of test or trial, depending on the criteria of qualification or disqualification that one observes. Starting from the point when the great stories or narrative myths—the "master narratives"—no longer function, as Lyotard used to say, but simply affirm or destroy other types of insinuations, other markers of the real are there to replace them. We're currently witnessing the deployment of something more subtle than any sentinel of logic or truth, that is, the deployment of something that disqualifies or corroborates, something that renders every previously posited truth as a provisional or even precarious truth. What interests me are not the great narrative systems that destroy or create a world ex nihilo, while letting us believe that it is possible or desirable to reconstitute the world without raising the question of the status of the "world."

A different relation to being (to what is not, to what is) is being instituted, one that is largely based on and governed by this phase of the technological disclosure, it seems to me. Scientific tests themselves are not as transcendent or as univocal as one might think; we have a tendency to associate them with expert results, with certainties, but as soon as we take an interest in the culture of laboratories, we see that reliability is never total, that we are only operating within a system of probabilities. It is rather a matter, as Hans-Jörg Rheinberger has said, of a sort of grammatology of laboratory writing; something else is involved, very subtle proceedings, framed by a sort of writing, decisions, traces that are there and not there, legible and illegible at once. A whole history of scientific literature remains more or less unexplored, but what counts for me is especially the way we have assimilated the culture of the test, the way we experience the difficulties and demands of trials, to the point of feeling a need to test ourselves, a need to supply proofs of our own validity or viability. Everything becomes a subtle process once again: there is very elaborate thinking about evidence, about the way an object is constituted, and at the same time a continual testing of that evidence. For example, the DNA tests that have legal standing actually pose many problems and open up new dossiers on law, medicine, pharmacology, the human body or bodies, artificial or partial animals. Even the pope has written about verifiability. Another route to explore, which I did not explicitly pursue in the book, concerns the relation of police laboratories—forensics—to criminal justice. The appeal to the scientific method and policing are of utmost importance, and the television series that proliferate around this alliance are not wrong to show their fascination, their narrative avidity, for laboratory techniques (and technicians).

> Could you come back to the idea of evidence after Kafka? Do you mean by that that we've lost the evidence of innocence?

After Kafka, we can no longer provide enough evidence to protest our innocence. We can no longer prove anything at all. The word "trial," in English, expresses this well, since it designates both an ordeal and a legal proceeding in addition to its scientific usage.

Kafka wrote a very fine text called "Die Prüfung" ("The Test"). In French, this has been translated as "L'examen," but the German word has a much broader semantic field and Kafka carefully pursues the gradations and degradations of the being that is tested, examined. The one who refuses to respond is the one who best passes the test. Kafka's prose is constructed around proliferating hypotheses that stage the limits of their own verifiability. There is first of all the Platonic trajectory in which the hypothesis of the examination is situated. All these mutations interest me, because they come from very far away, culturally and historically, and yet after long periods of latency they are resurfacing on a massive scale, as we can see today, when—this is at least my hypothesis—the test drive is intervening on all of life's multitracked semantic registers. These are the trajectories that Derrida dealt with in a different context when he wrote about the Germanness and Jewishness of Hermann Cohen, perhaps the greatest of the Protestants. The work of these mutations bears upon the status of the hypothesis, a hypothesis whose provisional logic, a logic that combats all dogma, is also that of the trial. Authority itself is called into question—any authority whatsoever, including that of God or father and their satellite entities.

Authority is henceforth linked, paradoxically, to repetition. That is, to the possibility of proving, of subjecting to examination, of testing and repeating tests before witnesses (hence the great importance of witnessing, testimony, in these reflections). Yet the repetition itself spoils any possibility of definitive authority, because it may at any moment be canceled out by another test. To sketch out the difference between inventors or alchemists, whose knowledge is connected to magic, to secret things, and scientists, we might say that the opposition between them bursts forth with this culture of experimentation in which everything becomes subject to its own possible destruction (although the opposition does not hold up in strict terms, it offers a new relation to life, to truth, that posits the possible in a completely different way). The movement of disclosure that passes through the alche-

94

mist, that is, through the author hidden in his study cultivating secret texts and formulae, carries out inadmissible maneuvers whose meaning and interpretation are tied to an inspiration that is often divine and shrouded in secrecy. The figure of the alchemist is receding, making room for that of the scientist who can put to the test and make known in the public light of day the value and the reliability of such examinations. This requirement of a trial was discovered and invented or delimited by Nietzsche as belonging to our experimental disposition, to our post-Christian origins, for in spite of everything it is Christianity that prepared the way for welcoming such probity. Christianity and art have prepared us to receive and act according to the experimental disposition, with all that this implies. One can no longer bear false witness about life, according to Nietzsche; everything is subject to the probity of the trial. Nietzsche understood that from now on we have to have witnesses, attestations, a concept of iteration—it is a gift, but nothing is given. His thinking about gifts is intrinsically connected to this understanding. When Christianity switched to the faith channel, it conceded the space that belongs to proving and testing things out. In this way, it opened a back door for the desire, enacted by Eve, to figure things through try-outs, even though severe punishment was sure to follow unauthorized acts of probing. But punishment can be exciting, and so one's scientific curiosity was aroused. The scientific testing depot was around the corner from the Christian prohibition.

At the same time, isn't there still a presupposition that there is a master who has the key to the test?

Even when the test purports to be able to find and localize the result or the truth of a scientific undertaking, on the basis of a trial, a countertrial will intervene and systematically destabilize all certainty. The master is a momentary prop.

We need results all the time, but results are systematically overridden. There is henceforth a different relation to time, and this is an essential reason why Nietzsche had to be interested in time. First, in the order of the eternal return—but Dionysus is at one and the same time the god of trials, of transformation, of self-destruction, and of extreme creation, and under conditions in which there are a lot of risks to be taken. My own reading of this, if I can say so with a straight face, is carefully restrained. We know that Nietzsche is an antidemocrat, but, for him, if there were a sort of paraconcept of democracy that could "work," it would be situated in the register of the test. The idea of democracy would not be something stable, it would not be without a relation to that which exceeds it; it would not be something simply subject to a categorical dictatorship, whether a dictatorship of concepts or a dictatorship of politics or ideology. Democracy would have to be radically democratic, able to host its own parasites, open to the disturbing adventure of its destructive tendencies.

Integral to the concept of democracy is a continuous defeat: democracy entails risks, threats, and massive instabilities. From the starting point of his thinking about the experimental disposition, about life itself as an experiment, Nietzsche emigrated to America to find a site in which self-testing abounds, spritely mutants are born, along with forms of governance and possibilities of different relations to the future.

According to Mary Shelley, the author of *Frankenstein,* democracy in America began with a violent break, one that has haunted America ever since, because this violence (as we are seeing today) keeps returning in a ruthless or ungovernable way. In the *Frankenstein* story, the monster, the unnamable monster, starts out as an autodidact. A whole theory of language, of memory, is developed because the monster has no master or teacher, no outline of knowledge to guide him. He is alone; he lives in a hut at one point and hides himself away. But a family lives nearby, an Arab family that reads, writes, and speaks; from this moment on, the Frankenstein-monster begins to learn. Moreover, his native language (his mother tongue) is French, because he is Swiss. He sometimes resembles Rousseau. At one point, the narrator has the monster say that the discovery of America was not delayed enough, not gradual enough. A form of violence caused a place that would be henceforth haunted to spring up or to be invented. The monster himself is an aspect of this haunting, the provocation of abrupt origination, and he identifies himself with the scientific invention that gave birth to him. And, for Nietzsche as for Mary Shelley, America is a sort of laboratory that contains and spikes monstrosity also. Now, one could say that democracy is being tested there, but for these two authors it was already, from the beginning, a test, a test-tube baby. It cannot be said that democracy is being tested only today, for it has always served as proving ground and part of a test; democracy has always included intrinsic problems of monstrous destruction and unavoidable self-destruction. Mary Shelley has her monster stress that the way America was discovered was too rapid, too abrupt. The technological speed involved was phenomenal, and deadly; in other words, this monster is already an effect of technology.

Mary Shelley was very interested in electricity, in the destruction of the world by shapeless forms, technological monstrosities, and she was very close to—probably in love with—Andrew Cross, the great theoretician of the era of electricity. For her, as for Heidegger, America was at once the place par excellence of technology and a place without ghosts . . . designating the monstrosity of something that had been untried, not yet been tested, that had no history, no childhood. For a monster has no childhood. We see this with Goethe, when he speaks of beings that are born without being born, without having developed a childhood and without having been able to ask initial questions. These questions have to be asked for there to be even the possibility of a history.

This invention of America, which was already modeled on a scientific discovery, interested Nietzsche and Mary Shelley specifically and explicitly, even if their milieus had little in common; this was true for Rilke and Heidegger as well, for America was a testing place par excellence, a proving ground or nuclear test site, even if one could not yet imagine this at the time, that is, a place where everything is at risk of blowing up because there is an excess of drives and of speculation, testing—a different culture of try-outs. At the same time, for Nietzsche, who always worked on a double register and according to a double rhythm, the site of these excesses is also, perhaps, our only chance. The notion, very celebrated in America, of "living dangerously," which is Nietzschean, comes from that context, that power to put oneself in danger, as people legendarily do in America; it provided, for Europe and for the world, a spectacle of unbounded risk, and at the same time it offers the only chance to make a break with history. And, in Nietzsche, there is a will to break with the monumentalism of history that weighs down, oppresses, lulls to sleep like a bad drug. In this view, America would be, among other things, a detoxification clinic for Europe. But we have to be careful: rehab doesn't always work.

I am also interested in something that the writer Laurence Rickels demonstrated a long time ago (twenty-some years ago, an eon in American time): the intersections and subterranean communications between California—the extreme site of America, of the concept of America—and Germany. Rickels has continued his work on Nazi Germany, showing that Nazi ideology continued to work on us; it was implanted in California, especially in the cult of adolescents, body builders, group psychology. It so happens that the actor Arnold Schwarzenegger is California's governor, and Larry Rickels sees Schwarzenegger as the third Austrian who has found a place in the active and living imagination of California, that is, of the future of the United States, after Freud and Hitler. These three Austrians, he thinks, direct the American imaginary by remote control.

97

But does he think that this is harmful, or does he see it rather as a stage that has to be gone through in order to come up with an antidote?

It may be the case that adolescence (and California) harbor the neo-Nazi tendency. Still, Rickels is much too ironic to see any sort of antidote here, or to recuperate anything at all. Moreover, for Nietzsche, irony attaches to a very important moment in the rhetoric of testing. Rickels's skepticism is quite Nietzschean, quite radical, but at the same time he has a disturbing diagnostic gaze. He has published a three-volume study titled *Nazi Psychoanalysis* that shows not discontinuity but continuity between Nazism and psychoanalysis—which is scandalous—and he does it in a way that is at once shocking and rigorous. But he shows that the Nazis had a psychoanalytic apparatus deeply inscribed in their system for several reasons; for example, psychoanalysis was supposed to make it possible to detoxify and unhinge the homosexual aspect of Nazism.

But is the cult of beautiful bodies, of the beautiful image, of purity, radically antithetical to the culture of psychoanalysis and the idea of the unconscious?

Perhaps; it depends on what unconscious we're talking about, of what and of whom, but Rickels's work is really gripping in this regard, and, even though it's hard to accept, hard to hear, I have to say that it shook me up a little, because what he says can't simply be denied, either. Rickels is powerful and persuasive; he has done his time in the hidden home front of Nazi desire. At the same time, we can affirm that Freud himself was aware of Nazism in its beginnings and, when one thinks of it, didn't seem to take much interest, unless we imagine that Freud saw outposts of nazification in every psychic apparatus and topology, in every social bond and the many murderous standoffs that he described. He certainly shocked the world with his close reading of human destructiveness. Still, he never pursued a detailed study of anti-Semitism, for example; on the contrary. At the end of his life, American analysts told him that it wasn't the best time to write *Moses and Monotheism*, because Moses was a beloved icon, a key figure for the Jewish people; they warned him that his *Moses* might well destroy an essential support, that it was not the right historical moment for iconic deflation, and Freud agreed, but he could not keep himself from kidnapping Moses one more time, taking him away from his "people."

Freud, who was so prescient, who had lived through anti-Semitic injuries and injustices, avoided confronting anti-Semitism head on. And even when he wrote about Dostoevsky and masochism, he said right away that he did not like Dostoevsky the man, but that if the author had been one of his patients he would have been able to endure and tolerate his delirium; then he listed Dostoevsky's faults, including the fact that he was thought to have raped a girl, or that he may have been a pedophile. This list has infuriated the literary critics who work on and in the vicinity of Dostoevsky. To be sure, Freud gives us a very clear, short, and simple list of the writer's flaws (he says that Dostoevsky will never be known as a liberator of humanity because he bowed to the czar), and he says nothing at all about the author's anti-Semitism! Rickels's work examines this painful and thoroughly discordant collaboration of psychoanalysis and the Nazi phenomenon with care—it's a vast undertaking. Rickels consulted archives, studied the psychology of sons of Nazis who underwent analysis and who received from their analysts a kind of welcome that is unspeakable even today. Nazism and psychoanalysis have spent some nights together, they have made use of one another and have loved one another . . . this is something that remains unassimilable.

Does something of Nazism persist today?

Absolutely, as soon as we see the effects of unconscious ghosts and transmission, and I am not even talking about the manifestations of small neo-Nazi groups. A whole segment of the former East Germany has never done this reflective work on its shattered history. I am not saying that those who have done the work are spared, but at least there we perceive a discourse, an effort, a nagging symptom. At the same time, the East Germans have easily evolved from Nazism to capitalism, and they have often maintained that fascism was identical to communism, as if they were refusing to "work through" and to see, to live, the nightmare. It is as if communism had immunized them for a certain period of time. I would say, to go back to Mary Shelley's words: it has happened too fast, the violence has been experienced and forgotten too quickly, even among those who have done the painful work, those who have suffered and reflected a lot.

In my case, if that's the right term, the resurgences of Nazism announce themselves regularly through all sorts of networks and calculations, conscious or unconscious. For example, I've come across this problem professionally. There are ghosts that come back out frequently, unconscious recurrences of scenes of persecution. Sometimes I feel that I provoke endless reruns of Nazi vs. Jew stories that get played out metonymically—there are unaccountable skirmishes among the phantoms that inhabit some of us. These outbursts of raw hostility have almost nothing to do with my colleagues and me; we're suddenly possessed by a historical exigency to persecute and prod, to cower, to exorcise each other's historical squatter populations. Something else . . . I've been the head of the German department at my university. Now, one year when we were recruiting, someone suggested appointing a colleague whose grandfather had been a very well-known Nazi, and the candidate had the same name. I expressed my reservations about peaceful cohabitation to a colleague who replied: "You can't say that *he's* a Nazi." True, but his family didn't reject the grandfather's name. Now how can this young man, unless he's schizophrenic (perhaps he is), maintain a real relation of refusal and rejection toward his own name? And even so, suppressing a family name is not enough. I fought my demons. We made the guy an offer, which he eventually declined. Friedrich Kittler told me that at one point everybody wanted to name his or her son Adolf, and the German state, the Third Reich, said no, people had to find other names. His own family name, Kittler, rhymes with Hitler. He told me that once his car broke down in the countryside, and he was lost; he knocked on a door and introduced himself; the people were very welcoming because they had heard "Hitler" instead of or with "Kittler." Moreover, his family was privileged: his brother had been given the name that Hitler's "friends" (if one can imagine that he had friends, and then what about the politics of friendship?) had given him: Wolf. Wolf is a common enough name and it is also code for Hitler. Problematic transmissions are unconsciously attached to this name, questions that stand out. This is the problem of a whole generation that did not know its fathers; my colleagues of a certain age, now in their sixties, never had fathers. A whole generation began with phantom fathers, Nazis who were both despised and idolized, and this effacement must work on the unconscious, including the national unconscious, in a way that has rarely been really studied, it seems to me. Starting from this determined and invested absence of the father, what modification of Hamlet shall we have to read? Because we'll still have to wait several generations for the visor to lift.

In any case, the United States, like other Allied countries, wasn't always so innocent with respect to Nazism. This history is beginning to be discovered. There are intriguing tangents as well to consider. For example, American universities routinely refused to grant tenure to Jews until not so long ago. Lionel Trilling, who taught at Columbia University during the 1960s, was threatened; he was given to understand that because he was Jewish he should not expect to remain there for the rest of his career. And then there are ties that aren't always acknowledged but aren't always denied, either, between science and racism. We need only think of the scientific support systems that have been recruited to keep racist assumptions alive. This intellectual habit of finding ground for one's prejudices has a long history and many access routes.

Nietzsche said that, in the end, every form of racism breaks down before the demand for proof. I try to show in *The Test Drive* that certain ways of testing and examining are problematic. For Robert Boyle, the way to test was also a laboratory problem, a disturbance of protocol. Alexander Graham Bell himself was very interested in American expressions and practices of racism. The scientific approach that includes a trial, a test, entails an examination that always requires proofs and cannot accept, for example, the a priori assumptions of different types of racism. Nietzsche says this openly, just as Alexander Graham Bell and Boyle invented protocols for testing, for subjecting objects (or non-objects, for not only scientific objects were at stake) to a trial, but, for them, an explicitly antiracist, democratic requirement was involved. With them, it was a matter of representing the results of tests, of experiments, in a way that invited criticism and annihilation of what had just been shown. They introduced, one could say—stretching a bit here and there perhaps but not falsifying—a progressivist scientific method that I would oppose to Nazi science and other types of state or corporate science. And it was also necessary, according to Boyle, to find a way to integrate an extreme, radical modesty into scientific and philosophical discourse, because in his day, when natural philosophy was dominant, philosophy and science were still too closely coupled and too sure of their premises, too arrogant, even contemptuous, and this contempt permeated the tone and content of research, which was not open to public scrutiny, staving off the more democratic temper.

Today, if we really weigh the "test attitude," what duties or tasks does it imply for philosophy?

Philosophy is still detaching from all sorts of dogmatisms and authoritarian stances—it is still pulling out shards from significant battles about the meaning of meaning. For Nietzsche, subjection to the test is a question of modesty, and pride in allowing oneself to be shaken up, in being a genuine noble warrior who can affirm his own defeat in the face of something that would be more true, more noble, than any dogmatism. And at the same time he issues a challenge: *Versuchen wir's*, let's see if it works. We can imagine a punk gangster who would say, in English, "Try me," in other words, "Go ahead and put me to the test." This is a challenge masked as a green light, but it's also establishing a border that one must not cross—despite the invitation to do so—by making an attempt, by issuing a challenge. Nietzsche says, in effect, "Show me someone who would be strong enough to tolerate the possible consequences of such a challenge"; time and again he introduces the hypothetical temper of *versuchen wir's.*

> But today, at the beginning of the twenty-first century, have we taken up Nietzsche's challenge? Don't we have a tendency to leave that attitude to science?

The whole problem lies right there: it's too costly for us to leave the benefit of the encroaching doubt to science, and I am trying in my modest way to move closer to the danger. We've absorbed the lexicon and the history of the attitude I have described with respect to the test, the trial, but we've also given up the effort to bring the necessary reflection to bear on the matter. Husserl had already pointed out the peril, that is, the fact that science was winning out by overemphasizing objectivity and would impoverish our lives, devitalize them, and kill forms of invention that could enchant, give delight, create new galaxies of joy, as Nietzsche says. Science should be the source of joy, surprise, support; that is why Nietzsche calls it the "gay science," because knowledge or science, the scientific approach, whether underwritten by the state or not, now, is glacial and frightens us—it has to frighten us.

The field of thought shifts from one solid block to another, first literature, which is deemed qualified to judge the themes and the topoi I'm discussing with its own form of rigor, then science, dedicated to tests, verifiability and falsifiability, and finally philosophy, whose assignment would be to conceptualize or give up on politics.

In *The Test Drive,* I also wanted to talk about Husserl, because his book *The Crisis of European Sciences and Transcendental Phenomenology* ends with the word "test." My friends, that is, my best fiends, begged me not to bore them with a chapter on Husserl, but I stuck to my plan. Even though the interlocutors I'm privileged to have in my life are somewhat skeptical about his "relevance," I am going to do it anyway, I thought. But I'll go about it differently, I told myself: I'm going to write as if I myself were Husserl. I am going to do more or less what my friend Kathy Acker did when she wrote *Don Quixote* and *Great Expectations,* among other looted titles, following the path of her friend William Burroughs. Burroughs asserts that, as far as literature is concerned, everything must be stolen: "Steal everything!" he writes or orders at one point. I plan to steal the personality, if he has one, of Edmund Husserl, my double. I'll comment on today's philosophies, starting by talking about "my" attitude toward science and philosophy, and I'll give my opinion about Martin, who was, finally, an infidel.

This method has allowed me to slalom from one biographical and critical pole to another. I've found astounding postcards exchanged between
Husserl and Heidegger. During World War I, in the trenches, the unhappy
Heidegger received postcards from his mentor Husserl, who said to him:
"Listen, my dear student, the *Vaterland* needs you, so don't make too much
fuss! It's very important, you're letting go of philosophy now because you've
been called by the fatherland. As for me, I'm making enormous strides: I've
just discovered how the phenomenology of this and that comes up against
. . ." There's a touch of sadism in their relationship that I bring to light. I
interpret their correspondence with a certain ferocity, and I let Husserl
criticize me in his own words. He doesn't always condone the logic of
my philosophical attacks, or the somewhat perverse angles, the somewhat
feminist and compulsively antiracist aspects of my thought. Husserl also
accuses me of not acknowledging my debt to him and for ignoring his
start-up engine on performativity, which he argues that my friends and I
have neglected to mention. "Does no one do real scholarship anymore?" he
rails at one point. I let him comment on Derrida's texts about his work.

To say "I" in Husserl's place also allows me to express things for which I
would otherwise find no expression, in particular about the fact that Heidegger was a censor during World War I. Husserl is my kind of weapon of
mass destruction. He can observe and say things that I don't believe I'd get
away with. He has the authority to express dismay about where philosophy
has been going and, on another level, he can put the screws on Heidegger. In World War I, Heidegger filtered letters and censored them. He was
called *Front Wettermann*, because he also worked for the weather bureau.
So he had the job of general censor during the war. He was in charge of
war hermeneutics, of deciding when and where to censor letters. Some
thought that he read all his colleagues' letters, as well, and could hack into
their private exchanges. Well, I'll leave it at that for now.

Husserl began by developing a reflection about tests, but then he stopped,
and the editor implies in a note that he took up the text again several months
later. Since I am Husserl, I use his voice, I can comment on what Avital is
doing and say that she exaggerates a lot. Stopping my own text, too, at the
point where I pronounce the word "test" also allows me, according to a
heuristic strategy that I develop, to speak of Husserl's subtle racism. I take
his entire corpus and play DJ: I change sequences, but I show that he is the
one who pointed out to us the danger of letting science work all by itself,
in isolation. This rift, this break between science and the "real" world but
also between science and the narrative voice, to go back to the literature

of Mary Shelley, is thematized in Husserl, and that is what gave birth to the monster. In Shelley's text, there are two persons, one representing poetry (Elizabeth) and the other the scientific drive (Victor), and they pull apart from one another: this is what creates the technological monster that Victor Frankenstein can no longer control. The monster is formless; it is a monstrosity of pure science deprived of poetic and literary reflection, devoid of any other understanding and logic, deprived of the logic of the other, which science has not known how to incorporate into its efforts. (Victor's best friend, Henry, also gets eliminated, and he represents natural philosophy—another booster that science relied on and denied, according to Shelley.)

Science, in brief, enfolds at once the scientific method, natural philosophy, and the work of poetry. It invents an ever-surprising relation to the world. Sometimes literature itself finds a new stylistic figure for which science then goes on to get a patent. For example, we can consider that William Gibson, who writes cyber-punk novels, invented virtual reality. It's now a tool of warfare in addition to its other qualities and uses, but this invention first appeared in science fiction. Although this may seem bizarre and very "American" to the French, we have to recognize that science fiction has been the site of considerable inventions; the fiction, literature, cinema, and poetry of the scientific method are imagined before our eyes, as in the film classics *The Matrix* or *Total Recall,* where mutants appear and stake out their territories. Science, for the most part, now goes it alone, often subordinated to the destructive needs of war, of institutionalized hostilities. Nietzsche reminds us that science was connected, in the beginning, to astrologers, sorcerers, and music, and so science, when it still belonged to the realm of the imaginary, made promises, and it promised too much. In astrology there is an excess of promise, a hypercomprehension that always surpasses the knowledge base from which it stems.

When science was not yet working for corporations, governments, states, it knew how to inflate the rhetoric of promise, and this was very important for our *Dasein,* according to Nietzsche—he doesn't yet say *Dasein,* but he's almost there. Nietzsche is the thinker of scientific transformation, and of all types of alteration, of what can become other, of a becoming that implies and needs destruction. We can attempt to analyze this rhetoric of promise as a rhetoric of irony, and designate science as an entity that, today, following the trajectory of that figure of speech, does not keep its promise—as Thomas Pepper, the author of *Singularities,* and others have argued, irony may not be a figure, however.

But what is a promise?

Nietzsche demanded that we conceptualize the rhetoric of promising as that which, following the trajectory of irony, can never fully promise its own realization, and which is already, from the get-go, crumbling on its own foundations. Because a promise, condemned in a Benjaminian sense to its own ironic destruction, and inasmuch as it is a speech act (something that can endure further questioning, but I'll let us off the hook for now), affirms itself in the present but is made to act on the future. It exists only in that tension between the present (of its proffering) and the future (of its accomplishment).

A promise can only promise itself, or cannot even promise itself. A promise is always, structurally, a promise broken, an oath violated. As for irony, there are "figures" related to it, such as anacoluthon or parabasis, which express this rupture in different ways and with all sorts of ethical implications.

The thinkers of a gay or joyous scientific method were also great ironists, with the possible exception of Karl Popper. Irony is what rejects the coincidence of speech, its *Bedeutung*; irony demands and constitutes a pressed relation to time and is based on tangible ruptures, commitments that are impossible to fulfill to the degree desired or posited. Kierkegaard should also be mentioned here, because he conceptualized experimentation and irony together in a single framework. To put it briefly, irony overtakes thought; this is what Stendhal taught us. Neither experimentation (the passion for tests) nor irony respects assigned limits; these can explode, burst open, and break apart a world. Nothing is guaranteed when one is confronted with the destructive run of a test; everything happens at top speed—there is no safety zone. Speed and the velocities of testing connect up with an ironic tempo that tends to run on fast forward. But what interests me, too, is why, given the proliferation of test sites, the hegemony or the exuberance of tests, since Perceval, let us say, the sites of testing are now arsenals tied to loss, to deserts, to pollution. Nietzsche says—Nietzsche shouts—that the desert is expanding. The so-called Third World, the former colonies, are being transformed into test sites. The sites of scientific probes, like those in Nevada, are uninhabitable places, shattered, broken. Nietzsche calls for sites that would be welcoming expanses of abundance, places that would be able to affirm life without ceasing, however, to be places without shelter or ground. In Nietzsche, there are two sorts of homelessness, places without shelter. The first is a place of impoverishment, exhaustion of the planet;

it comes from a shrinking of all that can nourish, all that can induce and sustain pleasure. The other form of homelessness is the happy, dynamic rootlessness of what has been separated from metaphysics; this is probably what Deleuze tried to identify in his nomadism.

Why do we have a rather unhappy image of these places, a picture of sterilization?

A crucial question. I'll begin by answering it from an unconventional direction, in particular that of the painful and unhealed, unreflected, separation between poetry and science, going back to the eighteenth century at least. I start with Goethe, who was both a scientist and a poet, and whose true passion was science. He loved poetry as well as prose and highways, but this was not where he proved his authority as a man; he became instead rather proud and vulnerable in the realm of science. At the same time, science depended on poetry to keep intact its dreams, its original softness—I am thinking of our habit of elevating the "hard" sciences.

But this forgetting that overtook poetry spread in other forms, probably because, in science, flowers of evil spring up no matter what. Nietzsche needed science to sharpen and pursue his thought, leaving aside the fact that science is after all an heir of Christianity. As we began to see, it was because of Christianity that the scientific spirit was able to declare itself, manifest itself—and it was the great flaw in its rise that Christianity insisted on scientific integrity at least in relation to moral truth.

Christianity was so compulsive and obsessive that it couldn't help but give up its God. Christianity bequeathed itself its own almost organic losses, and since then the scientific, experimental spirit has become an orphan in relation to its God. It was necessary to go on without God, without the mendaciousness and also without the support of an overflowing spiritualism. By separating themselves from their metaphysical roots, the sciences and their adherents had to sterilize the material worlds that they have dominated ever since. At the same time, a large sector of Christianity has been obliged to abdicate its dogmas, while faith has been constituted as a prohibition against science and the scientific method; religion and faith have always had trouble tolerating science.

I'm trying to establish a possible and appropriate genealogy, and also to protest, to denounce what we are going through now. One can begin anywhere in the empirical and practical realm: in stem-cell research or gynecology, for example. At certain periods in history, the objects that science was to focus on were constructed on the basis of formidable ideologies. Let's consider the pain that women experience during menstruation: texts

106

obviously authored by male signatories claimed that this was of no scientific interest. In contrast, the fact that some women cannot procreate, cannot have children, has been an urgent problem to be solved. I try to show how the sites of experimentation have been circumscribed and chosen and how the objects of scientific study have been isolated.

> Do you agree with Negri's analysis when he says that science, overall, has become bioscience? In relation to the medical realm, what is at stake is the integration of living things into the heart of that matter.

Yes, but we can also say that biology is no longer principally interested in living things, as Nietzsche predicted. I know that Agamben, Negri, and others are working in this area, but I wonder if reflection on the promises of bioethics and biohermeneutics should not be pushed further, for here too it's a matter of putting into place exhausted sites in which objects are in no case opposed to death. As Nietzsche says, and Husserl in another way, science is no longer positioned on the side of life, the affirmation of life. Off the top of my head (although I wouldn't be able to improvise very much on this subject), I'd say that we should look more closely at what they're saying, but in any event laboratories are dead sites. Rheinberger affirms that experimental science today has an excremental structure: it involves writing, traces, and numbing absence. When one says that nature is the very sign of life, that it is part of what is living, the laboratory for its part finds itself on the side of writing death. Which generates anxieties on the ethical level. In the seminar posthumously published on animals and sovereignty, Derrida offers a harsh critique of the notion of bare life and its tie-in to bioethics. He really stomps on some of Agamben's premises. Ouch!

> It took me a long time to understand why such prohibitions were established, for genetically modified plants, for example. Beyond the fact that they are tampered with (but everything is tampered with, and this has been true for a very long time—in antiquity plants were already being tampered with), why does this cause such anxiety all of a sudden? I finally understood that, if transgenic corn is planted in ordinary soil, the harvest is twice as resistant, and it's certain that no disease will attack it, but the seeds don't reproduce themselves, and the next crop has to be started from newly purchased seed. The plant exhausts the soil and doesn't reproduce itself. Something may be gained, but at what price? When one begins to think about it philosophically, it seems completely terrifying.

Indeed, it so happens that this development constitutes the major tendency and ideology of the ultrascientific approach. We have reliability, strength, production, but we don't have life. It would be very tempting to affirm, as Heidegger noted, that science most often doesn't take the trouble to reflect on these presuppositions. In other words, it does not ask questions that would put the test to the test; there is no "meta-test," neither children's questions nor wonder that open up related fields of corn or thought. But only, afterward, the cry of remorse like the one we knew with Oppenheimer, who has given his name to scientific impeachability. Moreover, scientific research has all sorts of motivations for world-historical guilt-pangs, because it is largely tied to the military-industrial complex; it's a death machine, once again. At the same time, given the "advances" or revelations of technology, one can no longer refer to Nature or to the prevailing constructions of our mother Nature without preambles and considerable precautions, and one cannot content oneself with condemning science, which would be regressive, foolish, and endangering, pushing science (and its startling multiplicities) off into another corner of isolation.

At the end of your book, from what angle do you approach the conclusion?

I dedicated my book to the memory of Jacques Derrida, but it can be said that, in a way, the seed of the book came from Alan Turing—from the Turing test. Alan Turing decoded the "Enigma," during World War II. He was a great British scientist whose knowledge made it possible to access the Germans' secret codes and save the Allies. But he was unable to save himself. He was homosexual, but this had never been disclosed. One day, he went to the police because he thought that someone had tried to break into his apartment in a burglary attempt. The policeman, one of his friends, asked him if he had any suspects in mind, if anyone had witnessed this event. And Turing replied: "No, you know, only Roger and I were there." The policeman then responded that it was too bad he had said that, because he (the policemen) was now obliged to denounce Turing. And Turing thought he was joking. They were in Cambridge, in a major laboratory in which he was viewed as the master thinker. But despite Turing's fame there was a national trial. It was very humiliating. Even Turing's brother wrote to the newspapers to denounce him. As a child, he allegedly never thought about others, had always been horribly selfish, disgusting, and so on—and then the law against indecency brought him down in flames. As it was he who, in a certain way, had won the war (World War II was already in large part a war of computers), they gave him the choice of punishment: he could either be imprisoned or be castrated by hormone injections. He chose hormone injections, because he couldn't bear the idea of having to abandon his research and his laboratory. His body then developed feminine features, and he experienced terrible side effects. He fell into a depression and committed suicide. He had been humiliated before the nation, and that can never be eradicated. I think that is why he is not as well-known as he deserves to be. He should have been a national hero—if there has to be one; he should have been admired at least as much as Wittgenstein and his circle.

I think this homophobic gesture—the destruction of Alan Turing—continues unconsciously to haunt the social sciences on the terrain of wars and even touches the tests I am studying. Persecution of scientists has always been part of my analysis. I make an effort to localize the cries of ghosts in the history of science itself. This method is not entirely foreign to philosophy, which listens in silence and doesn't believe very much in positive histories, which have been emptied of the parasitic noises traceable to the subterranean chains of History. Each technological episode convokes its own ghosts, communicates with insistence, holds spectral colloquies beyond pure empiricism. Every time I write, I obey, I respond to a phantom that is locked up in its solitude and is not yet being heard. And the ghost who made some noise, who called out to me this time, was Turing's. Because I find that we owe him a great deal. Even if the Normandy troop landings were very important, painful, tragic, heroic, the outcome of the war was decided by technology, and—dare I say so—was dictated by the essence of technology and even quite specifically by the intricacies of computer technology. It was Turing, after all, who broke the unreadable German code.

# X

# A Mutant Splice
# of French Theory

Can you tell us about French theory, a critical frame of reference or philosophical offshoot of which you have become a major exponent?

What is known as "French theory" has undergone a major development in the United States. This development—which has been very costly to me personally—is also the history and the appropriation of a resistance. Obviously, it also involves the university: in other words, the institution has endured constant renovations and undergone major house-cleanings in an attempt to domesticate something that comes to us from elsewhere, that is, now as often in the past, from France. The relations that Americans maintain with France are complex and tortured; there is a fascination with and a deep love for France, but also a real suspicion, especially with respect to the unabashed intellectualism of the French. The fact that French presidents and ministers have written books or poems is proof that they can't be trusted!

It is necessary to say something, too, about the unprecedented heterogeneity, including effects of homosexualization and feminization, that French theory has brought to America. Such enrichment of our home ground is especially surprising when one considers that the French are for the most part not gender-sophisticated or outstandingly feminist as a culture. All this comes into play most of the time in literature departments, not so much in philosophy departments: there is a significant displacement here. Philosophers, Anglo-macho types, continue for their part to advocate rejection of so-called Continental philosophy, but not always and not all of them, because certain other philosophers, such as Habermas in Germany and the late Richard Rorty in the United States, have begun to create a postwar zone where they are reconciled with Derrida's works, if not with Derrida himself.

Has the great reconciliation between Habermas and Derrida finally taken place?

It was a troubling reconciliation for those close to Derrida, and even for the warriors that Habermas has sent out, consciously or not, to make trouble for everybody. Many problems arose in German and American university contexts at the time, because Habermas or his representatives came across as particularly malicious and imperialistic.

It was Habermas who took the first step, in New York, I believe. One could write an entire history of great men or women (though this may call for a different angle, I'm not sure yet) and their disciples, a history of as-sociations and dissociations, of gravitational pull. Many disciples gravitated around Hans Georg Gadamer, too. Small groups quarrel and suddenly their leader, Mafialike, perhaps, proposes a truce. In any event, what is called French theory marks an interesting and suspect displacement of philosophy: "French theory" is already an inaccurate name, for it means that what is in question is not entirely philosophy. Perhaps an analogy be-tween the categories of concept and notion is in order: a notion is vaguer than a concept, and French theory presents itself more as a notion than as a concept. So what is this displacement? One no longer says "think" or "philosophize," one says "theorize." At the same time, one can be tempted to affirm that something else is indeed happening. This movement, if it is one, pursues an interesting politics by opening itself up to dissident scenes and paradisciplines, giving rise to noncanonical constructs but at the same time anchoring its research and taking responsibility for an entire tradition, some of which was en route to oblivion.

This new order of priorities and the intensification of a particular field within the history of criticism have stirred up a serious reaction. An epide-miology of forms of thought persists in universities. People may feel easily invaded, infected, weakened. At the same time, they are strong enough to tolerate some parasites and some new innovations, even major overhauls. Nevertheless, the partisans of French theory sometimes go too far and de-stroy the comfortable "gentlemen's club" that a university takes it upon itself to protect in some outposts. These partisans are at once overly serious and overly seductive through their own pleasure in the text. They are perverse (this is why I approve of them); they eroticize university work, mixing genres and presupposing philosophical knowledge. A well-known Harvard professor, for example, once wrote, in the *New York Times Magazine*, I believe, that deconstruction was a problem, because it presupposed extraordinary intelligence on the part of students. Thus, even within the university, which sees itself as a "temple of knowledge," it is acknowledged that there is something untenable in requiring such a level of thought, of intensity, of intelligence, and that it may be harmful and dangerous for students. (Kant would agree that there's something like overstudy or strained intellectual pursuit, but I am not really talking about that here—unless I'm mistaken!)

This is also why I have devoted myself to the study of stupidity, because in the United States, as elsewhere, no doubt, the anxiety of intelligence is frightening. Even in meetings of German scholars, I'm bound to say, I have found myself the target of a sort of disparaging group psychology. To my great surprise, I have heard people say: "We shouldn't have invited Avital, she's spoiling our fun, she's casting a shadow over our peaceful meeting: she sees problems in the texts, everything becomes problematic with her, it's really this cosmopolitan, Jewish tendency, not devoted to great works but 'hyperintelligent,' irritating, that bothers us." This happened during a professional conference and not at the home of friends where people might have gotten drunk and insulted one another in a friendly way.

To put matters quite soberly, French theory has created problems, has undermined the illusion of innocent and agreeable readings. It has altered the somewhat aristocratic habits of the academic workplace. (I am talking about the ego-ideal of the American university and some places of privilege where imitation-aristocratic clubbing is still taken seriously, but for the untenured and adjunct population it's the gallows.) In the tiny context of my German conference, it was even considered distasteful that I had taken on Musil—the most honored author, faultless with respect to Nazism, and whom I found problematic for my part even so. I have tried to analyze these problems with the greatest politeness and with irony (characteristics which are—no doubt wrongly—viewed as French). Thus I did not attack Musil with a Panzer, with massive and cumbersome (although effective) weapons, but with a light touch, with finesse; still, my approach remained unacceptable, as he ranks among the flawless writers of the time and the discipline. I have learned from my French teachers to *enjoy* the sparring sessions with exquisite texts and runaway concepts. I relish these encounters and assume an intimacy with these authors, my friends and support group.

Pleasure remains a great underlying theme in French theory. The category of pleasure should be analyzed in detail: how is it that the French take pleasure even as they appear to master what they are talking about?

They have done their homework, the heavy lifting of serious study and, when they're in the mood, archival research. They come out unscathed. This constitutes an insult or an injury to the hard-nosed, that is, to the Germans, the English, and some Americans.

*Was the fact of constantly going back and forth, in French theory, between philosophy and literature seen as something new?*

I think it would be interesting to analyze, first of all, the fears, the phobias, and the apotropaic strategies that are invoked to handle French theory in the United States and elsewhere. Because they create both a desire and the repression of this desire. They are the site where desire as such is discussed, analyzed. Now there is also a great repressive tendency among Anglo-Saxons with respect to desire, and a real suspicion of it, because— pardon the expression—what does desire have to do with philosophy, even if regional articulations, philosophical dialects, speak about desire? French theory, in this sense, is a site that stokes the trouble of high contamination, a site welcoming contaminants that should not be seated at the table in the presence of adults.

*What do you include in French theory?*

French theory exists first of all as a product of exportation from France; cheese, wine, things connected with pleasure, or "French kissing," or, for the Germans and the Swiss, "French beds"—when Germans want to have an extrawide bed, queen- or king-sized, they have to import one from France. The label "French" connotes pornography, or at least exces- sive exploration, disordered morality. At the same time, there remains a trace of phallocentrism, but this is different. I know that you want names and addresses. Let me consult my black book. OK. I feel like I'm being asked to turn over these names to the authorities! On the French side of things, French theory includes a list of well-known suspects: Rancière, Balibar, Lyotard, Cixous, Major, Torok and Abraham, Deguy, but above all, obviously, Deleuze, Derrida, Foucault, Kristeva, Barthes, Bataille, Nancy, Lacoue-Labarthe, Kofman, Althusser, Bourdieu, Lacan, sometimes Zizek, sometimes Badiou (even if he tries to escape the label and to shoo away some of the rival schools, Badiou attempts to be serious and conservative in his own way). So, in broad strokes, French theory entails a conversa- tion and engagement with these names and their damages, their intellec- tual insurrections—which are often extremely compelling. In many cases, French theory takes off from and stunningly engages German thought, whether this involves a remix of Hölderlin and Celan or sidebars with Hegel, Schelling and psychoanalysis, or resignifications of Marx, Nietzsche, et al. The relationship to German philosophy is inexhaustibly yet solidly circumscribed. I need not emphasize the importance of Heidegger in this context of replenishment and exchange. The French often introduce, even in the driest deserts of thought, an aura of seduction and sensuality that students appreciate. I've looked at some of the books published on French theory in the United States and in France: they all carefully avoid speaking of the "sexual" aspect of the French label, whereas it's an aspect that has to be located and expressed, for, after all, the other great man who was welcomed into the French-American zones of thought was Freud. To set aside the subphenomena of desire and the effects of seduction about which Barthes, to take just one example, has spoken so well would doubtless be a repressive show of ignorance.

Not all teachings with qualities of insurrection and the demand for resignification come out of French theory. I'm not saying that Jesus Christ was sexy, or French, but after all he was hung, almost naked, in a sado-masochistic staging that was thus very attractive and fascinating as a body presenting itself. To this can be added the fact that children follow him and are seduced, as they are by Socrates. Everything that attracts young people seems potentially harmful from the standpoint of power, and often someone, or the State, has to get involved by condemning to death those who put young people in danger or thrall.

Women who write about Lacan, for example, have often been perceived as seductive and scandalous. I am thinking of Jane Gallop, who made each of her lectures a sort of performance; once, it is rumored, she wore nothing but men's ties—so she was almost naked—in order to stage the double bind, the Lacanian knots. So the story goes. She also wrote a book not only about castration motifs but about a grievance procedure for sexual harassment in which she was the principal accused party; she described this with Lacanian refinement and critical finesse. A number of supersexy, bold, bizarre women showed up like surfers on the waves of French theory, and in fact during all those years we witnessed the emergence of splendid women, but also of women who were entirely "WASP," respected and outwardly conformist. Within universities themselves something happened in relation to these women, something that appeared as a pure effect of French theory. Certain women, Naomi Schor and Cynthia Chase, for example, presented very provocative work even without undressing.

So we're also talking about women, about the women who were able to emerge from French theory, for this theory gave them a space where they could live and breathe, whereas departments of philosophy—but not only these departments—are relatively unlivable for women and minorities. I am thinking of a woman of extraordinary beauty and talent, Gayatri Spivak. She was the first translator of Jacques Derrida; she translated *Of Grammatology.* She became very famous; she helped introduce the concept of postcolonial studies, studies on minorities—African Americans, Latinos, Asians, or "subalterns." But even Gayatri had her menu of struggles to go through and had to reopen doors for herself and others time and again.

It is undeniable that a sudden, possibly irreversible space opened up owing to French theory. All the subversives of this country, among whom I hope I may count myself, are indebted to the French thinkers, but they are also interested in the profoundly serious side of philosophy. Some of the more subversively inclined are reactively bound to French theory, which they repeatedly tear down—they also have a strong relation to it and a form of debt, for the fuel of negativity gets them going. There are skeptical philosophers as well, who are both inside and outside the main currents. These are people who are a little bit French themselves, but not entirely, people like Rodolphe Gasché, who is something of a policeman at times, because it is very important to him that properly philosophical requirements not be forgotten, and for him French theory seems to represent the bastardization of something more authentic, more sober. He is quite serious, and I very much appreciate what he does (I have worked with his texts and have been trained by them), but his sober appropriation necessarily lacks the somewhat savage, accidentally brilliant, unexpected aspect of an "American" approach. We are witnessing many different movements and offshoots, some of them subterranean, or latent. Levinas, for example, has become very important. He is part of the French wave that heads toward the Germans before landing on our shores. American Germanistics could be more vigorous if it didn't turn away from some of these edges. Indeed, Paul de Man said that the way Friedrich Schlegel is cited, that is, without reference to his great text *Lucinda,* decisively influences the discipline of Germanic studies in the United States, in Germany, and everywhere else—in fact, the studied lack of attention to Schlegel's work constitutes *Germanistik,* according to de Man. Schlegel wrote a famous essay on "unintelligibility," or "incomprehensibility" ("Über die Unverständlichkeit"), but he was severely criticized for it. Let's think about the possible relation between Schlegel and Bataille, for example, because the way Bataille got himself attacked by Sartre recalls Schlegel's own situation and fate. Bataille and Schlegel practiced a pornography of the *cogito,* as Peter Connor writes of Bataille; Schlegel, for his part, was attacked by everyone, by Hegel and by Kierkegaard. Moreover, this was almost the only time when Kierkegaard suspended his war with Hegel and joined forces to combat Schlegel. Dilthey and Carl Schmitt slammed him too, among other more contemporary thinkers.

Why this consensus?

A consensus is always suspect, but in this case it's quite startling. I think Schmitt goes pretty far in his denunciation, for he accuses Schlegel of being a sexual exhibitionist. What Sartre reproaches in Bataille, and what all the others reproach in Schlegel, is finally that they put together two incompatible codes. It's one thing to describe pornography; it's something else again to do philosophy. Moreover, Schlegel acknowledged authorship of his own text, which was completely unexpected: no one of his stature would have signed (or written) *Lucinda*. This was a provocation, according to eighteenth- and nineteenth-century readers. But if we follow Kierkegaard's logic, Schlegel isn't pornographic enough. We owe him a lot, because he made domestic love erotic, but at the same time his text is too abstract, not sufficiently pornographic in the end, not explicit enough. The crime is the interweaving of two codes that should never meet, the philosophic and the pornographic. For reasons that are at once overdetermined and transparent, the choices of discursive register and noncanonic movements that are nevertheless linked to the canon cannot be accommodated.

Bataille is always relegated to the sidelines by the philosophical coterie . . .

If Bataille had been able to separate the two, to say "Here we have philosophy," I bet he would have been pardoned and allowed back into the fold; he would have had the code enabling him to settle into it and to be respected. This is more or less the effect of your own French theory, the exclusion of Bataille by the Sorbonne philosophers, an exclusion underwritten by a defensive reaction, and this is what should be analyzed: what is forbidden, what is defended, what and where it resists and why. But I think that Schlegel's case is much more obvious. He should never have let philosophy and pornography share the same bed. Friedrich von Schlegel is too French even today; to top it off, in his "Über die Unverständlichkeit," he asks what people have against theory, against the incomprehensibility of a difficult and speculative philosophy. He says that without this unintelligibility people would be afraid, would become anguished and suicidal, for comprehension would announce the end of the world: if one could understand friends, families, nations, one would immediately commit suicide. And Schlegel began to speak of the unconscious. He tried to disclose a protective unintelligibility that, harbored somewhere in the mind, is needed and that inspires the generation, the engendering, of thought, literature, fiction.

This pre-Nietzschean gesture expresses our need for fiction and art, our need for illusion and artifice in order *not* to think about or commit suicide. And comprehension and reality, when they're looked at squarely, are finally too destructive. I mention incomprehension, or unintelligibility, because the staple criticism of French theory is that it isn't intelligible enough. People have a desire—a very debatable but quite vigorous desire—for transparency. They need an accessible grid, and definitive answers, not the interminable aspect of thought that is always ambivalent with respect to its own objects and possible conclusions. Even educated people want things to be expressed clearly, without residue, and to be unquestionably clear. And this desire has had unfortunate implications with respect to politics in America.

In addition, I would say that the French have not always had the "look" of serious academics—this aggressively superficial remark is connected with the theme of pleasure and the mixing of genres. Either one is serious-looking and ascetic, or one has not known the exhaustion of research, the pallor, even the ugliness stemming from this work that vampirizes the body. The very fact that the representatives of French theory are often rather attractive makes the Anglo-Saxons and the Germans uneasy in this respect. A beautiful woman such as Hélène Cixous, well-dressed and wearing makeup, is always somewhat disturbing in the milieu of literary and philosophical criticism. Moreover, she insulted American feminists a long time ago: on one of her early visits to the United States, according to a well-founded rumor, she made fun of the shoes feminists were wearing.

It must be said that, at the time, being a feminist in the United States almost required disdaining makeup and more generally the presumably seductive aspects of femininity, and it created quite a lot of confusion to witness the arrival on American shores of elegant, handsome people who spoke with unprecedented eloquence. It was as if we were watching a play with seventeenth-century refinements that were almost impossible for some of us to assimilate.

Obviously, if a man were making statements about French theory, I don't think he would talk about Hélène Cixous's eyeliner, lipstick, or perfume, but all those cosmetic artifices and the elegance on display played a significant if unspoken role, because they were no doubt perceived as an affront to what remained of the puritanical values that were deployed somewhere between Baudelaire and Nietzsche. It is a matter of beauty, of makeup; one hides, one presents oneself, there is a *Darstellung* of the person, the *haute couture* of a work, whereas, before the French invaded us yet again, we had probably thought that it would be best for the thinker's body and the *Dasein* in flesh and blood to pass unnoticed, on the sidelines of a provocative aesthetic.

> One has the impression that, before French theory, analytic philosophy had an unchallenged hegemony, and that there was a real (post-Wittgensteinian) suspicion regarding the great metaphysical questions, in particular the question of meaning. French theory succeeded quite skillfully in taking a tangential approach, by conceding that there was no metalanguage while still asserting the validity of raising questions about meaning.

There is no doubt a perspective according to which the French are seen as the great enemies of meaning even though they are obsessed with its range and limits. When Bataille says that "we have to stop producing meaning" and have to settle up with what he calls nonknowledge (*le non-savoir*), the proposition is still relevant today so far as work on *Bedeutung* and *Sinn* is concerned. I've made a connection between Schlegel, his work on incomprehensibility, and Bataille, because the affirmation of a brilliantly elaborated rejection of meaning imposes itself here. This is not simple, puerile anarchism, but the manifestation of a different dimension, of another viewpoint, already connected with the unconscious, with a place, a site of production of meaning that is breaking up, shattering, going elsewhere, and that is dangerous for those who are continuing to demand meaning in other areas. Wittgenstein's breakthroughs are not negligible, and he ought to be welcomed as a team player, a solid ally in our tactical upsets.

> Doesn't the proliferation of books on French theory indicate that this movement—if we can call it that—is already over, in a way? Because, finally, what have thinkers like Derrida and Jean-Luc Nancy brought you?

Oh, nothing! Maybe a smattering of *non-savoir.* (Laughter.)

> You're the only person with whom Derrida shared the podium in his seminars, and you're close to Jean-Luc Nancy . . .

The attention and credit I've been granted surpass me, it's true. My instincts for communion and empathy have allowed me to work with exquisite and always singular thinkers—people of incomparable goodness, of legendary generosity. How can this be translated in the still-contested statutes of French theory? What are the specific politics of friendship and how do particular personalities continue to shape its advent (or drill its edges)? As for its peculiar death grip . . . On the one hand, the death of

118

French theory or deconstruction is announced as imminent; on the other hand we're told that it was already dead at the outset! (Certain diagnosticians used to say that, like the Big Bang, it was in any case reaching us too late and that it's the future to which we no longer have access; we don't even know whether the past or the future is at stake.) It's very important that there has been this endless putting-to-death, this infinite finitude projected onto French theory. French theory possesses the structure of contagious diseases that have a latent phase: but while one knows that one is infected, when the disease breaks out with all its manifestations, will we be able to manage them, suppress them? Finally, as Freud emphasized, as soon as the father or some other powerful figure is dead, authority accumulates. And in death that father, or that power, is finally much more present than in life, and thus mortally forgettable. If the event (or the person) has arrived like a ghost, it (or he) is already so powerful that it is capable, like Hamlet's father, of governing the devastation of the household by remote control and capable of telling us in what disaster we are living—which is very frightening, after all. Confronted with such an indeterminate power, we cannot decide if it arises from death, if it is something that is always already dead, if it has just died, or if it is going to die a few centuries from now.

Obviously, after Hölderlin and his interpretation of Greece, we know that even the most splendid movements, histories, and inscriptions are finite. But at this moment there are surely seismic events, forgettings, repressings, of which we cannot be aware. I don't know how to locate myself in this whirlwind; sometimes I find myself at the imputed center with respect to French theory, sometimes on the fringe. As a Germanist, I am marked by another destiny of thought, moreover; it involves, to be frank, a special elixir, something Kant himself developed, that is, popularity.

The popularity of French theory remains an enigma, so we need to reflect on the very concept of popularity, on the aporias according to which philosophy, despite its ridiculous aspects (we may as well acknowledge these), has become recognizable and inexplicably loved (especially) by those who don't read it. Kant raises questions about popularity, and he wonders why the most difficult matters, the least understood, are "in fashion." French theory is not only what I have just said about a very beautiful, rich, and seductive language, it strains the mind insofar as it is bound to a real difficulty. It entails quite difficult readings and analyses, traversals of texts by Hegel and Husserl that are almost too demanding. And this is the question Kant raises: having renounced style, "sweetness," elegance, he tells himself he will never be popular, he will never be able to attract a sizable readership.

From now on philosophy has to renounce the delicious and extravagant *Darstellung*; it has to forget about style, rhetoric, and appealing accessories. This complicates the itinerary of popularity, which is growing despite the arid minimalism introduced by Kant, even while opposing it. Kant, for his part, is popular. But there are two sorts of popularity: the vulgar sort, in which one gives people what they want, one presents oneself in a calculated manner, and the other sort, which is much further removed from philosophical marketing strategies. If we had to choose, it would not be hard to vote out vulgarity—but questions arise when the two forms of logic intersect.

Why is it that two thousand or five thousand people used to come listen to Foucault or Derrida?

America is an immense reception desk, eager to sign up the new arrivals. We create rock stars, and we idealize the picturesque, even passive, activity called thought. Especially when it can't be reduced to meaning or to use value. What accounts for Einstein's enormous popularity? We don't understand a thing about what he said, and yet, like Picasso or Derrida, he was a popular figure. Everyone knows who Rembrandt was, even those who have never gone to a college or visited a museum: they're also aware of Nietzsche and his quarrel with God. Kant says that popularity raises problems within philosophy because philosophy *is* popular. A question remains: who is afraid of philosophy?

How is that question transformed into its opposite? What does philosophy have to accomplish in the United States in departments of English, American literature, and especially comparative literature? French theory became so popular that, when President Clinton was harassed by litigation and impeachment, he alluded to deconstruction! When he was told: "But you lied, you had sexual relations with that woman," he replied: "It depends on what the meaning of the word 'is' is," that is, it all depends on the way "there is" is interpreted in Clinton's statement "there's nothing going on between us." In some sectors deconstruction was then accused, through a distortion of meaning; blame was deflected onto the French and their copula, but let us not forget that Bill Clinton was a great rhetorician among the American presidents, something that hadn't been seen for a very long time. Here again, the two popularities intersect in someone like Clinton, who knows how to use the English language, who studied for a spell at Oxford, strayed into sexual promiscuity, had a finely honed relation to language, shed a tear openly and often, sexualized his office, and made necessary a reading of what power is, its relation to law, and the "there is" of this relation. It was a matter of politics, and it was necessary even so to refer to the French, in order to compare these worlds impregnated by the meaning or the critique of practical reason. In France, it was possible to observe that François Mitterrand had a mistress and a daughter hidden away while he was president, even though he was married—but these are only surface effects. At the same time, what is called French theory is by no means pure, certainly not one hundred percent "made in France," but outsourced and subcontracted in telling ways.

What I want to stress is the interaction between Germany and France and the texts that have intersected and duked it out. There would be no French theory without the German texts, through the intermediary of Heidegger, Husserl, and Habermas, via Sartre, Beaufret, Kojève, Deleuze, Derrida, Lyotard, and others. There have been constant intersections, repressions, denials, and we in the United States are the belated heirs of these phenomena. And I feel like a DJ with two or more records going simultaneously. Still, to say "belated" is to say too much (or not enough), for what happens in the United States and Latin America launches French thought and allows it to emerge in an often singular and unprecedented way, unique every time and thus for the first time.

In the United States, I'm not part of the political orthodoxy. I'm a renegade, in a way, whose research and publications are sometimes seen as subversive. At the same time, I could be situated squarely in the tradition of the ironists. It's not just that I would like to be the Mme de Staël of philosophical strains and French literature in the United States; it's that in my case, without the works of, and the violence done by, Derrida, Deleuze, Irigaray, Foucault, Cixous, and other feminine writing, I truly would have been crushed by the massive, often misogynist, racist, and conservative apparatus of the American academy.

I don't know whether it would have been a reciprocal leave-taking, some act of extreme courteousness that would have made me withdraw politely from the scene; in fact, early on, I was often let go. But as for the serious, unparalleled work that the French have carried out, and not only on German texts, it's a good thing they've done it, because in my particular and perhaps uninteresting case, it was a pretext for me to hang on; otherwise I wouldn't have had a key that let me into the house of being. I was given shelter. In the United States there are shelters for battered women, and French thought has had that function for me. There is such a thing as a professionally battered woman—that is the term Paul de Man used in conversation with me when I was down and out. His help was of both a theoretical and a practical nature, and I remain grateful for the active concern he showed me. My plight has something to do with the "resistance to theory" as well as the mark of gender and other downgrades, I believe. Let's not forget that Descartes explicitly opened the field of philosophy to women. In a very concrete way, the Germano-French cartography opened up priceless possibilities for me—we are talking about me now, correct? It gave me the right to remain audacious even as I was carrying on my little battles and my campaigns against the dominant institutions and values, against traditions stupidly limited by defective memories (Gore Vidal calls us the United States of Amnesia).

Finally, even when one reads the canonized authors—I began by writing a book about Goethe, after all—so many things in them are tidied up and distorted by the sanitation departments of traditional disciplines. The French incursion allowed me to become more "profound," more serious philosophically, and more intransigent. I am known among friends and colleagues for not making many compromises; where "hard-core" readings are concerned, I always wanted to practice the pedagogy of anacoluthon, of syntactical disturbance. I threw myself into this idea and used to arrive on the scene often dressed in a bizarre, postpunk manner, that is, a little outrageous, theatrical; I would surprise and annoy people with very difficult passages, readings, analyses, without alibis, without excuses. But certain people seem to need this stimulation, and teaching and reading often refer back to a problem connected with American culture: its systematic infantilization. At one and the same time, children are mistreated and everything is addressed to children, Disneyed down. But here we are dealing with a strategy that is much more complex than one might think.

Now, we need difficulty in thought, we're starved for it; this is perhaps an addiction in which all self-evidence, all relations with totalization, have to be broken, challenged.

> It must be stressed that in France the French thinkers behind French theory broke through thanks to May '68. Twenty years ago, Derrida and Nancy were much better known in the United States than here—this was the American boomerang.

Yes, everything started with this original translation, through the betrayal of origins, the "return to sender," boomerang effects. America is after all a text that endlessly reads Europe, that is read by Europe, that comes back to Europe, that tries to separate itself, to become independent time after time. There are round trips, very important networks of references . . . and various Americas, north and south, west and east, conservative, anarchist, leftist, radical subversive. Unless I'm dreaming.

There was a moment when Derrida, for the French, was more American than French, at the time of the invasion of French theory from the United States. Because of his impact abroad, people in France said that there was a revolutionary in their midst; without such an exceptional circumstance, the institutional smoothing effect is so powerful that every dissident voice is stifled.

Here's what has changed for us since they've disembarked: in universities, now, there are women, people of other nationalities, different colors, who are gaining access to a certain power—and this has a direct relation, intended or not, to the French thinkers who have opened up new fields, even if they themselves were linked only unwillingly or unwittingly to this new phenomenon. This is part of an immunopathological logic because the university has become much stronger in its capacity for resistance, despite its susceptibility to invasion by parasites, patricides, and "Parisianisms"; it has produced exceedingly powerful antibodies, but there is a cohabitation that is not always hostile, moreover, and not always easy, a cohabitation that has radicalized the possibilities—which does not mean that we are where we should be. By now the freshness, even the Frenchness of French theory has gone underground in some instances, so that even purportedly non- or antitheoretical stances owe their energy to the French, beginning with New Historicism—a movement now largely not so new, if not already obsolesced. New Historicism started up its engines in adversarial gear, in reaction to deconstruction, from which it only superficially severed. One could trace similar histories of cohabitation and disavowal in other important areas of study such as gender studies, postcolonial studies, disability studies, and so forth. Everything that struggles with referential authority, the traditionally evicted utterance.

Nonetheless, we really have to continue to destroy, to deprogram, and to deconstruct. There are enormous problems, people without jobs, people and languages being crushed. Those associated with French theory have become something like the imaginary elite at this point. It is strange, for, as far as my own curriculum vitae is concerned, I used to be really marginalized, and people now seek me out when they are rejected, expelled, as if they're turning to a recognized strategist. I try to help them, because I know that those who have been abandoned and even the survivors need new academic strategies; I feel that I too am a sort of refuge for the others. Finally, I'm perfectly aware that my domain is limited and that the pathos that I import into it functions as a catachresis, nothing more.

Still, as the university (and the universe) is being attacked by the Republicans, even and especially in their defeat and destructive legacy, the help one offers colleagues is a political act. We have learned this thanks to the institution building of the French intellectuals. They are everywhere, in any case. One must never scorn the little stirrings in the academy, even if (or because) the university sees itself deprived of any aura. French intellectuals have often energized the university and similar institutions in an exemplary way, though this practice may have ended. In any case, we are so saturated, so impregnated, so marked by French theory that we can no longer even isolate an example; all terrains everywhere have become indissociable from our various instincts of philosophical investigation.

When you undertake textual analyses, do you work on English and French as well as German texts?

Yes, and Spanish, now, too. It's increasingly clear that we have to reckon with Latin America, from the standpoint of literary or poetic vigor, from the standpoint of history, and also owing to the highly tormented and inadequate relations that the United States has with South America. I think that the choice of a text is already a political choice, as it were; this is part of the responsibility I feel; I have the impression of having agreed to be the guardian of forgotten texts, or of texts that are not even forgotten but rather too much in evidence and thus overlooked for that reason. But I deserve very little credit for this reputation, because my languages and my reading lists remain very limited.

At the Sorbonne, there are no faculty members of color, and women are in a very small minority.

I find this inadmissible, utterly unacceptable; around me, in my university, this couldn't happen. I'm not saying that this is always the case, but even on the evening news, for example, we have alternation between a man and a woman reporter. Even if it stems from the bad conscience of our era, even if it isn't "authentic," that doesn't matter to me; I want to see different colors, I want to see breasts in front of me. I don't care if this is done to hide real misogyny or not, let them fake it 'til they make it: I want to see something on the screen besides white men. And today, in periods of crises and wars, there are only men who make decisions. All this is to say that, although there are problems in French theory, some undercommitment, a lack of rigor in some contexts, nevertheless an exigency and an ethic are also present: these cannot be reduced to ethics, but they do entail an appeal to

124

responsibility, including thinking about persecution, very deep and broad thinking, because every being subject to the reality principle is persecuted from the outset and is stuck in a paleonymic trap. Who better to ferret this out than a hard-core deconstructionist? There are of course problems to be dealt with, and yet there is a persistent concern for the debilitated and underprivileged regulars of philosophical discourse and social practice.

This thinking is not simply politically correct, far from it, but it is *also* politically correct. I find in it an unstinting thought, fundamental and shocking and also restful in a sense, because one can also withdraw with it and into it, as Rousseau did—this isn't repose in itself, but in my view the only people who relentlessly underwrite a literary space, or a writing that would justify itself—or not, for that matter—are the French.

> I find that your books have style, in relation to American writing, which is always very efficient; you have truly European stylistic effects, if I may say so. Your manner of writing is no different from what you write, not in the sense of pure rhetoric, but in the sense in which it matters whether one introduces an idea, a thought, in a neutral way or with a certain tonality.

Everything I used to be ashamed of in my life is useful to me, even though nothing can be calculated and the relation to work remains, in my eyes, essentially noneconomic. Nevertheless, I think I'm one of those rare people who are interested in French theory and practice it without resentment and without compulsion, either; rather, with gratitude. I'm not the only one. But in the academy, as in other places where this sort of work is practiced, I see traces of great resentment toward one's own "object," maybe stemming from a Kleinian apprehension and bailout plan. Not always, but often. As far as taste and style are concerned, I often follow the law of the streets, appropriating the rhythms and presentation styles of hip-hop or rock or the occasional oratorio, or those of street theater, as the earliest philosophers did, moreover.

> Psychoanalytically, one could say that real gratitude makes one free, whereas resentment binds us to the object of resentment.

You are indicating the aporia of gratitude, then, if it enables one to detach from the object. Let's pursue that elsewhere! For me, this relative absence of resentment is a gift, or rather let's say that it manifests the capacity to suspend a powerful mistrust of others and to allow the various trajectories—which are at once very European and unquestionably American—to do their work. Which is normal for a Martian.

125

**Because you aren't into jealousy; you have your own thought.**

Or else I've given up the idea of having my own thought and I'm assimilating, absorbing, being a DJ. And everything I've been ashamed of in my life—being an immigrant, growing up in poor neighborhoods, empty suburbs, with no culture and little pride—I've used or revamped all that as well. At the same time, I've understood that I had parents who were relatively cultured but at the same time broken, German Jews who were driven out of Germany when they were eighteen and thirteen years old and weren't able to complete their studies. In Palestine they had to participate in the war for independence, they had to sleep in tents; later, they became diplomats, and I was born in Prague. At the same time, they wondered what they were doing in that desert when they were European, anti-Zionist, and pretty much pacifists. Finally, we left for New York, but we were without resources, we began with an empty apartment in Washington Heights—a place where German Jewish immigrants lived at the time, now populated by people from the Dominican Republic—and then my parents bought a piano.

That was it: no bed, nothing but a piano, and books. This is the most powerful thing they were able to pass on to me, even if I didn't see them reading very often, since they had to work overtime all the time. My mother was a secretary; my father, who read Greek and Latin texts and knew them by heart, was a truck driver. Later he did office work. They were humiliated, and I was very much alone, abandoned, and at the same time I was ashamed to be so poor, so acutely bereft in my existence. What people appreciate in what you call my style is that I can veer between slang and a phenomenological discourse, between different zones of new vitality, as Husserl used to say. Moreover, Nietzsche said that we must dance, and street dancing and break dancing are dances that I learned in the streets of New York.

**Did your parents understand you, follow you as you evolved?**

I was in the minority in my family. I was the Jew in the family, and they wanted to become Americans. So I'm the one who entered the forbidden city: I learned German, the language that was both adored and taboo. At the time, the idea of becoming a university professor was a crazy one, because the pay was too low; it meant studying for no benefit at all. In addition, my parents were seriously hysterical; they were fearful, anxious, and at the same time generous, with interesting values, because they didn't give a damn about, or really get, American values. I was in a state of major confusion.

I had the impression that I owed them for what had been taken away from them historically. My father was a writer, but when he went to Israel, he worked for a while for the radio and they told him: "No, this has to be done in Hebrew; it can't be done in German." And this remark broke him; he never really mastered Hebrew, he had a very pronounced accent in English as well, and when he asked for something it was hard to understand him; he had to repeat himself several times and asking that we pass the mustard sounded like a poem from Celan. I was ashamed—that's what happens to the children of immigrants. I myself could speak English, after a while, but my parents, finally, well, yes, but . . . My mother was quite gifted, but she always had a little accent. My father had an accent you could cut with a knife, and so even later, in restaurants, for example, it was hard to listen to his attempt to converse with the waiter and order food.

I've been able to overcome my prejudices, take on things that were very painful. But, to get right back to the point, something enigmatic and painful happens when children and parents speak different languages, or speak languages differently, but especially when a child masters what is foreign to the family and manifestly surpasses his or her parents in this area. I was ashamed of my progress, of my apparent adaptation skills. (I hear myself saying *a-parent*, without the parents, against the parents; I hear myself saying *s-kills*; OK, I'll stop. This is what happens in my head, but I'll shut it off.) Freud speaks of the depression that ensues in his note on the Acropolis ("A Disturbance of Memory on the Acropolis," 1936). This story about not understanding, about understanding too much, about loss without recuperation, punctuates my work. I write like a poor fool, sometimes, and in my book on stupidity I really act like an imbecile, like someone who needs to say things but doesn't find the words, who has an intense relation to stupid things and to my own stupor before things. I understand nothing and at the same I exhibit sort of gangsterish narcissism: if I'm the one who says so, it's OK, but if someone else tries to crush me, it's because he hasn't understood who I am.

The very fact that I have survived in the university system remains a miracle, because, as I've said, I've been rejected, fired, mistreated, thrashed, beaten down, thrown up. I'm like a cartoon character who explodes in all directions and comes back in one piece—on the surface, which, for a Nietzschean, counts considerably.

And I was always in a situation of struggle, insult, humiliation, like a character in Dostoevsky's work and Rousseau's at the same time—especially when my so-called career bogged down. In that period, Derrida supported me personally. In America, everything had become impossible and difficult, but there was still a sense of the sacred, somehow. Jacques was a god who appeared like a character in a Kleist play. He vouched for me, in a way, shed his light on me. At certain moments there were difficulties between us, silences, clouds, but the fact of being the recipient of such powerful light was decisive and incradicable for me. His benediction was an *Ereignis,* an event that I didn't even suspect. I was in proximity to the gods—I put this in the plural because there were also others who manifested themselves, especially at a time when I had no job, little hope. Now I tell myself that, happily, I had receptors—I mean that these encounters, for me, were prophetic, part of a destinal deal that was struck for me, always over my head—which, when reflecting on these things, I tend to keep bowed (I am thinking of Levinas here, his relation to poetry, and the humble warrior pose).

# The Disaster of Childhood
## A Textual Prompt

It's very moving, the way you talk about your childhood—the effects of shame, the relation to culture and exile. Childhood is important, not to explain someone's thinking, but to see what nourishes it, where it comes from.

Obviously I was a baby philosopher. When I was two I was bossing people around and I led ethical raids and know-it-all intrusions on my poor parents. I already had that Socratic finger in the air. The ethical impulse seems to have come first: I had a very strong sense of right or wrong, as do most children, since we rail about what's fair and what's not fair very early on. Apart from baby ethics I was quiet, never whimpered or complained, not a peep, kept it all inside. I was also a caretaker from day one or two. That's still the attitude or inclination that makes me feel safest. I have no idea where the compulsion to think came from, if not in order to get out of trouble quickly, find excuses and fire off grandiose arguments to stave off angry parents. I started stacking up on my rhetorical arsenal from my earliest days. But parents turned out to be only the first wave of assault, the first smack of a relentless reality-principle; there was still school and world to contend with. There was a catalog of shame to go through, the severe shakedowns that awaited my brother and me. Before encountering philosophy in early adulthood, especially French philosophy, with all its ambivalences that pay tribute to Germans and German Jews, I experienced my parents' expulsion from that culture in shame; they were like the trash-bodies of that mysterious, cruel world, always threatening to make a comeback and close in on us.

Two years ago, an Argentinean friend and writer, very competent in his rhetoric and rather flamboyant, fell into a sort of melancholy after drinking a little and said to me: "The only thing that bothers me in life is that I'm not Jewish." I almost fainted at the idea that someone could regret that—a whole history of pounding and shaming was suddenly overturned, especially considering that my own mother is anti-Semitic. And I commented on this to Claude Lanzmann, because during our discussions I had the impression that for him there were the Jews and the innocents on one side, and evil on the other. He nodded his head, indicating to me that he recognized this angle of the "Jewish problem," that of the incorporated persecutor. I found the same phenomenon in Kafka's "Letter to My Father": one doesn't always need to leave home to be treated like a little Jew, a dirty Jew. Kafka's father, Herman, had only contempt for Franz's Jewishness and made him endure endless shame on that account.

Your mother is anti-Semitic?

There are more paradoxes than your philosophies have dreamt of! The complexities of self-hatred are probably inexhaustible, especially in my household. She came from Berlin. When she was young, my mother's class went every day to stand under the Führer's balcony, and for her he was a rock star. When he appeared at the window, she became hysterically giddy; she had his picture in her wallet. When her mother (my grandmother) noticed this, she was furious and told her she was crazy. She tore up the Führer's photo right in front of my mother, who was angry and ashamed.

Were your Jewish grandparents aware of the danger?

No, I don't think so. My mother's grandmother was French, and she hid the fact that she wasn't exactly Jewish; she was apparently unaware of what that meant, until after the war. When she was asked how it happened that she wasn't deported, she answered my grandmother: "Your father asked me not to say anything, but I am in fact not Jewish." My mother adored the Führer and would have joined the *Hitlerjugend* in a split second if membership could have been extended to her; she was deeply wounded at being torn away from the idealized, sunlit space that was the Aryan world, and she was wounded for life in her self-esteem. To my great astonishment, she even claims to be grateful to Hitler, because thanks to him, she said, she finally became solid: she experienced boundless humiliation, incomparable disaster, and thus was readied for "real life." As a child, she was extremely wealthy, assimilated, superficial, and ditzy, according to her own account, and she had followed a pretty normative path for the well-to-do. By the time she was a tween she had internalized all the pronouncements against Jews.

130

Hers was the first family on the block to own its own airplane; Claudio Arrau and Vladimir Horowitz began their careers as pianists in my grandmother's living room. My grandparents had a salon, received many people, and had a very powerful cultural aura. Prominent in the cultural life of Berlin, they had a quite considerable influence. My mother was deeply hurt when her friends told her they couldn't play with her any longer because she was Jewish.

Coming from one of the eminent families in the city, she underwent this change from one day to the next, and her emotional life stopped there, in a way. She has told me the same stories about her early childhood over and over. For example, one day she told her best friend: "I'll lend you my bike," and her friend answered: "I can't, I can't play with you anymore." Once I was walking through a museum with my mother and she was saying only stupid things, very far removed from her aesthetic and intellectual capacities, for example: "Oh, the way that woman is pushing up her hair in Rembrandt, I don't like that at all, she could have . . ." In short, completely idiotic remarks when compared to her general culture and level of articulation. I allowed myself to say, for the first time: "But Mama, I don't understand, usually you're quite brilliant, and now you're talking nonsense. Why are you talking about hairdos in Rembrandt—you grew up in Berlin, after all!" She replied: "Ah, but you know, the Jews weren't allowed into the museums in Berlin. When I was little, I never went to a museum, and even going to the movies to see Shirley Temple wasn't allowed. To go into a movie theater, my nurse took big risks, she hid me under her clothes." So images, for my mother, are still unreadable things, worrying, stupefying, marvelous, over-invested, underdeveloped, prohibited, and so she confronts them stupidly, she understands nothing, unable to *see*. To this day she does not feel that she is allowed to set foot in a museum.

This was the first time I dared to criticize my mother and I was punished by extra guilt, because since then I've had trouble moving freely within museums and galleries and speaking about art. Although my parents were sometimes violent, persecuted-persecuting, impatient, brutal, illogical, with built-in psychotic episodes, I have never really dared counterattack them or defend myself seriously, and I think that's why I've developed a certain rhetorical capacity.

You found a different path. But you instantly internalized your mother's own exile. The culture that rejected her—why would you have a right to it when she doesn't?

When I got my doctorate at Princeton, my mother told me that, in our family, it had taken two generations for us to be established as intellectuals. Everything I do that isn't too awful is already burdened with a debt: it's something I owe her, I've stolen it from her; historically, it was all meant to be hers. She belongs to a sacrificed generation. And whatever I've been able to "acquire" I owe her forever. I get it, and I have no argument to put it differently. But there's something especially hard-hitting about the way I owe her everything a priori and forever. It's not even about something borrowed, the way little girls sometimes borrow their mothers' clothes: everything belongs to my mother. She's always told me: "It's thanks to Hitler that you are where you are." She thinks that by rights everything I experience, any honors I may receive, ought to have gone to her; she would have crushed me by her greatness—and this may not be entirely false. But can you see the enormity of making me Hitler's beneficiary, the perversity of this logic? It's crushing, still today. I live according to an impossibly cruel paradoxical logic that has me paying eternal taxes to Hitler's destruction each time I am seen to have "made it."

I wanted to keep a piece of furniture that my grandmother had in Zurich, a very fine eighteenth-century desk with hidden drawers. As I was still too young to have any money, I asked my mother to keep the table for me, because one day I would write and I would need it; I told her I'd pay her ten times what it was worth. She refused, countering with the astronomical cost, according to her, of transporting furniture to the United States. And I still feel the lack of that desk.

It was the break in filiation that was in play, not the cost.

Yes, that must be right. Since then, I've been writing on ordinary desks or in bad armchairs, and I tend to have back trouble. Back trouble is said to stem often from psychic distress. And it's very interesting, because I still feel that where friendly ghosts—close at hand and at the same time far away—have been withdrawn from me, I won't be able to converse with the specter of my grandmother in the shadow of her secretary . . . and keeping the writing desk from me also threw me into an acutely sustained mourning for Europe, because my grandmother remained very European to the end of her days.

How did she live through the war?

My grandmother went to Zurich. She took my mother very late, almost at the last minute. She belonged to the comfortable, cultivated class of people who thought they were protected. She used to say that Hitler was crazy, excessive, an unsavory madman, terribly unappealing; she thought that no one would take him seriously, and she even sometimes found what he said bitterly amusing. She wanted to stay in Germany, to enjoy the familial splendor. She stayed until the last moment, and my mother still has a sort of hatred for my grandmother's frivolity; while Hitler was at the gate, my grandmother had huge parties with all the Berlin queers, queens, and artists. She was beautiful, wealthy, and fabulously frivolous, qualities that I've always appreciated. My mother also detested Freud and psychoanalysis, because, obviously, psychoanalysis was part of my grandmother's life, part of what the century had to offer that was exciting and new. My grandmother may have been of the series that included Dora or Anna O, we don't know. She evokes those figures, and she sent my mother to an analyst when she was still quite young. It didn't work.

> George Steiner writes that Freud's great hysterics no longer exist, not because the neurosis has disappeared but because an extraordinarily brilliant language was in use in Vienna in the early twentieth century, a language saturated with double and triple meanings, literary allusions, irony, and a very solid knowledge of texts and culture; according to him, this language of the hysterics has become so impoverished today that psychoanalytic interpretation, which also presupposes these multiple meanings and allusions, has nothing left to sink its teeth into. When Freud alluded to Hamlet, the hysteric knew exactly which scene—it was double-talk the whole time!

This is true, and in fact my grandmother spoke at least five languages fluently, as does my mother. For my grandmother, the fact that I became a university professor was a bit of a disappointment and rated as vulgar, because she suspected that there was too much brute work, ambition, competition, publicity, and publication. She said to me: "My dear, do you really have to kill yourself working that way?" And I answered: "In America, as an immigrant, I have the choice between a sort of absolute fall in terms of the so-called class relations, and university life. I don't see any other way out." Because one *can* fall, very easily and very hard. And in fact, in America, we had really dropped to the bottom of the ladder, and the only access code, or at least the only way to simulate a slightly aristocratic life (or, let's say, the life of the upper bourgeoisie, not to exaggerate, or even the lower bourgeoisie, to be perfectly honest, and in some respects, OK, the working class, I mean how many hours and how much work does one put in to get a class taught or a puny article out, how much perishing pressure can a girl take?), the only way not to find myself completely crushed was, I thought, to aim for a university position. My mother became a secretary, my grandmother became a secretary, so I was haunted by that cultural and social decline, and somewhere it also attracted me: I've been a waitress and I have done other more or less degrading little jobs that I prefer not to mention but that have (de)formed me as much as the university. As a writer, I have made it clear that I remain a secretary, a secretary of the phantom, taking dictation from a whole corporate and incorporated partnership of phantoms.

My maternal grandmother left Germany, then, at the last possible moment. In Switzerland, she was safe(r), but had lost everything; she lived in a little studio. She hadn't been able to take anything from her former life with her, it was too late; she'd had to flee, and the Germans and the Swiss had had to be paid off so that flight could take place. When she arrived, she had nothing left but the desk-that-I-lack and some jewelry.

She took a nosedive in social terms; she didn't know how to cook, and my mother still holds a grudge because her mother really didn't even know how to boil an egg. They lived together in a single room; my mother was thirteen years old at that point, and very distressed. They went to Lausanne first; my mother was very happy there, her best friend was the pianist André Previn. But then my grandmother had to leave for Zurich—she had been appointed to an executive position with the social services for the Jewish community— and at that moment my mother fell into a permanent depression.

She never got over this event, in my opinion. The arrival in Zurich was a shock: for her, it was a humiliating destination, the mark of an irreversible fall. This fall, in my family, has been repeated ever since. For a long while my brother and I kept on getting torn or kicked out of our contexts, finding ourselves in front of various hiring and firing squads, in some regards unstable but so far capable enough to climb out of troubling circumstances. But there were and are lots of close calls that suggest repetition compulsion or something. Maybe unresolved first-generation survivor's guilt. If you call this survival. Well, yes, of course, survival but often not that much more than survival, which is great, I don't want to seem ungrateful . . . Still, survival shouldn't be considered enough for anyone.

Where was your mother's father when they emigrated to Switzerland?

In Switzerland; he was waiting for them to come join him.

And your father?

My father came from Mainz, from an Orthodox Jewish family. It is important to remember that in the household he had been recruited, in a way, by my mother, he had become her representative; my mother was the phallus of the family. It was a complete double bind on so many levels. My mother no doubt believed that my father was the aggressor, whereas in fact he obeyed her. In Kafka, in the famous "Letter to My Father," one finds this same structure, but reversed. He says that his mother was like a pack of dogs in a hunt, attracting the children into their father's line of fire or pushing them away. My father was my mother's hunting dog: either he chased us so my mother could shoot at us, or else he lassoed us and struck us in her place. In Kafka, it was different, because the mother *seduced* the children and they were oblivious to the looming parental danger. It's another method of hunting. The children, magnetized by the mother, became all the more vulnerable, and the father could then fire freely on them.

My father has a very moving story. He kept a journal in which he relates that one day he summoned his friends by means of a password they had all agreed on and that translated as "We're going to meet in the forest." This was a signal among them, an imperative order. So his friends came; they were seventeen years old, and my father said to them: "Listen, guys, I'm leaving." They asked him why. He answered that what was happening was too serious, too dangerous. They asked where he was headed, and he answered: "Palestine." They thought he was joking, and said: "But Paul, you're basically German, you'll never feel at home there in the desert; don't leave, stay with us." He explained that not only was he leaving but that he was urging them to leave with him, because Germany had become too dangerous for Jews and the Reds. And he tried to convince them. Only one of them said: "Yes, why not? I'm fed up with being here." "But why are you doing this?" the others kept asking. The day he had taken his baccalaureate exams, the flags on his school had changed, replaced by the swastika. And he answered: "This change is our fate."

So just one followed his lead. Fritz Blum, whom I later knew in New York. I always felt sorry for his daughter, Phyllis, but now I am distracting myself. My father left, and Phyllis's eventual father, Fritz, joined him later. (The others all died in concentration camps.) The same day, my father said to his parents: "We absolutely have to leave together; I want you to come with me!" His parents made fun of him, and said: "You're leaving because you're a socialist." And my grandfather was stupefied; he had earned medals during the First World War, he couldn't get over it. It's true that people who'd received decorations felt protected by their history of national loyalty and acknowledged heroism . . . Finally, they didn't listen to him and they let him go. So my father describes in his journal how he left: his family had prepared a special breakfast, the dining room table was all laid out; they accompanied him to the train, and he cried a lot. It was in '33, and he left in tears because he loved Germany, it was his first trip ever, and he was close to his mother.

> As early as '33? So he was like some others, Zweig and Malaparte, who guessed very early what was going to happen.

Yes, and no one was willing to listen to him. He went to Switzerland; it was the first time he'd left his country, his neighborhood, he was heading for Palestine, and he got sick. He was living in an attic, and he was somewhat delirious; he saw the Swiss flag outside his window as it unfurled slo-mo and wondered: "Oh no! Is there going to be a swastika in the center of this flag?" But it turned out to be a white cross. In the end, he didn't stay in Switzerland very long. Before he gave up on Europe, though, he wanted to get a medical degree. An excellent student, he had his sights set on a medical school in France. He was heading to Nancy, but eventually had to go to Palestine when the Grand Rabbi rejected him for being a "Bosch" (a Kraut). He was ensnared in a historical double bind—too Jewish for the Germans, too German for the French, nobody for everybody. He had nowhere to turn. He made it to Palestine, where he became a truck driver. He was a driver for British troops at the time, and he hid weapons under the seats—he was a sort of Zionist terrorist without being a Zionist; he was a more inclusive socialist, that was his program and wish for the future state of Israel.

He left Europe, and one day my mother, who had nothing but hatred for her mother, left too—something that no one ever understood, because she could have managed pretty well in Switzerland; she and her mother were beginning to be integrated, and she could even have lived in relative comfort. But one day she left for Palestine, without any preparation, as she was going home from school. She had been under pressure from a Zionist group to take the only transport ticket they had for someone under eighteen. One day she said to herself: "Today I'm not going home; it's time for an adventure." She had no brothers or sisters; she faced the crossing all alone and headed for Barcelona where she would catch a boat. She picked up the ticket, but by the time she got there she was eighteen, so there was a snag.

In Palestine, life was very hard. She was quite courageous, but while she was living in a tent there, in a camp, she came down with malaria. She had just met my father.[1] She went back to Switzerland after the 1948 war and prepared to become a secretary, which is what women of a certain milieu who had fallen off the grid did—it was remotely related to writing, to offices, it was remotely respectable and doable. She learned shorthand, a writing

136

technique that I have wanted to use for some of my writing. And it was Max Brod, Kafka's friend, who shuttled back and forth between Palestine and Switzerland, carrying love letters between my mother and my father. I know this because one day I went to visit my parents with a book by Max Brod in hand—I was a graduate student at the time—and my mother exclaimed: "But that's my friend, he was our messenger!" This is how I learned this story, but there were lots of others, some of them quite fantastic. My mother worked for the Legal Advisory Board of the Israeli Foreign Ministry and translated for David Ben-Gurion; I was born in Prague because my parents were Israeli diplomats. In Israel, my mother must have been no more than an assistant, but she overstepped her role. She got herself fired one day when a group of Zionists, or rather ancestors of Zionism, spoke about the need to kick the Arabs out of the territories that Israel would get. My mother, who was supposed to limit herself to taking notes, had the audacity to say: "But that's immoral, you can't think of doing that! That's not why we're here. If we commit an injustice like that right at the start, it'll be a mistake, a fault that will mark Israel, and we'll never get beyond it." Apparently, the men (there may have been women, too, I never asked her) looked at her with stupefaction. It didn't sit well with the group. Ben-Gurion was furious. She was fired on the spot.

For my parents, losing Germany and then Israel was a terrible wound in relation to the idealisms of that time. Freud, when he wrote "Mourning and Melancholia," began the essay by saying that mourning does not apply solely to deaths in the human realm, but to the loss of a country, a language, an ideal. I think my parents were also true sufferers from melancholia, home-sick for their countries, with their languages, their cultures, their climates, coffee klatsches, and so on; it was much more than their native land that they lost twice over, after which they stuttered through the world.

Did they go back to Israel?

From Prague, yes. But they left again, and almost in secret. At night, the way people had left Nazi Germany. There was apparently some friction between them and the government under which they worked. They decided to make a break for it. For me, this abrupt departure represented the first shock-break, from which I've probably never recovered. I was only four years old, and I didn't get to say good-bye to my grandmother, to my aunt, to my half-brother. He told me a few years ago that the next day he had looked for us everywhere and wept in the streets. As for me, I didn't know what the hell was going on—there were no subtitles, no preps, no meds, not even baby aspirin.

*And did your father's family stay there, in Palestine?*

In fact, almost my entire family was wiped out in Germany during the war. My maternal grandmother escaped, and also one aunt.

So this departure from Israel for the United States was a quasi-clandestine act, and traumatic. I was sent to a nursery school right away, but I had left a universe where I belonged to a safe-feeling community—a world that, for Israeli children, was particularly indulgent and kind, this is well-known, before they are fed to the army machine—and here, in America, I suddenly found myself alone with my brother, who never stopped screaming and crying, and my parents didn't want or know how to deal with it. He was two years younger than I, and he was my responsibility. They should have been happy to have a son. But I was the son, the little soldier, from day one. It's incredible that they left like that, without explaining anything. By plane, by ship. It was a KLM plane, I remember. We arrived in New York like new immigrants, well that's what we were, immigrants: we were poor as church mice, I guess; we wound up in Washington Heights. It was winter in New York, and as soon as we arrived we all promptly came down with pneumonia. My parents were demoralized, ill, alone with two very young kids in a foreign country.

It was in 1956; everything was gray, everything was hard, and my parents' anxiety was omnipresent. At that point, after all, my father was already forty-one years old, so he never completely mastered English. He told me that he had lost everything in Germany at the age of eighteen, including his ambition; it was my mother who was ambitious and determined, for him and for us all.

She always pushed to make things happen; she was the driving force behind their successive departures and crash landings. She was bossy, glacial yet dramatic, a real hot spot: she was rough on me, she wanted to control something in my life and my vocation, but at the same time her narcissism kept her from knowing or investigating my case in detail, so this may have given me the slack I needed to bolt or, when I couldn't, to build imaginary refuges. I was free to work out the ground plans for my internal empire. But I'd have to snap to. I actually had no time for myself. Sometimes it was like being brought up in a boot camp, but I have to acknowledge that she was also harsh and demanding on herself.

*She wanted, for you, everything she hadn't managed for herself.*

Yes, for sure, but no. That kindly paradigm doesn't really work here,

I'm afraid. For at the same time, every time I "succeeded" in something, I had to overcome the image she had of me, the things she berated me for: I was, let's see, an idiot, an imbecile, slow. I think that's why I ended up writing on stupidity: I worked on my relation to my own stupidity, to that systematic inadequacy that she discovered in me.

I have pictures of myself in America when I was very small; it's clear that I'm protecting my brother. I look like a depressed and weary little girl. I was already tired at age five; I stooped a little. But it's also obvious that my fists are clenched, as if to say "watch out, don't mess with me." My brother blames me now for having always been overprotective of him and thus castrating. I mean, I never let him fight his own battles, never stepped aside at the spectacle of an oncoming beating. How was he supposed to "become a man" under such circumstances? Where we lived, we often got beaten up because we were Jews. And what's funny, perhaps, is that, coming from Israel, I thought everyone was a Jew. Man, was I ever confused.

I remember one boy who came up and asked: "What are you, Jews?" I replied: "Yes, like everyone else." And he retorted: "What do you mean, like everyone else?" He was furious, provoked, and he beat the crap out of us. I was bleeding, and I said to my mother back in the apartment: "But how can that happen?" I hadn't understood that sudden flare-up of hatred. She said: "Next time, you tell them that their Lord was Jewish." Our neighborhood, at the time, was very Christian. There were lots of Poles, in particular, and those kids were pretty anti-Semitic. Irish, Italians as well. With them you could negotiate and carve up new identities accordingly. And where we lived, people more or less lumped Blacks and Jews together. The so-called Whites were the ones who were always spoiling for a fight, every day. It wasn't the Blacks. With the African Americans, we were friends; we shared Moses, after all, and the fantasy of being liberated. When a gang of little roughnecks came back to get us, I stood in front of my brother, because he wanted to fight back, and they called me "the boss girl." Then they started tossing around insults about us being dirty Jews. I replied: "If we're so dirty, how come the guy you worship as your God was a Jew?" For them, this came as a shock, but it wasn't good for me, because they were indignant that I had dared to treat Christ as a Jew, and they took it out on us with even more rage than before. I told my mother that I didn't think this was a good strategy! She replied, as if this was supposed to make sense, that people didn't like those who were too intelligent.

One day, I asked my father when he had had news of his father for the last time, before Auschwitz, and in what form. He answered that his father had sent them a postcard from the camp, and I almost fell over. A postcard? How? In my own defense (and I'm ashamed I said it), I responded ironically: "Did he write: 'Wish you were here?'" My father wasn't flustered: "No, he said that all was well, that I shouldn't worry, that things were fine." I asked him how the card could possibly have reached him. He answered that the Red Cross had distributed mail. The idea that my grandfather could have written a postcard from Auschwitz tormented me, and since then I've never been able to let go of my obsession with that correspondence and its recipient, that strange logic of the *courrier,* the *Schicksal* and the *schicken,* the impossible destiny and destination bound up with the destruction of history. Obviously, Derrida's *Carte postale* arrived in this site of injury.

> Your father did not succeed in convincing his family to flee Germany; that's really the tragedy of the survivor. When one leaves by twos and threes, one isn't saving oneself alone. When there's only one in a family, the guilt is almost impossible to overcome, even if it's not one's own fault; he was only seventeen. But the story of the postcard says the same thing.

This helps me understand something, because, for me, the theme of recurrent dreams and scenes that are repeated in institutions, in sites of authority, is always: "Am I going to succeed in convincing them? Will my rhetoric be strong enough to outrun older types of reality-testing?"—I mean, the reality that my father had foreseen was unthinkable, certainly inassimilable for his family, who rejected his "exaggerations." I often have his tape running in my head and wonder, "How will I prove my point in the face of extreme distress and impossible odds? Will I be able to unstick my interlocutors from their denial systems?"

> Your mother may have detested her own mother because they got away together. The love/hate relation is very structuring: we are two, we can fight to the death, to the grave; it's a form of love, of connection. When one is the sole survivor, I think one never gets over it; it takes place in a reality that defies formulation.

This may well be true. But she felt suddenly stuck with her, thrown into her mother's custody, saddled with a merciless warden. I understand this feeling of no escape and carceral isolation. One day, my father tried to hit me, and I was overcome by a sort of rage. It was during a period when there was no place where I could manage to write, and there were power tools and bulldozers everywhere—all the houses were being renovated; construction noise was a side effect of Reaganomics, by the way. I'd moved in with my parents for the month of August because the place was quiet and calm—I wanted to finish a book. So I went back, and for fun I would take writing breaks to tint some locks of hair orange or blue, I would dance in front of the mirror for a few minutes trying out my new look, and then return to work. It was really an innocent gesture, not at all outrageously punked up or offensive to the arbitrary laws of the house, I thought, but to my father my blue or orange highlights were beyond the pale. He went berserk. My brother turned up just when my father was about to hit me: he was red-faced with anger, calling me a slut, a whore, really losing it. My brother had to restrain him, because he was huge, like Kafka's father. On the sidelines, my mother was saying: "Look what you've done to your poor father!"

It was impossible to know when I would commit an infraction or get busted—they would swoop down on me without much warning, except for the permanent alarm that sirened in the back of my head at all times, day or night. I was really cast as the misfit of the family, the cause of violence, of domestic troubles, and even in my family's foreign politics I was the cause of all the problems. But, one day, all physical aggressions against me stopped, I was already grown at that point, eighteen or twenty years old, and my father had found a stick and was raising it, in slow motion in my memory, to strike me. I thought he was really going to kill me this time, and I said calmly: "If that thing touches my skin, I'm calling the police." All the violence stopped; my father was crushed, and I said to myself: "Did it really take all this time to understand that he was afraid of the police?" And the idea that there could be an outside force or figure or even fiction, a third party who would defend me, *me*, dealt an irreversible performative blow to the family custom. From that moment on, there were no more physical threats against me. The steady verbal cannonade was another matter.

It seems that at a party—I was two years old, my brother had just been hit—my father had given him a spanking, I think this was the beginning of the moralist aspect of my texts and my performances—I stood up in front of everybody and faced my father and said to him, in Hebrew: "Aren't you ashamed? If I ever see you raise a finger against this baby who has just come into the world, if I ever see you touch him, you'll have to deal with me." And apparently everybody was taken aback, because it wasn't an acceptable discourse at that point, certainly not coming from a tiny squawk box, and, anyway, who or what was ventriloquizing through the child, who installed the moral law so early on?

> But I think this is an extreme version of Oedipal love. People have no idea about father-daughter love: it's an atomic bomb. For fathers, especially when they've had a daughter late in life, the only way to sublimate their

love for her is, paradoxically, through aggressiveness. And the more the girls become young women, the more the fathers break them. There's a lot of incestuous love in that violence. At the same time, the girl receives from her father the certainty of being loved, but because it's too hot to handle, this love is transformed into brutal rejection.

When I helped my father die, so to speak, sadly and melancholically helping him to cross over to the other side, I offered to lie down on the floor by his bedside so he wouldn't be alone at night. He was already delirious, and he said: "But I'm not going to sleep with you now." And I replied: "Don't worry, that's not going to happen; I'll be on the floor and you'll have the bed." He insisted: "Yes, but I don't want us to sleep together," and I reassured him: "OK, OK." But at the same time, why didn't he want this? Thus even in his delirium there was censorship. Something else: a friend pointed out to me that as the first person to be born with this new family name it was I who was founding a dynasty, so to speak. Because in Israel, the law of the culture required that a Hebrew name be found, so my parents chose the name Ronell, which means "musicians of God." I have Gd etched into my own name, with which I am at war. But I think that for my father it was dramatic to be deprived of his own name, of his own language.

Because his name wasn't Jewish enough?

His name was too Jewish, in my mother's eyes. For her, it was out of the question to call herself Mme Goldstein, this was her own anti-Semitism at work. They found a sort of semiground for agreement. At the time they chose the name, they thought that Israel had a chance to be basically a non-religious, non-Zionist country. Modern Hebrew was supposedly conceived, concocted in the New York Public Library. This was a language where so much was supposed to be new. It was a way of affirming a new beginning; there were initiatory forces behind such choices. And as I was told that it was a huge thing to be the firstborn in this family under the new, chosen family name, Ronell, this logically meant that I was the father. I had a certain symbolic, if often unconsciously conferred, authority in the family, often scorned, to be sure, but despite all the brutality I experienced, I was in other respects quite untouchable. My brother must not have been invested in the same way; he suffered a lot because of this. And I have to wonder if my work on castrated sons and their relation to their fathers has anything to do with all this at some level of desperate arbitration.

I think castrated sons are sons who have suffered from noninvestment. Your relation with your father, even if it was violent, was particularly invested, a very powerful form of father-daughter love. And your brother's problem was instead a problem of noninvestment: this is castration, for a son. Even a son who has been beaten nevertheless constructs himself in very strong opposition; in the best of cases, he revolts, or breaks down, but he is something.

Yes, and although I don't want to reduce the work we do to so many efforts at working these things out and through, the project I have now, after writing *Test Drive*, concerns "loser sons" (*Loser Sons: Politics and Authority*)—and in a first phase I didn't realize that, as with other disseminated and hidden articulations, my own family could also be involved. The disinvested sons, under my microscope, end up on the world-historical stage as those who are really the terrorists. Mohammed Atta, George Bush, Osama Bin Laden, and others were all noninvested sons who have been destroying the world. To be sure, this is putting it a little crudely. Extend me a credit line on this, please, because I do work it out scrupulously in the book. I move it through Hannah Arendt's essay, "What Is Authority?"

I have been thinking a lot about the vanishing of authority and about the ways in which power gets wielded, specifically articulated these days. Maybe we need to talk a little about the concept of authority in Hannah Arendt and about Kojève's book, *La notion d'autorité*. I'd like to talk about these matters by taking an unusual route, in particular from the starting point of the contract signed between Kant and Goethe, in the eighteenth century, just when the genius, the writer, the poet, began to have a kind of perverse but constitutive authority. At the same time, in his book, which he was unable to finish, Kojève observes several types of authority, of which four are pure, while the others are blends, combinations. There are the father, the judge, the leader, and the master. The father as source of authority is central to his project and at the base of a political contestation. But I had to note that his sense of who bears authority is limited, even in his dozens of hybrid formations; he eliminated or took no interest in the authority of doctors or therapists, whereas even Kant often compared philosophers to doctors, inasmuch as they both prescribe regimens for health, at least on the register of symbolic health. They diagnose. And Nietzsche positioned himself as an epidemiologist—one could even say, now, a cultural "virologist."

I would like, somehow, to find a way to talk about this omission on Kojève's part, perhaps also on Arendt's and Hegel's. Whereas in our day it seems to me that medical, or philosophico-medical, authority still invites consideration. The medical field and the figure of the doctor exert a lot of pressure on the symbolic organization of things, whether or not you "believe in" doctors, follow their orders, or take your medicine. It's still an arena of monotheistic intensities—just listen to the way people talk about their doctors. Of course, like all monotheisms, it's quite prepared to fall apart. Well, it always was, I guess, which is why Gd often came rumbling down on us in those dramatic states of rage. Well, let's get out of the way and move on.

This is a bit of a leap, but I do want to turn our attention to the ever-crumbling authority of the poet, the one charged with being an exemplary carrier of language. Baudelaire projected that there would be no room for poeticity even among those who proved capable of appreciating linguistic power plays and positing stunts. What is the stature of the poet? This is not a lame question or merely arbitrary when one remembers that revolutionary vision is often instigated, sustained, and in the end—for there is an end, my friend—commemorated by the poetic word. From the standpoint of what is at once disinvested and exalted by the cultures that we share, I think that we should talk about the figure of the poet that was thematized for the first time in a literary work, that is, the ur-portrait of an artist—an often ill-tolerated parasite. Even for Nietzsche, the artist or the poet was, in the best way possible, an evil figure who had to be tolerated like a parasite or its antidote—a vaccine.

The portrait of the artist in what sense?

During a seminar in 2004, Hélène Cixous spoke about the status of Bergotte in Proust and she wondered at what moment literature first showed hospitality to the figure of the poet, and staged the plight of the full-fledged writer. This is a question that had intrigued me, for in poetry and dramatic works—let's think of Molière here, or Cervantes—the poet was an object of derision, really an embarrassment. This low estimation of the figure of the poet carries over to our day, but with a slight difference. Things changed in Goethe before they traveled to Joyce's *Portrait of an Artist.* The first time there was an attempt to take poets seriously, from the starting point of Kant's aesthetics while prefiguring some of Hegel's theories on the death of art, was in Goethe's play *Torquato Tasso.* This text is worth recalling; it brings us back to common places or territories, sites that fruitfully link or dissociate pathology, because Tasso, who was seriously paranoid, when taken up in Goethe inaugurated the way in which literature stages its own premises, or rather its abysses, even as it touches on philosophy. Goethe did not suppress Tasso's uncontainable edginess, but ran with it as a way to get close to the figure of the poet, often enucleated, emptied, and strained yet capable of delivering the sacred word. Yet Goethe did not spare Tasso in his dramatic depiction of a poetic destiny.

144

What is going on here involves disappropriation, or a monstrous appropriation, that literature carries out on itself, in which the very authority of the poet's relation to language and world is questioned and pathologized by Goethe. It suits Goethe's purposes that the name Torquato (since we were speaking of proper names) means "twisted." No need to recall that Tasso was the greatest poet of his day, and Goethe's. He *counted,* the way Shakespeare does for us, and commanded an absolutely untouchable authority; nevertheless, Goethe constructs a drama that is at once poetic and true (I am thinking of *Dichtung und Wahrheit, Poetry and Truth,* his own autobiography) around Tasso; among other things it implicates the forces at war within the "Goethe" corpus and the entire set of effects for which his signature is credited: Goethe the scientist, Goethe the historian, Goethe the doctor, Goethe the poet, Goethe the fantasy and the phantom, Goethe who began the tradition of thinking of the poet (or poetess—there was Bettina) as a vital, fragile, eviscerable being, defenseless and all the while "historial," as Heidegger would say.

Quite obviously, Kant himself studied the figure of the poet even though he presented poets in the third *Critique* as puerile, childish, more or less mentally disturbed. Goethe took on a frankly pathological story in order to carry out an investigation into the nature of poetic speech. And Blanchot said that he would never be pardoned for having escaped the shipwreck that snuffed out his compatriots, the madness that struck them all twenty years later: Hölderlin, Kleist, Lenz, and others. Even though Goethe escaped drowning in pain or being pathologized, he understood that the poetic word belonged to such abysses and bore witness to incredible dissociations with which he appears to have been intimately familiar.

When Freud says that the possibility of uttering poetic speech is connected with hysteria, he cites Goethe for several reasons, and for several inventions or discoveries. Goethe established and questioned the poet's authority and began a study that continued up to Benjamin at least, a study seeking to identify the place, the site that houses the poet, to discover the intersections among pathologies, illnesses, and at the same time the authority that accompanies poetic utterance. Heidegger disinfected the site of this questioning, which grounded poeticity in instabilities of the greatest order—he withdrew the poet Hölderlin and the philosopher Nietzsche from the sanatorium. In this way he also spared them the lexicon of immaturity with which so many are saddled. Poets in much of philosophy, and in literary settings as well, never make it out of childhood but are chronically left back, kept out of historical loops or theories of self-development and growth. They tend to resist *Bildung* or the narrative of formation. Their language may acquire authority but they themselves don't ripen in this way, and if they have material effects on the historical event these are often seen as accidental.

I'm moving too fast here; these converging issues could be put in different terms. Kojève, for his part, examines the notion of authority with a sort of, let's say, Hegelian sobriety. In his own particular way, he cleans up the site of his interrogation: he stabilizes his field and decontaminates the figures of his analysis. He leaves little space for the mentally unstable figures who have exercised so much authority without "having" or commanding authority—Hitler, for example. He doesn't interrogate those patients whose claim of authority has become a worldwide symptom. At the same time his entire effort is based on the impossible emergence for which Hitler stood—the perversion of authority.

> This is problematic, moreover, because it means that one can only attach oneself to pure reason and to the way it expresses its authority, but not to the ruses of reason, or to the way reason is undermined from within by madness. Is there not, even so, an avoidance in this?

Yes, there is no room for the unconscious, for a consideration of what props up reason or strengthens the economies on which it feeds. In this section of *Loser Sons* called "What Was Authority?"—it resonates with Arendt's important essay, "What Is Authority?"—I wanted to explore the multiple terrains that would come out of this repressive constellation and so, to begin with, I also wanted to look closely at the authority or lack of authority of poets, doctors, or philosophers, and the authority that often goes hand in hand with what is most disavowed: the ridiculous. What authority do poets have today? Do they still have any? I don't know which of the two would be the mask of the other, the ridiculous or the serious, the modulations of the Nietzschean "buffoon" or the poet in times of distress. I come back to this question: does the ridiculous take on, by a certain number of strategic manipulations or inadvertent maneuvers, the profile of authority?

Does authority necessarily tip over into the ridiculous, into the pitiful, and has this scale always been part of the phenomenon? Socrates was simultaneously ugly, ridiculous, troubling, and, according to rumor, a man of great authority in the streets of his city. So starting with these knots, these textual and extratextual references, I wanted to ask questions about certain manifestations of power from the standpoint of authority, because we think we can pinpoint the collapse of authority, whereas authority may have always been collapsing and may have always presented itself to us as such. Kojève wouldn't agree completely with us. At the same time, he thinks that

146

authority needs power and institutions for its own preservation; otherwise it no longer represents anything. So authority would already, in its essence and by definition, be devoid of power and support. Here is a foreshadowing of the Kojève of the Lacanian text—and its contrary, Authority not crossed out. And since things shift quickly, authority in turn becomes very fragile, strangely in need of support.

> The idea is rather Nietzschean. The true powers are the most exposed and thus the most fragile. And the weak reign with all the instruments of power.

Yes, the weak, the Christians, the "cretins" (etymologically related, this is not my doing)—but also the nobles; there is a whole Nietzschean parade here. In fact, in French, I wanted to call my book on stupidity *Le crétinisme et son destin* (Cretinism and its fate), after *Le christianisme et son destin*, a famous book on Christianity, starting with the notion of the idiot king about whom Lacan warns us. This would be situated somewhere between a pathological history and a moral failing, something that flies beneath the radar of any ethics governed by a reflection on poetic acts (and passivities), where "literature" torments itself even as it presents itself, exposes itself, with a cruel honesty—without alibi, Derrida would say—toward itself, always on the verge of faltering, looking for its voice, a child thrown against looming figures of adulthood, those wearing the mantle of authority—those, such as philosophy, telling it what to do or how to mean or change, or urging that it grow up already.

## Note

1. During the translation process, Catherine Porter asked for some clarification about the sequence of events here. Realizing that there were gaps in my French narrative, I called my mother. This is what she emailed me five minutes later: "So, after sitting a few weeks in Atleeit (the British screening camp for new arrivals) next to Haifa, where my cousin Gideon Shomron could glimpse me and I him, separated by barbed wire, each surrounded by hundreds of others in the same situation, I was released and shipped with my group to Ramat David, a kibbutz close to Nahalal (where Daddy had worked with Moshe Dayan in 1933/4), and worked 8 hours a day in the fields, distancing myself from my group and listening to the natives chatter in Hebrew. I then received a 'deal' from the kibbutz, namely working only 6 hours a day and getting daily Hebrew lessons from a professional teacher, member of the kibbutz. At that time I graduated from a dorm with about 12 people to a room with a roommate, Dr. Ruth. Ultimately, in 1948, I volunteered for the new Israel Air Force and after the war landed in the Legal Adviser's Office of the Foreign Ministry."

# Saying Good-Bye to My Teacher
## A Home Video

don't want to crowd out the possibility of saying something here. A lot rides on it, on making language turn toward the emptiness; yet, on some essential level, nothing matters anymore. After all this time, I am not getting it together. But let me see what can be said—because I should try, I tell myself, to break through the debilitating muteness. I feel duty bound to bring up some language, not to cover anything over, but to expose my own incapacitation here, in the twelfth chapter, as if I were moving through a program, propelled by a trauma from which one can only and never recover. Let me try to put the scald of an endless mourning out there. I feel that I am messing up.

There is no doubt that I am unable to show tact or follow the metronome of a proper mourning. (Freud gave you two years to get your act together, to deal with the loss and move on before you were pathologized or diagnosed with a mourning disorder.) There is the matter of discursive courtesies and prescriptive nuances as well—the protocols of timely affliction. By now the time for eulogizing has ended and one is well into the phase of mourning that demands some reflective sobriety, perhaps a scholarly intervention. My other work will attend to this exigency and I have in any case, from day one, written on and with the formidable intricacies of Derrida's oeuvre and shown, I think we can safely say, exegetical zeal to this end. I guess the question now is how to constitute and assume his legacy. My fatigue and dispiritedness make it hard to offer lucid assertions or prophetic clips at this juncture, so I thought that I would roll back the curtains on recent and faraway scenes, observing some of the traumatic episodes that bound us these past months and years. Or, ditching traumatic punctuation marks (assuming this to be possible), I might screen some moments that, given the relentless intensities of the two years and a half, I could not until now read—I just went along, pulled by a lethal logic, once in a while able simply to acknowledge the squeeze it put on me. Inevitably and anxiously, I am inserting myself in a narrative in a way that unsettles me. I should have preferred to expunge my story, efface my traces, when writing of Derrida, clearing the runway for the singularity of his narratives. I don't at all like the narcissistic surplus that I see spilling ahead, I should have removed or recused myself, but then this ducking action might have required of me in turn a sort of critical essay—or that I keep silent. Also an option: silence. Still, I am taking a call by which I feel obligated, even if it unravels the nobler pose that I would like to have held: no narcissistic annexation ("he's a part of me"), no abandonment to his own, incomparable stature ("he doesn't need me"), just a silent vigil, responsibly strong, deliberate, and solemnly detached from the often noisy regions of telling.

• • •

*March, 2004.* It was at breakfast one morning. No, mornings were hard for him. I did most of the talking—the prompting, actually. It must have been lunch. The French consulate, I think it was, had asked him to choose an American university at which to announce the publication of *L'Herne*, the last publication of his that he was to live to see (they keep coming, living-on style). At lunch, we had just done some meditating and bodywork, he said: "I want it to be at NYU, I've chosen New York." It was to be his last stopover. He wanted to say good-bye to us, the American contingent, to give his last class—give *us* his last class—and on some afternoons we'd sit together in Ris-Orangis to plan the seminar. (I had just given a seminar on the figure of the orange that led from Goethe's "Passionate Trilogy" to Ris-Orangis.)

He, Derrida, had given seminars for several years at NYU, one on forgiveness, recently, and another on memory, in which he revisited, with sharper language, some of his thoughts on the work of Paul de Man; his critical review of de Man had stirred some controversy, the atmosphere in the bloated NYU classroom was tense, excited. Hundreds of people from all over the country would flock to hear him. One student drove every week from Ohio, another from Virginia; others flew in from Canada and the West Coast to study with Derrida in New York. Some people even came from Brooklyn, possibly the biggest frontier to cross. This time he was going after de Man, and with laser precision. Not everyone was ready to see that happen. He was attacking (the politer term would be "commenting on") a gigantic branch of his American empire, that of rhetorical deconstruction. In March '04 he proposed to offer lectures this time on Sovereignty and the Beast. At least that's how I had translated the course title, wrongly but purposively, I thought. On closer inspection, the title ought to have been The Sovereign and the Animal, nuances that in English were quite weighty, in any case. Actually, I had inverted it: the title should have been The Animal and the Sovereign, but that didn't sit well with me. Who knows how many hours I had spent sizing up the pros and cons of different versions of each title I'd skim off of his blueprints. He was pursuing his line on animal exclusion from conventional philosophical holding pens, scanning traditional determinations, including, according to their peculiar idiomatic swerves, those demarcations separating man from beast that prevailed in the works of Levinas and Heidegger. He planned to start up the speculative engine with a reading of *Robinson Crusoe,* whose protagonist's last name (I saw this when preparing the novel for the joint teaching venture) had been transformed from the German "Kreutzer." He was going to go after the notion of "bare life" and take Giorgio for a ride. I had taught together with Derrida every fall semester for the past several years. It made me nervous, excited, worried. Typically, I'd prepare the class by presenting pertinent materials, training the audience (not all students: there were some professors, some freelancers, a number of artists, curators, filmmakers, literate residents of the metropolitan area) how to read some of Derrida's most recalcitrant works. I figured they could handle the more accessible commentaries on their own, without my somewhat authoritarian intrusions. Though I was earnestly on the job, prepping the class, priming the syllabus, I'd inevitably pervert its course. I'd start off, almost always inadvertently, by taking the course off course. Not planned but nonetheless executed. This time, I thought, I could warm up the class on beastliness by jamming on the German antecedent, the translation or transformation of a name from German. How many of us had followed that itinerary, unloading a German name to find ourselves isolated, starting from scratch, abandoned by the world! It took me into Derrida's thought on forgiveness, traced via Jankelevitch: can "we" forgive the Germans? (Actually, nearly every word here should be in quotation marks, especially "the" "Germans," but all other semantic markers as well. Obviously.)

At NYU, October was known as "Derrida month," ever since the year we had organized a whole series of events around his oeuvre and person. Ben Binstock, now a Rembrandt specialist at Columbia and Princeton whom I had known since my Berkeley days, devoted himself to rebaptizing October in 1998, turning it into our own, very cherished Oktoberfest, inclusive of Nietzsche's birthday. He filled every day of the month with a Derrida event or, strictly speaking, not an "event" as such. Or, even more strictly speaking, maybe an event—who am I to say? How would I know what lay behind or ahead of these manifestations? An event would lose its eventness if I were able to say that it had or had not occurred, or landed, or arrived, or been determined, or sparked futurity, or opened the past for the first time. So destructive of our determined efforts to pin it down, the event sometimes "passes"—yes, it passes for something other than itself, passes us by, or it just passes. In any event, that was the year that I gave the lecture called "Abraham! Abraham! Abraham, Jacques & Martin" in the ancient downtown synagogue. At the end of the delivery—I was nervous, Jacques was sitting right next to me, looking over my shoulder, reading along while I read aloud, it was an impossible scenography—when I was done, he planted a kiss on my forehead, in public, punctuating the presentation. That was the way he'd greeted me, each time, when the moments came for the hellos and adieux. But now he took my forehead and kissed it in public, after my delivery.

The very day I was supposed to pick him up at JFK, he left us, Jacques Derrida left his body. I had a visitation that night, but I am not prepared to talk about it. I still don't know how to say it and until three months after his departure I didn't believe it, still hadn't revved up the engines of reality-testing, and I would simply not have it—even though I had attended that austere ceremony without ceremony in October. That he was gone, not of this world, no longer among us: Ha!—None of these phrasal injuries meant anything to me; yes, there were pretend memorials, and I played along, making as if he were gone, faking summations and call-ups, feigning distress, affecting shock, the whole bit, but I knew it was *all a lie* and he was still with us, wouldn't leave me, and I held this knowledge close until I walked into his house one day, months after the burial, at Christmastime, and saw his briefcase—a book bag he'd carried, always too heavy, noticeably worn—waiting in the corner. It hit me then.

If I had the courage or capacity, I would turn this writing over to him now. Not only in terms of a citational mode that resurrects the other, restoring language to the now voiceless one. Yes, clearly, that is his due: that we sing praise to and in his words, retoning and releasing them, to be heard according to different pitches, weighted by sorrow, lifting on a note of inextinguishable awe. Derrida! Derrida! I would want to have had the courage of addressing you, or at least to deliver a storm of language that could be addressed to him or seen as coming from him. There were times when I thought I caught him on the telepathic channel—we shared a whole network of superstition and taboo as well as private mysticisms—he was cleared of that clandestine interference with the others, I observed, very straight up, socially fit (uncannily so for a philosopher, O those brutes! but that's another story), but with me, he let me get spiritual and, let's just say, philosophically weird, remote-controlled by an unlocatable command system but, then, who isn't when it comes to subjecting oneself to greater things such as freedom, love, sacredness: how do we even know what or who it is that prescribes the categorical imperative, as I believe Jean-Luc once asked. I see that I have approached themes that weld transmission systems, parasitical utterance, and ghostly formation. These themes, not always thematizable occurrences, actually, are disclosive of the way I'd sometimes cable over to him, according to the secret algorithms of our encounter. Other times, I'd have to be down to earth and downright classical in the matter of language usage. He'd have suddenly switched tracks on me and expected a kind of uncompromising clarity from me. I'd feel the strain but endeavored to deliver.

If I had more strength, I would want to write a series of *cartes postales* whose destiny and destination, forever suspended, would alight on your name, maybe I could take as my main or at least initial theme something like the Age of Derrida—how to measure, calculate this still-pregnant age, where it began, how they begin, he and "deconstruction" (for brevity's sake). In my own work, if I can call it that (he: mother and father, baby and friend, "O my friends there is no friend," but that's another story), he was the fateful site ("father" and "fate" are irrevocably linked by Freud: I might add that to the *Carte postale*'s lexicon of Heideggerian *schicken, Schicksal, Geschick,* etc.), the materno-paternal engine of my so-called own work—I stutter, I stagger, tripped up by the presumption of positing that pushes me on or down, can't tell, same difference—I'll pull myself together and push on. In my "own" work, then (ten-minute pause about whether to put the vampiric bite marks around "work" or not; I try it out: "work," work, Work, "work," work, "my" work, well you get it), I had tried to measure and calibrate the *Goethezeit*—the time, timing, temporalities of Goethe, a blockbuster time zone for what is known as Germanistik. When I started thinking about the age of Derrida, a few years ago, for the purpose of another paper honoring his work, I did not know that the mortality timer was on, even though I had moved in to help care for Derrida when he got ill. We didn't know how much time he had, but we thought it would be more. *Mort.* The night before he left us Marguerite had called and we spoke for an hour about his operation, the way he held her hand, the two years ahead of medication, recovery, the treatment plan. I was in New York, she called me very late her time. The time difference belongs to my effort to read off and determine the times of Derrida.

• • •

*Flashback.* It was August in Berkeley. Most of my colleagues were in Europe or Hawai'i and I was wrapping up endless footnotes for *The Telephone Book,* the extensive "Yellow Pages." So it must have been 1989. The phone rang. Someone from the university president's office was asking me if I would host the minister of culture from the Republic of China. Me? Well, no one else is around and we ran out of options, I was told. For three days? I don't know. It seems like a lot and I'm not prepared. I'd need to do some research. Besides, I have to finish a book and wash my hair. An hour later the minister greeted me. He expressed delight, offering generous expressions of awe, for I was owed, he said, the respect that only a disciple of Confucius could expect. I was the student of Jacques Derrida! At the time, in the mideighties, Berkeley itself was not prepared to embrace Derrida, much less a mutant offspring, or what Derrida himself would come to call his own rogue state or territory (he'd link territory with terror and *terre*, earth, uprooting the concept of nation-state, the *voyou* Avi—he translated my name as saying, "for life," as in he was stuck with me for life, *à vie*). For my part, I felt more like an early Christian than a disciple of Confucius. There was a lot of solitude and theory bashing in those days, a lot of intimidation and punishment. Low salaries and mocking colleagues—assuming one managed to get in or on anyone's payroll. Not only that, but, once inside, Freud was KO'd at least once a month, Lacan was spun out of our orbit, and, with the exception of one or two troublemakers, the theory girrrls hadn't even shown up yet on the boy-scanners. I was the fastest pun in the West, but that was nothing to boast about in those days. The only one who had some holding power was Foucault, cleaned up, straightened out, and identitarian. So the dispatch, the postcard and *envoi* came to me from China—the news of the fate of deconstruction. For me, the report of its destiny and destination came from an altogether unexpected horizon, and the minister, who became my friend, opened the scene for an alternative "Purloined Letter," pointing to its location right there, in front of my nose yet resolutely invisible. As in a Kafka parable, I received the broadcast of Jacques Derrida's fate as philosopher from a sentinel who held the secret of a genuinely possible and strongly inflected future. As Derrida has taught us, there are many futures and even more returns.

Toward the end, he turned his thoughts toward politics, summoning up the democracy *à-venir*, still ahead. Already quite ill, he went on television to advocate, in his special way, for gay marriage. Actually, the state should butt out of marriage sacraments altogether and leave that to religious officiants. Everyone should have access to civil union and those who additionally wanted marriage—an inescapably religious institution—could turn to their local synagogue or church or mosque. He had agitated on behalf of the homeless, illegal immigrants—the famous *sans papiers*—and recognized literature as a space for unprecedented dissidence. What may seem to Americans a disjunctive or disproportionate alignment inclusive of literary clout belongs to the dossier of his achievement—putting literary power right up there with other effects of referential authority, restoring to or seeing in poeticity an unstoppable register of resistance (he writes in the book of that title that *résistance* has always been one of his favorite words, whether politically inflected, historically promoted, poetically enacted, or psychoanalytically toned). He had gone, years before all this, to Prague ignoring that government's warnings not to accept an invitation to speak. He felt his duty resided in *not* declining the invitation extended by a group of blacklisted philosophers. The authorities busted him on trumped-up drug charges; he was thrown in jail.

On the home front he had never joined the French Communist Party as such, though that was the way the wind blew in his milieu, the direction that magnetized most of his peers at the prestigious École normale sup. Still, he wrote for *L'Humanité* and was friends with its poet-philosopher adherents such as Jean Ristat, whose recent obituary pages and public tribute reminded the readers of Derrida's support and contributions, particularly an anniversary article stating "Why I Love *L'Humanité*." So there were street smarts and philosophical skirmishes, risks taken, including those of uncool nonmembership. Without succumbing to Maoism or communism, like some in his crowd, he never reverted to the Right, like some in his crowd. What is important and confusing to American readers is the way he remained resolutely on the "Left," in a vigilant and demanding sort of way. Once in a great while he may have blinked, as when he and Hélène Cixous perhaps gave too much credit to the new socialist government at the time Mitterrand came into power. They joined in and up momentarily but this had its good side, too. Besides arranging his jailbreak, the Mitterrand government gave him other breaks, as when he got the permit to create the Collège international de philosophie on rue Descartes—the only premier French institution, as far as we know, that is open to cosmopolitan contamination, cleared for foreigners to teach and think and profess in France. So, besides his writing and lecturing, Derrida also resignified the university in crucially significant ways, creating solid and traceable rebound effects from the United States to Europe and back again, mirroring pedagogical imperatives and institutional innovation like no other. On his home territory he was denied professorships or a chair at the Collège de France, even though they made him apply and present his work and humble himself before committees with the assurance beforehand that it was a done deal, all you have to do is show up. (I was at his thesis defense, the entry ticket for beginning the whole process, and I was there when he carried a box-load of his books and papers to present to the grand committee. One of the undeclared side effects, at least from an American point of view, of Derrida never getting a completely appropriate job in France is that he had no assistants or secretarial help so he had to locate, photocopy, collate, and carry everything by himself in days and cultures where there were no friendly neighborhood Kinkos and such. Well, I am attentive to material concerns such as these, seeing him schlepping his encumbering carton of books to subject himself to a committee's interrogation—that sort of thing belongs to my internal album of anxious reminiscence.)

He was, on some days, his own proletariat, at least according to the standards of American visitors and inscriptions. He told me that Harold Bloom, in the days when they were speaking (one day we walked past him, he was sitting on his stoop at Washington Square, it was a hot day in the year 2000, and Harold refused to get up to greet his old friend who stopped his gait, at the other's gate, waving and prepared to embrace, chat, remember their common past; Jacques was hurt and for awhile obsessed with the denied greeting. Uli, a young professor of German, was caught in the middle as usual, having worked with both of them, whereas I as usual had no split loyalties to tally)—well, anyway, when Harold met Jacques in the old days of friendly interlocution and active visitation and saw his house, especially the small attic into which Jacques had squeezed himself in order to write—a scant wire heater did little to change the teeth-chattering cold, in those days the master would write with a scarf wrapped around his neck, wearing sweaters, sometimes a coat—Harold Bloom expressed his dismay and surprise that this was where the great works signed "Jacques Derrida" got the green light, upstairs in an unheated attic. A lot of American academics of that generation, with their big old Victorian houses and comfortable studies were taken aback, some of them muttering about *pied noir* aesthetics or housing arrangements, and I heard this sort of thing from snobby French intellectuals as well. Derrida's personal architecture of study was modest—it was not until the last five or so years that he and Marguerite added a studio annex to the house, with a loftlike bed upstairs and a wide space for his two or three desks downstairs, his massive holdings. This was the bed to which he would repair on afternoons when he was sick, taking a book with him to read as he drifted into his two- or three-hour nap.

The books were unmanageable. Major pile-up syndrome. People sent him books every day. In the early years some books did not footnote him but the author instead wrote a personal dedication on the order of "without you I could never have written this work; my debt to your work is tremendous, inestimable," and once I asked Jacques about that—I loved reading the dedications, including those of Blanchot, and I remember that Paul de Man's *Allegories of Reading,* if that's the one, unless it was *Blindness and Insight,* said, very elegantly I thought: "Ineffaceably, Paul"—so I asked him about the debt named in handwriting but invisible in the public and published version of the text. He responded with an ironic smile that this happens all the time, people consistently disavow you yet sneak in their thank-yous. Maybe that's why I laid it on thick when it came to naming my debts to him, but it was something I wanted to do, and I'm not cheap about that sort of thing, I am a creature of gratitude, I am elated when it is possible to thank, even in the most thankless situations. I like to end my yoga practice with gratitude poses, something that I taught Jacques. How happy I was when reading the first time Heidegger's purposeful conflation of thanking and thinking, *danken, gedanc, denken.* But now I am getting off track, driven by a nearly compulsive desire to offer thanks, perhaps a reactive defense meant to stave off the depressive pressure of the incalculable loss I bear and toward which I remain thankless. I wanted to go on another ramp, following the micro- and geopolitical maps that Derrida had us read.

He had been thinking, via Marx, about political mourning and what we think we're doing when we celebrate the death of Marxism—or Marx. He was concerned about the repetitions in late capitalism that went into affirming that "Marx is dead," "Marxism is over," "communism is toast." Who was Marx, he asked, that his death had to be announced more than once? In *Marx en jeu,* a dialogic supplement to *Specters of Marx,* he observes, "When someone dies and the announcement of this death is repeated for more than one day—normally, when the papers announce a death, it is stated for one day only and thereafter nothing further is said—when it is repeated time and again, this means that something else is going on, namely, that the dead person is not so dead, or not dead enough. Saying 'Marx is dead' echoes formulae such as 'God is dead,' of which one has been speaking since the time of Hegel but also since the time of Christ and Luther, for Christ, too, is emblematic of 'God is dead' and that has lasted, that continues to last. Thus Marx is dead . . . is a symptom, a symptom of the work in progress of mourning, with all of its phenomena of melancholy, jubilant mania, ventriloquy" (1997). Before submitting this passage as a fairly accurate prediction of what would drag his corpse for a few extra rounds, I want to switch for a nanosecond to a largely sidelined aspect of his political inquiry, namely, the steadfast loyalty to America that Derrida has shown. For now I will skip the description of his marriage to Marguerite in Boston, or the fact that when others canceled us out, he flew to New

York in 2001 shortly after September 11 at a time when everyone expected that more was coming, or the division of his labor between the East and West Coasts, the many inscriptions of "America Is/In Deconstruction" or the famous "States of Theory" lecture delivered at Irvine, or his relationship with such arch-Americans as Paul de Man and Richard Rorty and Gayatri Spivak and Peter Eisenmann and the lawyers and artists and professors and curators and philosophers, reactive or hospitable, depending on who or where or even what was happening.

One day I said to Jacques that I found the utterance "God bless America" unbearable and I promised to puke if I heard it again. He looked at me, with a slight ironic smile and informed me that he didn't find it loathsome at all. Perhaps this isn't the best example of what I am trying to get across— Drucilla Cornell certainly had no patience for his putting the brakes on my expression of rage—but it indicates his ability to hold back on condemnation, one of the lessons that he brought home with elegance on many occasions. Reflecting on what he could have meant—he was not defending the utterance but saying merely that it provoked no horror in him—I realized that he himself offered blessings and in his last words, read over his grave, delivered blessings to his mourners. But that was not it, either. "God bless America," though put to pernicious usage and corrupted into a constative statement, has a more difficult itinerary to account for: is it a prayer, a supplication, a wish, a hallucination, as when one asks, may God please bless America? Does it name the *blessure* or wounding that states an absence of blessing, so that one has compulsively to ask for the blessing painfully withheld, and so forth? As Mary Ann Caws reminded me at the NYU memorial tribute for Derrida, one says "God bless you" to stop a pernicious spill, to lock out the devil, as when someone sneezes. "God bless America" could be a way of saying "Holy shit!" I'll leave off now, because I just saw in an email announcing a new article by him that Sam Weber has something under the title "God Bless America"; I'm eager to see what he's come up with but too lazy right now, or too tired, to email him and find out. So even as we were walking down the street and I was mouthing off, producing an easy target, Jacques was making me think about the blessing missing in speech action. From this small and modest example, one can metonymize upward and outward.

There are two more microexamples that I'd like to set forth because I don't see how they would otherwise have air time, so marginal do they seem. Sure, Jacques taught us to scour the margins, stay close to their purported contingencies, to shake up the certainties concerning the marginal and central concerns of occurrences. In France, one of his last public appearances involved taking questions from *Le Monde* journalist Jean Birnbaum, a highly intelligent interlocutor. Some issues concerning the American appropriation of his work came up, and Jacques, sensing the easy disdain for Americans given the recent Bush invasion of Iraq, told the audience to hold off on making wholesale judgments. The Americans that he knew were far more radical than any French person in the audience, and the struggle for democracy was real and deep in the United States. He said something about the exemplary vigilance of some Americans, their pain and steadfast commitment to justice, ending with the exhortation to help and support our American friends in their time of moral despair and true need. It was very tough and beautiful, a hard line to carry off. I will not speak here of the failure of the European Left to find something more vital or constructive than lame versions of anti-Americanisms (which are understandable but neither inventive nor very effective, and, frankly, turning a blind eye to their own fascistic areas of corporate and political behaviors is of no help either).

Finally, on the sofa, after we had been doing some visualizations, I had the opportunity to speak to him about the torture that Americans had inflicted on their detainees. No need to say how appalled we were, how depressing this fold of world history was becoming. Still, Jacques said that no one else had ever even tried to work at it the way the Americans were doing—we had been watching the hearings, the pounding questions that were thrust at those held accountable. I am not offering a naive version of asserted culpability, rating who got snagged and who got away or forgetting what gets swept under the rug of repressive state regimes. Nonetheless, there was a strong leakage of self-denunciation that the world had not seen in the context of other episodes of torture, a genuine struggle with self-accusation—not to say the need to expose activities of torture which, whatever more has to be said—a lot more has to be said and done—does not happen in other political states, not to the extent of televised legal proceedings. That Alberto Gonzales got appointed before he was finally removed from office, that Bush fixed another election—these are other matters. What Derrida was commenting on was the resiliency and courage that moments such as these hearings tend to demonstrate. Perhaps not good enough, but it is something, maybe a nano-something. I am looking for bigger trials for the Bush and Cheney crowd.

As concerns the supplementary reflections on Marx, the title that Derrida gave his intervention was "Marx, c'est quelqu'un." He asks, who is this burdensome, interminable Marx whom we know in some sense to be dead but who remains *increvable,* inextinguishable? He does not ask a question concerning essence—what—but *who.* I'd like to dwell momentarily in the subtle light of this question, stay with the shift it portends. So Derrida, for us, as he himself says of Marx, was somebody. He was someone and is someone. Many of us worked with him, shared meals, took walks, attended colloquia, called and read him, even fought with him.

But who bears the name *Derrida* now, and what does it bear—also, what contours the bearing of this name, this beautiful name, too often demeaned, persecuted in significant ways among American academic philosophers, even in death. Lacan has taught us what it means to want to kill the dead. A colleague of his tells me that the Berkeley landlord and philosopher John Searle started circulating an attack piece immediately after Derrida's death but that, given the outraged reaction to the nasty *New York Times* obit, he has refrained from publishing it for a while, until it's decent to pound the dead. As resentfully piqued as some of these unrelenting assaults may be, they are part of the narrative, not to be quickly discarded or overlooked.

As with everything else, America was bitterly divided around the value and consequences of Derridean thought; the more conservative set, especially, wanted to keep things proper and "serious." "Seriousness" became the tactical defense weapon against the French, and a rhetorical feint that Derrida confronted in "Limited, Inc." On the teaching front, many professors worried, moreover—and here one can begin to understand something of the reactive rage—that students would skip over more traditional training grounds in favor of Derrida's notoriously difficult texts. There was no backup or "substance" to their learning; Derrida became a kind of rock star upon which American students obsessed without a cognitive safety net. It is true that many of his followers skipped French or Greek or German or philosophy or literature classes and went straight to "Plato's Pharmacy" for their drugs, or to the "Double Séance" or "White Mythology" for literary and rhetorical tourism, sometimes working backward and construing a reading list from his prescription pad and idiomatic mappings. A more reliable institution of learning was in a certain way compromised; a more savage, utterly American mix of pedagogical intensity and wild intellectual unloading threatened to replace the university curriculum. Still, the professorial rage or "conflict of the faculties" (to quote a text by Kant on which Derrida had worked) exceeded any recognizable itinerary of motives or reason for such a level of defensive aggression. At this point one would want to cover up the story of warring factions, but they have not subsided or in any way resolved their differences. A palpable level of armored attack persists. The attacks on Derrida, as strange as they may now seem, are part of the portrait of risk-taking thought, and the violence of the gentlemen academics is only part of the package deal of genuine innovation, heart-stopping questioning. So, let us agree not to remove the stain or sting, the disruptive aggression on mourning. Keep it around. In America we tend to assassinate those we love, it is a national hobby of sorts. It is, according to a familiar Christian scheme, also a way of keeping something alive.

What bears down on us as Derrida's heritage? What calls us by this name, Derrida?

The heritage: we have to sort and sift, splice and split, unlock and scramble the codes of "legitimate" heritage, split heirs, defend, respond, read—certainly read, have him continue to read us and our rhetorical unconscious, our unconscious rhetorics, rhetori*tics*. Derrida was an outstanding symptomatologist and we would continue to benefit from his analyses and predictions, his sense of our aporetic inclinations and disturbed historical snags.

His name calls us, asking that we be vigilant, strong, that we understand why democracy has in a certain sense reverted to pernicious mappings and origins, a boy's club—the inescapable fraternity and brotherhood of man—that was bound to falter: he saw it, he called it. He saw that democracy, self-defeating and fragile at times, now needs our help, our often solitary and responsible resistance. At the point of horrific disintegration in crucial forms of American democracy, Derrida put democratic institutions and articulations on the line, started prodding and probing, making renewed demands and establishing contracts for something like a livable justice, a viable politics.

• • •

Maybe I should start wrapping it up, as if that were doable. It would have been nearly impossible for me to offer a dialectical summation of Jacques Derrida's accomplishments or to calculate his influence on the intellectual worlds around which he organized his thought, always inventively yet responsibly anchored, classically filtered. Some aspects of his influence or invention belong to a subterranean history, or are yet to be placed in a narrative of the alien unsaid. This may sound a bit sci-fi, but in some areas of his work it is as though Jacques were beaming signals from another region of meaning, speaking from new intelligibilities, as Schlegel might have said, that haven't yet arrived or whose significance has not been cleared for landing. I'm not trying to speak in code. And I'm not on medical marijuana. It's just that I assume that his irremissible bearing on legal studies, architecture, art, literature, pedagogy, medical ethics, psychoanalysis, philosophy, historical recounting, and performance has already been recorded.

So. Let me try to offer an aerial view here, if that is imaginable. Or perhaps it is *only* imaginable. So let me try, even if I crash and burn and ruin the mood of melancholic honoring that I wanted to establish. Sometimes melancholy tips toward something else. I have seen how melancholy makes me giddy and takes me off course. I'll try to focus.

So.

It's not even a matter a matter of debt. Something incalculable happened to us, something yet to be understood. Like any event, even a happy event, it was traumatic. Derrida: this name marks a catastrophic incursion, an end indistinguishable from a beginning. He was declared dead from the moment he walked in on us. In the university there are still some traces of the stages of anticipatory bereavement—denial, anger, bargaining, periodic punch-outs. In the few shots pledged to a statement on his legacy, I want to say one or two things that may not have been covered by other tributes.

I've tried to track a marginal perspective meant to be metonymized into the bigger picture. One cannot imagine how whited-out the academic corridor was when Derrida arrived on the American scene. There was really no room for deviancy, not even for a quaint aberration or psychoanalysis. Besides offering up the luminous works that bore his signature, Derrida cleared spaces that looked like obstacle courses for anyone who did not fit the professorial profile at the time. He practiced, whether consciously or not, a politics of contamination. His political views, refined and, by our measure, distinctly leftist, knew few borders and bled into the most pastoral sites and hallowed grounds of higher learning. Suddenly color was added to the university—color and sassy women, something that would not easily be forgiven. In him, Kant reemerged as a morphed and updated historicity, a cosmopolitan force that placed bets on and opened discursive formations to women. Derrida blew into our town-and-gown groves with protofeminist energy, often, and at great cost to the protocols of philosophical gravity, passing as a woman. My first translation of his work was "Law of Genre/Gender," where he reworked the grid to the rhythm of invaginated punctures. Not all the folks at the reception desk were cheering such gender intrusions into the exercise of linguistic pieties. Nonetheless, Derrida could be said to have quickly developed a substantial following, especially in America—Latin and North America.

The more politically based offshoots would occasionally disavow him. He regularly got it from the left and right, from those who owed him and those who disowned him (often the same constituencies). In some quarters Derrida's thought, whether Kantian or not, became associated with queers and women, and his poetic sparring with paleonymic language got quickly feminized, seemed somehow too girlie and slippery. Based on some of the things that came up, I wrote about the historical backslide of paronomasia,

161

its anal zoning ordinances and the returns, on all counts, to Shakespeare's Bottom. It is interesting how language play spelled trouble. Derrida's language usage, exquisite and replenishing, itself became an offense to the more strictly controlled behaviors and grammars of academic language. Perhaps unavoidably, Derrida, like all breakthrough thinkers and artists, continues to attract death sentences even after his announced death. The resentment that he stokes as he downsizes metaphysical strongholds is itself a text to be read—a massive reactivity that belongs to a legacy of a hard-hitting oeuvre. The traumatic impact of his thought—trauma arises from ecstatic opening as well as from catastrophic shutdown—makes it difficult to offer closural solace or to pin down what his work might "represent" for us today.

One of the things that I appreciated about Derrida from the start was the political punch he delivered, often stealthy but cannily effective. I missed the sixties but inherited their beat. I'm probably more politically anxious, faster on the trigger than most of the folks around me; in any case, I look for trouble and aporia in the most downtrodden neighborhoods of thought. Derrida suited my mood at once, though his political investments were more lucid and constrained perhaps than I was looking for, more aligned with Hölderlin's image of Rousseau—on the side of mediation and sober reflection, able to enact the *re-trait* of which Jean-Luc Nancy and Lacoue-Labarthe write. Still, he packed a mighty punch, I thought. He agitated for the poor, the homeless, immigrants, for Nelson Mandela and against apartheid, with the Palestinians, Africa, and every conceivable "liberal" cause. He traveled the world like no other thinker. On a more local station, he went on French TV advocating gay marriage—sort of, asking for the abolition of all marriage as a state-sponsored arrangement and the implementation of civil union for everyone seeking it. I know I'm repeating myself but I'm in mourning and have the permit in hand: I'm obsessed. Let us continue. Years before that, he tried to reform the French educational system by demanding that philosophy be taught early on, beginning in the second or third grade. He instituted the Collège international de philosophie, which is now the only prestigious institution in France to our knowledge that welcomes foreigners (let's face it, the French are in some ways hopeless xenophobes). As with the pressure put on the American university, he knocked down the doors and let all sorts of impurities like us in. By the time he finished his tour of duty, Derrida appears to have been respected in Europe as Aristotle must have been among the ancients. A master teacher, he was seen also to have historacular powers. Still, he never made it to the top of the line—my understanding is that he was denied a professorship and barred from the Collège de France. Even though I think he was considerably injured by such insults, it belongs to the catalogue of what I love about the guy, the way he took institutional assaults, stayed modest and generous and open and continued teaching to the end. When he taught at NYU, his office hours remained accessible to everyone who thought she had an idea to bounce. Now, writing this, I realize that the whole lexicon of his gestures, punts, and attitudes was radically democratic. He held doors open and welcomed nearly anything or anyone (it would be foolish to make a rigorous distinction between the thing and the one, given his work); he was impeccably polite to intruders, hospitable to dissidents of all stripes, and sheltered the intellectually homeless. Given that his last years were devoted to rethinking democracy, it cannot be a mere coincidence that the catastrophic elections bringing Bush a second term broke the hearts, again, of those who mourn him. One thing that Derrida did for Americans, for those who have to wander the ghostless cultures of abandonment, was to bring another Europe to bear, another atlas of "the rest of the world," and his praxis was to read us to ourselves performatively, which is to say, he constituted us by staying near, keeping an incomparable nearness as he marked his distance, his uncompromising spacing. Whereas in France he may have been at times classified according to internal protocols that I have not decoded, for his American readers he produced a prototype of a strongly held French imaginary—rigorous, uncompromising, learned, just, modest. Did I say "French"?

# Index

in Freud, 65; Nazi, 98; structure of, for
Lacan, 60; for technological invasion,
62, 64; for testing, 95; for a trial, 91
destruction, 5, 96, 103; vs. devastation, for
Heidegger, 3; and experimentation, 94;
of history, 140; for Nietzsche, 79–81, 104.
*See also* self-destruction
*Dichtung und Wahrheit* (Goethe), 145
*Dictations: On Haunted Writing* (Ronell),
12
Dilthey, Wilhelm, 116
disease: autoimmune, as metaphor, 2–3,
49, 73–74; contagious, as metaphor, 119;
and rumor, 67–70, 87. *See also* AIDS;
contamination; illness
disposition: experimental, 35, 95–96
"Disturbance of Memory on the Acropolis,
A" (Freud), 127
*Don Quixote* (Cervantes), 43, 102
Doppelt, Suzanne, 69, 91
Dora, 42, 133
Dostoevsky, Fyodor, 14, 66, 77, 99, 127
"Double Séance," 159
drag queen, 39, 71–72, 133
drive: death, 46, 49, 80; justificatory, 47;
test, 35–37, 81, 84, 91–109. See also *Test
Drive, The*

ear: and addiction, 52
Eckermann, Johann Peter, 11–16, 20, 37
economy: and anality, 45; of death, 51; of
decision, 43; libidinal, 4; logic of, 74;
narrative, 13; of parricide, 30
effacement: effects of, 24; discourse of, 53
*Elective Affinities* (Goethe), 8
electricity: in Freud, 66; for Mary Shelley,
96–97
Enlightenment, the: Goethe and, 21–22;
*The Magic Flute* and, 79–80
*Entretiens infinis* (Blanchot), 12
epidemic, as metaphor, 66–68
Eve, 42, 84, 95
excrement, 14, 45
experiment: in Nietzsche, 82–83, 88;
scientific, 101
experimentation: culture of, 94; and irony,
in Kierkegaard, 105; sites of, 107

father: absence of, 100; as authority, 143;
author's, 126–27, 134–43; death of, 119;
Derrida as, 152; Eckermann as, 13, 15;

in Freud, 8; Kafka's, 130, 135; relation to
daughter, 141–43; television as, 56. *See
also* parricide
*Faust* (Goethe), 92
feminism, 30, 84; and Valerie Solanas, 25,
38–41. *See also* transfeminism
feminization, 44, 47–48, 110
"Fins de l'homme, Les" (Derrida), 39
Flaubert, Gustave, 34, 59
Foucault, Michel, on AIDS, 69; American
reception of, 7, 28, 120–21, 153
*Frankenstein* (Shelley), 96, 104
French theory, 29, 110–25
Freud, Sigmund: on addiction, 60; on
aggression, 48; American reception of,
97, 114, 153; and anger, 26; on anti-
Semitism, 98–99; on apotropaic objects,
79; on contamination, 68; on Dostoevsky, 99; on father figures, 119, 152; and
Goethe, 8, 13, 18–19, 21, 78; on the house
of being, 62–63; and hysteria, 45, 65, 133,
145; on loss and mourning, 127, 133, 137,
148; on love, 2, 4; on Nietzsche, 85; on
technologies, 63, 66
friendship, politics of, 100, 118

Gadamer, Hans Georg, 26–28, 111
Gallop, Jane, 114
Gasché, Rodolphe, 115
*Gay Science, The* (Nietzsche), 81, 84
gender, 9, 81, 122, 161; in Nietzsche, 83
gender studies, 71–72, 123
*Gender Trouble* (Butler), 72
German language, 14, 19, 126; *Dasein* in, 24
(see also *Dasein*)
Gibson, William, 104
Glover, Edward, 19, 60
Goethe, August, 15
Goethe, Johann Wolfgang von, 7–17, 18–22,
122, 149; and the body, 24, 78; and Kant,
143, 145; on monsters, 97; on the poet
figure, 144–45; and science, 106; on the
tempter figure, 92; and time, 152. Works:
*Conversations with Eckermann*, 11,
14–15; *Dichtung und Wahrheit*, 145; *Elec-
tive Affinities*, 8; *Faust*, 92; *Sorrows of
Young Werther, The*, 8, 19, 22; *Torquato
Tasso*, 144
gratitude, 125, 156
*Great Expectations* (Dickens), 102
Guattari, Félix, 11

language: and AIDS, 69–70; ballistic theory of, 67; and the body, 19; Clinton's relation to, 120; creation of, 142; and Derrida, 151–52, 161–62; and French theory, 118–19; loss of, 123, 137, 142; multilingualism, x, 127, 133; vs. music, 79–80; phallocentric, 40–42; poet's relation to, 144–46; rhetorical and poetic dimensions of, x; subject's access to, in psychoanalysis, 60; and technology, 4; and testing, 88; theory of, in *Frankenstein*, 96; and trauma, 148. *See also* German language

latency: in illness, 76, 80; in technology, 92; in the test drive, 94

law: of culture, 142; and DNA tests, 93; of the house, 141; against indecency, 108; moral, 141; of philosophic learning, 27–28; and power, 120; relation to, 49–50, 65; of the streets, 125; and television, 52, 58; and war, 48. *See also* outlaw

"Law of Genre/Gender" (Derrida), 81, 161

"Letter to My Father" (Kafka), 130, 135

Levinas, Emmanuel: American reception of, 115; on the caress, 33; on human-animal distinction, 150; and poetry, 128; on responsibility, 14, 65–66

"Limited, Inc." (Derrida), 159

literature: birth of modern, 19; and the figure of the poet, 144–45, 147; and philosophy, 1, 21, 102, 113; Schlegel on need for, 116–17; scientific, 93, 104; as space for dissidence, 154; trashcans of, 14

*Little Red Book* (Mao), 5

logos, 33, 34

"Loi du genre, La" (Derrida), 81, 161

love, 1–4, 116, 140–43, 152

Lyotard, Jean-François, 93, 113, 121

MacKinnon, Catharine, 46, 83

*Madame Bovary* (Flaubert), 15, 59

madness, 41–43, 145–46

Mailer, Norman, 25, 39

manifesto, 43–44. See also *SCUM Manifesto*

Mao, 20

Marx, Karl, 8, 114, 156, 158–59

*Marx en jeu* (Derrida), 156

Marxism, death of, 156

master: as authority, for Kojève, 143; Goethe as, 16; and hysteric, for Freud,

45; lack of, in *Frankenstein*, 96; need for, 27; in testing, 95; Zen relation to, 30–32, 35–37

*Matrix, The*, 104

Medea, 25, 40

medicine, 73–74, 76, 88, 93

meditation, 26, 31–33

*Mein Kampf* (Hitler), 5

memory: Derrida on, 149; and oblivion, 2; primal, 84; and television, 53, 55, 57–58; theory of, 96; and trauma, 50

Mephistopheles, 92

micropolitics, 48, 71, 80. *See also* politics

Mirabeau, Octave, 4

Mitterrand, François, 121, 154

monster: in *Frankenstein*, 96–97, 104; Goethe as, 8; in *The Magic Flute*, 79

*Monster* (Warhol), 25

Moses, 98, 139

*Moses and Monotheism* (Freud), 98

Mozart, Wolfgang Amadeus, 69, 78–80, 87

music, 48; vs. language, 79–80

Musil, Robert, 5, 30, 81, 112

mutation, 23, 87, 94; AIDS and, 63, 69; drugs and, 60; technology and, 4, 54, 63, 69, 92

Nancy, Jean-Luc, 19, 33, 34, 66, 113, 118, 122, 162

narrative: economy of, 13; master, 93; televised, 52–53

Nazi, 5, 51, 81, 97–101, 137

Nazism, 4–5, 51, 98–100, 112

Negri, Antonio, vii, 107

Neurosis: obsessional, 14, 15, 27, 68, 133

Nietzsche, Friedrich, 2, 26; and the body, 32–33; and contamination, 69, 78–80, 85–87, 89, 143–44; on dancing, 126; on democracy, 95–98; on the ear, 52; on the feminine, 42, 81–84; Freud and, 85; and Goethe, 10–11, 13–14, 21, 23–26; Heidegger and, 67–68, 145; and madness, 41; and Nazism, 81; on promising, 107; on *ressentiment*, 9, 73; on science, 102–7; on tests and testing, 35–36, 81–82, 88–89, 92, 95, 101–2, 105; on the *Übermensch*, 80, 83. Works: *Beyond Good and Evil*, 82, 84, 105; *Gay Science, The*, 81, 84; *Human, All Too Human*, 81; *Thus Spoke Zarathustra*, 21, 69

night, queen of, 73, 79–81

*Notion d'autorité, La* (Kojève), 143

Avital Ronell is University Professor of the Humanities and a professor of German, English, and comparative literature at New York University, where she also codirects the program in Trauma and Violence Transdisciplinary Studies. She is also Jacques Derrida Professor of Media and Philosophy at the European Graduate School in Switzerland. In 2009 Ronell gave an eight-performance cycle at the Centre Pompidou, Paris, beginning with a discussion with Werner Herzog. She is the author of *Stupidity, Crack Wars,* and other books.

Anne Dufourmantelle is the author of *Blind Date* and other works and coauthor, with Jacques Derrida, of *Of Hospitality.* She is a psychoanalyst in Paris.

Catherine Porter, professor emerita in the Department of International Communications and Culture at the State University of New York, Cortland, is the translator of numerous books and essays, including works by Hélène Cixous, Jacques Derrida, Anne Dufourmantelle, Michel Foucault, Gérard Genette, Luce Irigaray, and Sarah Kofman. She is a recipient of the Palmes Académiques with the rank of Chevalier for furthering Franco-American relations through teaching and translation.

The University of Illinois Press
is a founding member of the
Association of American University Presses.

———————————————————————

Designed by Dennis Roberts
Composed in 10/13 Adobe Minion Pro
with Adobe Myriad display
by Barbara Evans
at the University of Illinois Press
Manufactured by Sheridan Books, Inc.

University of Illinois Press
1325 South Oak Street
Champaign, IL 61820-6903
www.press.uillinois.edu